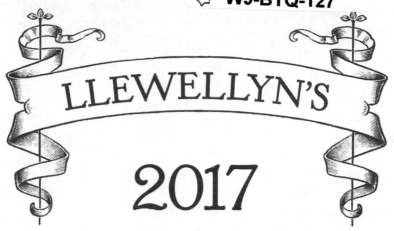

LLEWELLYN'S

2017

Magical Almanac

Featuring

*Peg Aloi, Elizabeth Barrette, Penny Billington,
Stephanie Rose Bird, Deborah Blake, Blake Octavian Blair,
Emily Carlin, Deborah Castellano, Alexandra Chauran,
Dallas Jennifer Cobb, Kerri Connor, Sally Cragin,
Monica Crosson, Autumn Damiana, Raven Digitalis,
Denise Dumars, Ash Wennsday Everell, Michael Furie,
Shawna Galvin, Magenta Griffith, Justine Holubets,
Hannah E. Johnston, James Kambos, Najah Lightfoot,
Lupa, Melanie Marquis, Estha K. V. McNevin,
Susan Pesznecker, Suzanne Ress, Cassius Sparrow,
Melissa Tipton, Charlynn Walls, Tess Whitehurst,
Charlie Rainbow Wolf, and Natalie Zaman*

Llewellyn's 2017
Magical Almanac

ISBN 978-0-7387-3762-1. Copyright © 2016 by Llewellyn. All rights reserved. Printed in the United States. Llewellyn is a registered trademark of Llewellyn Worldwide Ltd.

Editor/Designer: Ed Day and Lauryn Heineman

Cover Illustration: © Tammy Shane

Calendar Pages Design: Michael Fallon

Calendar Pages Illustrations: © Fiona King

Interior Illustrations: © Elisabeth Alba: 23, 26, 87, 89, 93, 215, 217, 279, 282, 285; © Meraylah Allwood: pages 66, 69, 71, 114, 118, 234, 237, 240, 276; © Carol Coogan: pages 35, 37, 40, 121, 123, 251, 254, 303, 306; © Chris Down: pages 17, 20, 79, 81, 84, 220, 223, 225; © Kathleen Edwards: pages 30, 33, 95, 98, 206, 209, 212, 288, 290, 293; © Dan Goodfellow: pages 44, 48, 51, 130, 133, 137, 268, 271; © Wen Hsu: pages 15, 53, 56, 77, 125, 127, 205, 273, 309, 311, 315; © Mickie Mueller: pages 61, 64, 101, 104, 227, 231, 295, 297, 300; © Eugene Smith: pages 108, 110, 112, 243, 245, 248, 319, 322, 325; © Amber Zoellner: pages 73, 75, 257, 261, 265, 328, 331

Clip Art Illustrations: Dover Publications

Special thanks to Amber Wolfe for the use of daily color and incense correspondences. For more detailed information, please see *Personal Alchemy* by Amber Wolfe.

You can order Llewellyn annuals and books from *New Worlds*, Llewellyn's catalog. To request a free copy of the catalog, call 1-877-NEW-WRLD toll-free or visit www.llewellyn.com.

Astrological data compiled and programmed by Rique Pottenger. Based on the earlier work of Neil F. Michelsen.

Llewellyn Worldwide Ltd.
2143 Wooddale Drive
Woodbury, MN 55125

About the Authors

PEG ALOI is a freelance writer and media studies scholar. She has written on diverse subjects ranging from color symbolism in film to aromatherapy to women's sexual health. She is also an accomplished singer of traditional music and an award-winning poet. Her blog *The Witching Hour* (at Patheos) explores popular media related to Witchcraft, Paganism, and the occult.

ELIZABETH BARRETTE has been involved with the Pagan community for more than twenty-six years. She served as managing editor of *PanGaia* for eight years and dean of studies at the Grey School of Wizardry for four years. She has written columns on beginning and intermediate Pagan practice, culture, and leadership. Her book *Composing Magic* explains how to combine writing and spirituality. She enjoys magical crafts, historic religions, and gardening for wildlife. Visit her blog, *The Wordsmith's Forge* (www.ysabetwordsmith.livejournal.com), or website, *PenUltimate Productions* (www.penultimateproductions.weebly.com). Her coven site is Greenhaven Tradition (www.greenhaventradition.weebly.com).

PENNY BILLINGTON is a Druid author, speaker, and ceremony and workshop leader who has had a significant role in the Order of Bards, Ovates, and Druids for many years and has edited their magazine *Touchstone* for fifteen. Her published work includes *The Path of Druidry*, a best-selling practical Druid study course and guide, and *The Wisdom of Birch, Oak, and Yew* (both Llewellyn). This year she has written on Druidry, ancestral connections, and meditative practice. Visit her at www.pennybillington.co.uk.

STEPHANIE ROSE BIRD is an Eclectic Pagan practicing Hoodoo, Green Witchcraft, and shamanism. Deeply into meditation and

yoga, she is a creative visionary. She has written five books: *The Big Book of Soul*; *A Healing Grove*; *Light, Bright, and Damned Near White: Biracial and Triracial Culture in America*; *Sticks, Stones, Roots & Bones*; and *Four Seasons of Mojo*. Her debut novel is *No Barren Life*.

DEBORAH BLAKE is the author of the Baba Yaga paranormal romance series (which includes *Wickedly Magical, Wickedly Dangerous, Wickedly Wonderful,* and *Wickedly Powerful*), as well as nine books on modern Witchcraft from Llewellyn. She has an ongoing column in *Witches & Pagans Magazine* and was featured in *The Pagan Anthology of Short Fiction*. When not writing, she is the manager and cofounder of the Artisans' Guild, a not-for-profit artists' cooperative shop where she also sells her jewelry. She can be found at www.deborahblakeauthor.com.

BLAKE OCTAVIAN BLAIR is an Eclectic Pagan, ordained minister, shamanic practitioner, writer, Usui Reiki Master-Teacher, tarot reader, and musical artist. He blends various mystical traditions from both the East and West with a reverence for the natural world into his own brand of modern Paganism and magick. Blake holds a degree in English and religion from the University of Florida. Blake lives in the New England region of the United States with his beloved husband. Visit him on the web at www.blakeoctavianblair.com or write to him at blake@blakeoctavianblair.com.

EMILY CARLIN is an Eclectic Witch, teacher, mediator, and ritual presenter based in Seattle, WA. She specializes in shadow magick, defensive magick, and pop culture magick. She teaches one-on-one online and in-person at events on the West Coast. For more information, go to http://about.me/ecarlin.

DEBORAH CASTELLANO writes for many of Llewellyn's annuals and writes a blog on *PaganSquare* about unsolicated opinions on glamour, the Muse, and the occult. Her shop, the Mermaid and the Crow, specializes in handmade goods. She resides in New Jersey

with her husband, Jow, and two cats. She has a terrible reality television habit she can't shake and likes St. Germain liqueur, record players, and typewriters. Visit her at www.deborahmcastellano.com.

ALEXANDRA CHAURAN is a second-generation fortuneteller, a third-degree elder high priestess of British Traditional Wicca, and the queen of a coven. As a professional psychic intuitive for over a decade, she serves thousands of clients in the Seattle area and globally through her website. She is certified in tarot and has been interviewed on National Public Radio and other major media outlets. Alexandra is currently pursuing a doctoral degree, lives in Issaquah, WA, and can be found online at www.SeePsychic.com.

DALLAS JENNIFER COBB practices gratitude magic, giving thanks for personal happiness, health, and prosperity; meaningful, flexible and rewarding work; and a deliciously joyful life. She is accomplishing her deepest desires. She lives in paradise with her daughter in a waterfront village in rural Ontario, where she regularly swims and runs, chanting, "Thank you, thank you, thank you." Contact her at jennifer.cobb@live.com or visit www.magicalliving.ca.

KERRI CONNOR is the author of *The Pocket Spell Creator, The Pocket Guide to Rituals, The Pocket Idiot's Guide to Potions, Goodbye Grandmother,* and *Spells for Tough Times.* High priestess of the Gathering Grove, she has been published in several magazines and is a frequent contributor to Llewellyn's almanacs. A graduate from the University of Wisconsin, Kerri holds a BA in communications and lives with her family, cats, and chickens in rural Illinois. Visit her website, www.kerriconnor.com.

SALLY CRAGIN is the author of *The Astrological Elements* and *Astrology on the Cusp,* which have been translated and sold overseas in a half-dozen countries. She serves on the Fitchburg School Committee (MA), teaches in the adult education program at Fitchburg State University, and is available to speak about readings, astrological or

tarot. Visit "Sally Cragin astrology" on Facebook or e-mail her at sally@moonsigns.net.

MONICA CROSSON is a Master Gardener who lives in the beautiful Pacific Northwest, happily digging in the dirt and tending her raspberries with her husband, three kids, three goats, one dog, three cats, many chickens, and Rosetta the donkey. She has been a practicing Witch for over twenty years and is a member of Blue Moon Coven. Monica writes fiction for young adults and is the author of *Summer Sage*. Visit her website at www.monicacrosson .com.

AUTUMN DAMIANA is an author, artist, crafter, and amateur photographer. She is a Solitary Eclectic Cottage Witch who has been following her Pagan path for almost two decades and is a regular contributor to Llewellyn's annuals. Along with writing and making art, Autumn is currently finishing up her degree in early childhood education. She lives with her husband and doggy familiar in the beautiful San Francisco Bay Area. Visit her online at www.autumn damiana.com.

RAVEN DIGITALIS is the author of *Shadow Magick Compendium, Planetary Spells & Rituals,* and *Goth Craft* (all Llewellyn). He is a Neopagan priest and cofounder of an Eastern Hellenistic nonprofit community temple called Opus Aima Obscuræ. Also trained in Georgian Witchcraft and Buddhist philosophy, Raven has been an earth-based practitioner since 1999, a priest since 2003, a Freemason since 2012, and an empath all his life. He holds a degree in anthropology and is also a professional tarot reader, DJ, small-scale farmer, and animal rights advocate. Visit www.ravendigitalis. com, www.myspace.com/oakraven, and www.facebook.com/raven digitalisauthor.

DENISE DUMARS is a college English professor and writer. She is cofounder of the Iseum & Lyceum of Isis Paedusis, a study and

worship group chartered by the Fellowship of Isis. Her botanica, Reverend Dee's Apothecary (www.DyanaAset.com) is the only Southern California source for all-natural essential oil and New Orleans–style magickal and spiritual oils and products. Find information on her writing and speaking engagements at www .DeniseDumars.com.

ASH WENNSDAY EVERELL is a Green Witch, writer, and illustrator who loves gardening almost as much as collecting punk vinyl records. They live in Los Angeles with their partner and an unruly kitten named Artemis and run the Witching blog *Theory of Magick* (http://theoryofmagick.tumblr.com).

MICHAEL FURIE (Northern California) is the author of *Spellcasting for Beginners, Supermarket Magic,* and *Spellcasting: Beyond the Basics* (all Llewellyn) and has been a practicing Witch for over twenty years. An American Witch, he practices in the Irish tradition and is a priest of the Cailleach. Find him online at www.michaelfurie.com.

SHAWNA GALVIN lives in Maine with her husband and son. Her novel, *The Ghost in You,* was released in 2013, and a collection of poetry and essays, *Mimi's Alchemy: A Grandmother's Magic,* was released in February 2014. Shawna's writing has appeared in a variety of publications, and she has edited short stories for *Brutal as Hell.* She works as a writer, publisher, editor, and part-time professor of writing and literature as she continues on a spooky publishing journey at Macabre Maine. She holds an MFA in creative writing. Visit www.shawnagalvin.com.

MAGENTA GRIFFITH has been a Witch since the 1970s, and a high priestess for more than twenty-five years. She is a founding member of Prodea, which has been celebrating rituals since 1980, and a founding member of the Northern Dawn Council of Covenant of the Goddess. Magenta, along with her coven brother Steven Posch, is the author of *The Prodea Cookbook.* She presents classes

and workshops at a variety of events around the Midwest. She shares her home with a small black cat and a large collection of books.

JUSTINE HOLUBETS, a Solitary Wiccan practicing ancient Egyptian sacred traditions, lives in Ukraine (Lviv) and is a tarot and lunar rhythms/astrology consultant for Zodiaclivetarot.com in the UK. A published author focused on philosophical, social, and gender issues, she also prepares courses to help women maintain healthy, dignified intercultural relationships. She also explores sacred architecture and symbols, Greco-Roman mythology and psychological archetypes, and chakra and energy healing. Visit http://www.zodiaclivetarotreading.com/tarot-reader?id=129.

HANNAH E. JOHNSTON is a Witch, mother, and musician. She has researched and written about young people and Pagan Witchcraft for over a decade and is the author of *Children of the Green: Raising Our Kids in Pagan Traditions*. For more information, visit her website at www.hejohnston.com.

JAMES KAMBOS is a writer and an artist from Ohio. He has written many articles about folk magic and enjoys sharing his thoughts about magic and mysticism with Llewellyn readers.

NAJAH LIGHTFOOT is a priestess of the Goddess. She is a Witchvox sponsor, a Lucky Mojo Certified Practitioner, and an active member of the Denver Pagan community. Najah is dedicated to keeping the Old Ways while living in these modern times. She enjoys movies, good food, and practicing the art of Shaolin Kung Fu. She can be found online at www.craftandconjure.com, www.facebook.com/priestessnajah, and www.twitter.com/priestess_najah.

LUPA is an author, artist, nature nerd, and wannabe polymath in Portland, OR. She is the author of several books on totemism and nature spirituality, including *Nature Spirituality From the Ground Up:*

Connect with Totems in Your Ecosystem (Llewellyn, 2016), and is the creator of the Tarot of Bones. Her primary website is http://www.thegreenwolf.com.

MELANIE MARQUIS is the author of *A Witch's World of Magick* and *The Witch's Bag of Tricks*. She's the founder of United Witches global coven and a local coordinator for the Pagan Pride Project in Denver, CO, where she currently resides. She is also a tarot reader, folk artist, freelance editor, and literary agent. Connect with her online at www.melaniemarquis.com or www.facebook.com/melaniemarquisauthor.

ESTHA K. V. MCNEVIN (Missoula, Montana) is a priestess and ceremonial oracle of Opus Aima Obscuræ. She has served the Pagan community since 2003 as an Eastern Hellenistic officiate, lecturer, freelance author, artist, and poet. Estha studies and teaches courses on ancient and modern Pagan history, multicultural metaphysical theory, ritual technique, international cuisine, organic gardening, herbal craft, alchemy, and occult symbolism. In addition to hosting public rituals for the sabbats, she organizes annual philanthropic fundraisers, Full Moon spellcrafting ceremonies, and women's divination rituals for each Dark Moon. To learn more, please explore www.facebook.com/opusaimaobscurae.

SUSAN PESZNECKER is a writer, college English teacher, nurse, practicing herbalist, and hearth Pagan/Druid living in northwestern Oregon. Sue holds a master's degree in professional writing and is cofounder of the Druid Grove of Two Coasts and the online Ars Viarum Magicarum, a magical conservatory and community (www.magicalconservatory.com). Sue has authored *Yule: Rituals, Recipes, & Lore for the Winter Solstice*, *The Magickal Retreat*, and *Crafting Magick with Pen and Ink* (all Llewellyn). Visit her on her website (www

.susanpesznecker.com) and Facebook author page (www.facebook
.com/SusanMoonwriterPesznecker).

SUZANNE RESS has been writing for many years. She published her
first novel, *The Trial of Goody Gilbert,* in 2012 and has since completed two more. She is an accomplished self-taught gardener,
beekeeper, silversmith, and mosaic artist. She lives in the woods
at the foot of the Alps with her husband, daughter, four horses,
three dogs, four hens, millions of bees, and an ever-changing
assortment of wild creatures.

CASSIUS SPARROW is a Hellenic polytheist and Witch, tarot reader,
author, and garden enthusiast. He is a devotee of both Hermes and
Dionysos and has been a practicing polytheist for over ten years.
He currently lives on the Gulf Coast of Florida with his darling
wife. In his free time, he can be found writing, baking, or working
in his herb garden. Contact him at cassiussparrow@gmail.com.

MELISSA TIPTON is a Reiki practitioner and professional tarot
reader who loves helping people discover their soul path through
energy work and tarot. She writes extensively about happy living
through yoga and Witchcraft on her website, www.yogiwitch.com.
When she's not on her yoga mat or hiking Missouri trails with her
husband, she's in her studio sculpting fake food for her dollhouse
miniatures business, the Mouse Market.

CHARLYNN WALLS resides with her family in Central Missouri. She
holds a BA in anthropology with an emphasis in archaeology. She is
acting CEO of Correllian Education Ministry, which oversees Witch
School. She is an active member of the St. Louis Pagan Community
and is a part of a local area coven. Charlynn teaches by presenting at various local festivals on a variety of topics. She continues to
pursue her writing through articles for *Witches & Pagans Magazine,*
Llewellyn's Magical Almanac, Witches' Companion, and *Witches' Spell-A-
Day Almanac,* and on her blog, *Sage Offerings (www.sageoffereings.net).*

TESS WHITEHURST is an award-winning author, feng shui consultant, and intuitive counselor. In addition to creating the Magic of Flowers Oracle, she's written six books that have been translated into nine languages, and her articles have appeared such places as *Writer's Digest, Whole Life Times,* and *Law of Attraction* magazine. She's appeared on morning news shows on both Fox and NBC, and her feng shui work was featured on the Bravo television show *Flipping Out.* Tess lives in Boulder, CO, with her longtime boyfriend, Ted Bruner, and their magical black cat, Solo.

CHARLIE RAINBOW WOLF is happiest when she's creating something, especially if it can be made from items that others have cast aside. She is passionate about writing and deeply intrigued by astrology, tarot, runes, and other divination oracles. Charlie is an advocate of organic gardening and cooking and lives in the Midwest with her husband and her special needs Great Danes. Visit her at www.charlierainbow.com.

NATALIE ZAMAN is a regular contributor to various Llewellyn annual publications. She is the coauthor of the Graven Images Oracle deck (Galde Press) and writes the recurring feature *Wandering Witch* for *Witches & Pagans Magazine.* Her work has also appeared in *FATE, Sage Woman* and *newWitch* magazines. Find Natalie online at www.nataliezaman.blogspot.com or at www.broomstix.blogspot .com, a blog aimed toward Pagan families.

Table of Contents

Earth Magic

The Magic and Mystery of the Forest

by Penny Billington

Mysterious, whispering, thrillingly alive—trees stir our hearts. As a Druid, I go to the forest for my magic. But as an urban Druid, the forest is often represented by my local park: if we become sensitized, just pausing under a large tree allows us to tune in to the magic of root and branch and the slow growth of the seasons.

Our species's relationship with trees goes back millennia: trees have had a significant place in every major religion as symbols of immortality, fertility, and nurture. They are examples of service to humanity, supplying fuel, shelter, and food. With their longer lives, they speak of an underlying stability and continuity of life that we need in these frenetic times. Also, they are miraculously beautiful. They have witnessed our own and our ancestors' pasts and can be regarded as our spiritual elders. And just being in their presence, with the Sun diluted through their ambient greenness, is to conjure a feeling of verdant nature leading to a magical otherworldness that feeds our souls.

We may find the aura of ancient trees challenging or scary. Yet what draws us on our spiritual journey but the need to connect to the mysterious? And how can we expand beyond the five senses into superconsciousness without that frisson of intense awareness and strangeness that we feel in the atmosphere of the forest?

When we become familiar with the trees, we will recognize this sensation as anticipation. It is part of being at home in nature, which is the aim of all students of the nature religions; it is part of being open to magic. And, taken gently and slowly, accessing the magic of the trees

can be an ongoing process that benefits our practice immeasurably.

Stage one is in acknowledging our connection—try thinking of the trees as wise family members. We are human people; they are tree people. We will have to find a way of speaking together that transcends language, but we can communicate. With this in mind, we must first slow down to become more in tune with our leisurely cousins.

When we are making a new human friend, we tend to mirror the person—and this is exactly what we do when communicating across species. The trees are slow and still, so we will be also. And this gives us ample time to engage with the world of the five senses to experience the life of nature around us in a deeper way.

Most people rely on sight too much, so when you go to meet your local trees, focus on the other senses to view the world afresh. Feel the atmosphere of a tree-place through the breeze on your skin; the smell of damp, moist greenness in your nostrils; and the rustling of leaves and song of the birds in your ears. Then use your slowed-down sense of sight to gaze deep into the patterned bark. Imagine the serpentine roots thrusting through the soil. Now you are slowing and opening to the atmosphere of the forest.

Sit on your park bench and just take your time. Say hello and state your name and purpose: ask silently to be known. Then wait and check the response. A good way of gauging this is asking yourself how you feel in the moment. If you're not comfortable and in the right place, just say thank you and move on to another tree, another space. Relax into an awareness of the beauty and usefulness of your particular friend, the miracle of its slow growth, and rich canopy, and thank it for the way it shelters you. Slowing and expressing gratitude by our attention and thought is one gift we can give, from a fleeting moment of thanks to a poem or drawing. In a reciprocal exchange, you can ask for any gifts the tree is ready to give you, then remain open and allow time for intuitive impressions.

You might be suffused with peace and calm or realize that your blood correlates to the sap of the tree, or, in the tree's aura, you might experience a timelessness that colors the rest of the day. There are no rules. These are lessons that go deeper than the logical mind and feed you at a profound level. You might feel a spirit of the tree—a dryad—representing its green life and acting as a bridge to communication. If so, you don't need to justify or explain anything to yourself or to others. You just have to accept the reality of the imaginal realms and take the magical connection at that level: just go with it. As with all communication, it should feel comfortable and mutually beneficial, and if it doesn't, then you terminate that chat. But if you are communicating well, then, as with making a friend in the human world, stay in contact. It need not take long: nod to your tree in passing; take a walk by it;

notice it through the changing seasons, recognizing its winter silhouette as well as the glory of its summer foliage.

On our less frequent, long forest walks, we will meet many charismatic cousins—the ancient trees of our lands. That is the enriching and deepening experience into the forest ambience that is an intensive for our spirituality, suffusing our senses in the heady aura of deep, ancient life. But we are nourished daily by our contact with the next-door neighbors: the trees in our yards and parks. Take a leaf or nut home and repay the tree with an impromptu verse or praise for its fruitfulness. We are not anthropomorphizing the tree by doing this, just realizing that we can only respond in the way we have learned as humans. And our sincerity of intent, to make a relationship, is what matters: it more than makes up for any mistakes or clumsiness in approach.

The beauty of this incremental approach to magical relationship is that it is accessible: we don't have to go on big, expensive trips, and all but the most physically impaired can reach one, with the help of family and friends. And if getting out at all is a problem, then there are still resources (nature programs, art for our walls, CDs of the sounds of nature), and others can bring trees into the home as presents, like the first catkins or budding twigs in a vase, scented pine cones, a walking stick made from found wood, or a bonsai tree.

The Forest and Magical Practice

How does becoming in tune with the forest relate to genuine magic? Well, making a connection is the bedrock of magical working. Spells are not just the words on the page, the timings of astrological signs, or sigils focusing our intent, though these can be important components. But without the belief in our *relational* nature—our capacity to connect to the larger forces of the universe, to

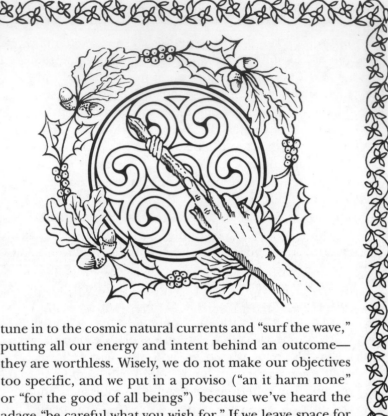

tune in to the cosmic natural currents and "surf the wave," putting all our energy and intent behind an outcome—they are worthless. Wisely, we do not make our objectives too specific, and we put in a proviso ("an it harm none" or "for the good of all beings") because we've heard the adage "be careful what you wish for." If we leave space for the magic, the universe will understand our *core intent.* For example, our limited mind might think we want a specific situation, job, or person, but underneath, those wishes are fueled by our needs for respect, security, or love, which might be met in a myriad of ways. Relax into the *feeling* of the quality you aspire to before doing any magic.

The trees are ideal helpers when we formulate our spells because their unhurried, wise influence helps us relax into an expanded mindset and a wider perspective. They connect deeply to gain nourishment directly from the elements, which supply our power. Their roots thrust deep into the earth; they breathe the clarity of the air, drink the water, and gain nourishment straight from the fiery Sun. They are repositories of green power—and they all have their own qualities. For strength for your spell, incorporate the oak, holly, and ash. For the long view of eternity, use a wand of yew. Try the dancing birch, rowan, and willow for grace and flexibility; hazel for wisdom; or bramble or vine for tenacity. For the secrets of faery, use blackthorn, hawthorn, or cut into an apple. Using the trees in this way begins to synthesize our magical and everyday worlds, for the trees exist on every plane and are always relevant helpers.

~

Within our imaginal realms, we might visualize a dwelling around the huge trunk of an ancient tree, and imbibe its strength during meditations. Or, drifting to sleep, we may travel the astral seas in a boat of stout oak planks. We can float, cushioned in the feather-lightness of a birch bark canoe, safely to the shores of morning. And, back in the everyday world of work, we take our lunch break on a bench. By our favorite tree, we practice simply being. And then we repay nature when the park is threatened by development, for all relationships should be reciprocal.

In a way that is too deep for the surface, logical mind to understand, the trees have connected us to the beating heart of the earth, and we have been refreshed by the sounds of nature that we crave. Returning to work, we stroke the acorn in our desk drawer and thank the spirit of the tree it came from. We smile to the forest giant outside the window before turning back to our desks, invigorated by green magic.

From Care to Karma: Inspiring Our Kids to Care for Mother Earth

by Hannah E. Johnston

Pagans consider the world to be a beautiful, complex, animate entity. We try to spend as much time as possible attuning to her, giving and receiving energy, and attempting to restore the balance that mankind has skewed. As the human population surpasses seven billion, we strain the resources of beautiful Gaia. Despite her inexhaustible resilience, teaching our children about our reliance on Mother Earth is fundamental to our survival. By seeing all of nature's creations as an intricate part of the whole and that together this great buzzing mass of the world is sacred, we have a responsibility to do our part to ensure its healing and its continuation.

Before taking care of the world, we must first learn how to care of ourselves. Our basic job as parents and as educators is to keep our kids alive until they can care for themselves. As such, when we do everything for them, we do them a disservice because we interfere with their capacity to self-care. Today so much is done for our kids that simple tasks can become a battleground—but taking the rubbish out, tidying the bedroom, and laying a table are important life skills to learn. Unless we value our kids and remain consistent in our approach, they will not see these basic tasks as a sign of self-care. To learn, children must be motivated and be allowed to approach a skill by their own volition and see how the task or skill fulfills a greater purpose. It is hard to teach a kid to clean when you hire a cleaner. When we ask children to undertake self-care and household work, we can reward them, acknowledging their meaningful contribution to family life.

Putting Ideas into Action

Rewarding positive behavior is great in theory, but it is always a bit more difficult when it comes down to brass tacks. Here are some pointers to get you and your family buzzing with care for themselves, for Mother Earth, and for all who dwell within her.

Our first step is to make it fun! Eco-guilt doesn't work, especially with kids. Neither, necessarily, does turning recycling or conservation into an art project. At best, choose ways of being that are easily integrated into daily life. However you want to approach caring for the earth, make it part of life's pattern of joy. "Conserve, conserve, conserve!" I heard this sung as a chant to an improvised ditty by a mum at playgroup as she taught her two-year-old to turn off the water after washing her hands. Simple yet so effective. Use this when switching off lights, turning off water, or saving food for the rabbit. Whatever it is, if you sing this mnemonic, you will quickly find your kids doing it. (Well, as long as they are under seven. If they are older than that, they will think you have finally gone crazy!) Pagans are so good at creating little snippets of doggerel rhyme. Make a few in your family that accompany little tasks that bring our wee ones' attention to conserving energy.

Reduce, Reuse, Recycle: Respect

These three R's are a literal interpretation of the means to tread gently. Reduce our consumption; reduce the unnecessary waste of energy. Reuse: can you use that old T-shirt as a duster? Can your rubbish become precious in another's hands? In the natural world, everything has multiple functions and goes through stages so that even in death it brings nourishment, shelter, or use to another life form. Consider whether your rubbish can be transformed into something new. And if it cannot be reused, then recycle. We need to ensure that our kids know where waste goes by educating ourselves about our local waste networks or visiting a waste center. We should inform our kids that there are whole cities built on our waste because our waste gets sent to developing countries. When we weigh the energy costs of recycling commercially, it doesn't always give us the warm feeling we hoped it would. If you show children the results of such waste disposal, unencumbered by the lackadaisical attitudes we adults have developed, they will cut to the heart of the matter, and, before you know it, will have organized their school and their friends to campaign for local recycling.

However, there are some simple ways to recycle. First, donate clothes, toys, and household objects. Compost everything—get worms! If worms aren't your thing (though they are for so many Pagans since they are truly nature's magic makers) co-opt other animal allies. Consider keeping scrap-eating animals—chickens, goats, and, of course, rabbits. Rabbits are wonderful when properly kept as pets and are allies in recycling. They eat a lot of your scraps, are good for cuddling, and require less space than a goat!

Be conscious of packaging. Try to buy goods that have little packaging or compostable packaging. It's worth those extra pennies. Importantly, cook only what you need, and encourage kids to finish their food. Part of this for our family has been to bless every meal. By blessing meals, we help kids connect to and show respect for what they eat, which leads to being less inclined to waste it. In our home, we bless the food by acknowledging the communities that have brought it to our table; the elements of earth, air, fire, and water; and, most specifically, the animals, farmers, factory workers, packers, supermarket, and delivery people:

> *Blessings upon all who bring this food to our table* (allow your kids to extemporise here), *and blessings upon Mother Earth, who nourishes our bodies and souls with her gracious bounty.*

Trust me, whether the blessing is long or short, younger and older kids waste less when they acknowledge what has gone into bringing a meal before them. (Boo, my little one, likes to thank the people who made the cutlery!)

Respect, a crucial Pagan ethic, becomes a natural extension of these approaches. These actions demonstrate our respect for the earth, for ourselves, for each other, and for the planet.

All things are connected. Teaching and modeling conservation—whether this is helping a four-year-old turn off a running tap whilst brushing his teeth, or allowing your teenager to hang out at the local park as long as she has an old plastic bag to clear some litter as she loiters—demonstrates the connection between our relationship with the world and our relationships with each other. It also builds self-respect. To conserve something means to keep, to protect, to work *with*. Conserving is dynamic. Conservation means working to protect something that is valued. Conservation is the perfect model of care, as it fosters an approach based on guardianship. Encourage your kids to be modern-day knights, healers, and witches. All these roles were created to help conserve the well-being of a place.

K Is for Karma

The three R's are building blocks to understanding karma, or the law of eternal return. By karma, I refer to the ancient

belief that as all things are connected through their relationship here on Earth, we meet all things with respect and consideration. In doing so, we hope that such respect will be reflected back to us and the balance of the world maintained. Many people misinterpret karma as a "tit for tat" understanding of the world, as if to say, "If I do something bad, something bad will happen to me." Boo, my youngest at age five, saw the world entirely in these terms: "If Julian hits me, then I hit him back." Essentially, what we attempt to foster in place of such clumsy justice is the law of consequences, which suggests that for every action there is a reaction. We have the capacity to choose that action and thus accept the consequences for ourselves and others. If we successfully do this, then we have established an ethical and moral framework for our children to test.

Karma is a map enabling us to see the consequences of our actions before they bear fruit. As such, karma is a means of understanding the future, as powerful and insightful as any tarot reading or crystal ball. For many Pagans, with our love of threes (and our backdoor adoration of old occultists!) when we discuss karma we refer to the law of threefold return—whatever you do comes back to you threefold. As adults, we understand that this is a safety measure to ensure that we fully consider both our magical and mundane actions. This is not to quash our ability to make decisions but to help us maintain an awareness of the world's interconnectedness and perhaps to help us think about how our own actions may ripple beyond our immediate sphere.

I often think about this law when I think about our old family car, Silver Fin. I love beautiful things (I am a Taurean after all), but I also have a compulsion to give my belongings to people when they need them. I mentally catalogue our belongings, and when we get to what I consider overload, I give them away. I enjoy the feeling of lightness it brings me and the frisson it creates between my husband and I as he tries to guess what I will get rid of next!

With two growing boys, we gave their outgrown clothes to friends whose son was a wee bit smaller than ours. One of the most wonderful models of the threefold return came when we finally realized we needed a car and these same friends gifted their old car to us. A strong friendship and all those months of ensuring their son had our boys' outgrown clothes were recognized in one extraordinary act of kindness and generosity. Such a model of threefold return may not always be your reality, but to show our kids that what you do comes back to you is an excellent way of inspiring them. Thus, recycling, conservation, and respecting take on deeper levels of meaning. Recycling becomes a spiritual act, conservation a duty of care, and an attitude of respect a modus operandi for relating to people, places, and all beings. And, as we cultivate these qualities, the Goddess smiles upon us.

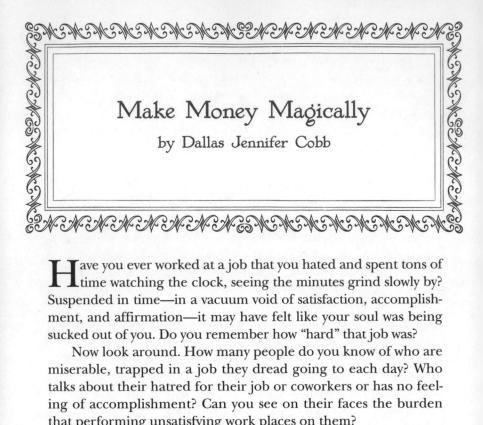

Make Money Magically
by Dallas Jennifer Cobb

Have you ever worked at a job that you hated and spent tons of time watching the clock, seeing the minutes grind slowly by? Suspended in time—in a vacuum void of satisfaction, accomplishment, and affirmation—it may have felt like your soul was being sucked out of you. Do you remember how "hard" that job was?

Now look around. How many people do you know of who are miserable, trapped in a job they dread going to each day? Who talks about their hatred for their job or coworkers or has no feeling of accomplishment? Can you see on their faces the burden that performing unsatisfying work places on them?

Statistics show that many people in our society spend the majority of their waking hours doing something they hate and spend their best years in drudgery, working toward the elusive freedom of retirement. A 2013 Gallup Poll surveyed 150,000 working Americans and discovered that only 30 percent actively enjoyed their job or boss, 52 percent described themselves as "disengaged," and 18 percent were "actively disengaged" and openly expressed their discontent. The statistics suggest that a combined total of 70 percent of working Americans don't like their jobs.

There are many reasons cited for dissatisfaction: workplace harassment, abuse, unsafe working conditions, poor pay, little opportunity for advancement, and a lack of growth, learning, or positive engagement. And surely there are many more.

For a moment, imagine what all that hating, drudgery, clock watching, and dread is doing to the physical, mental, emotional, spiritual, and social health of all those people. Now consider the havoc that it wreaks on their relationships with family and friends. And what are the spin-off effects—how is work dissatisfaction impacting our larger society?

New World Economy

With a failing economy, the disappearance of manufacturing jobs, and the rise of Internet-based enterprises, the ability to make money magically will help you to stay flexible and financially manageable through the coming tough times.

I see these as the important factors: shaping your work around your life, creating multiple sources of income, getting paid to do what you would be doing anyway (and might be paying for right now), making money from the tools or things you already own, and learning how to maximize your income by writing off all appropriate expenses. If you can write off some of your "hard" costs of living (like food, clothing, shelter, and transportation), then you will actually save more of your hard-earned money.

Make Magic

We all need to make money to pay our bills and provide for ourselves and our loved ones, but does work really have to be so hard? What if it were possible to live and enjoy life while working at things we love to do? What if work was something enjoyable, engaging, and rewarding? What if we could seek pleasure, and make money magically?

If the old quote from Dion Fortune is true, then "magic is the art of changing consciousness at will." Popularized by Starhawk, who added that sometimes it is called "the art of evoking power-from-within," magic is our ability to change our own consciousness at will by engaging our personal power of choice and then acting upon that.

Think about using magic to change your relationship to work. Imagine the real and lasting changes it could bring to you, your health, and your life. And pause and think about the ripple effect it could bring to your relationships and all arenas of life and society.

We can transform money making from work to pleasure.

Endings and Beginnings

I used to overwork. I had a job that I liked and made good money. But it was all that I did. Work dominated my life. I worked long hours, banked lots of money, and did little else. I was single, alone, childless, and lonely. I came home each evening after work and prepared so I could return to work the next day. Work consumed all of my vital energy.

Sometimes great beginnings come disguised as dramatic endings. It can be forced job loss through firing, downsizing, or company closure; it can be ill health or an injury that renders us unable to perform the job; it can even be emotional or mental health that demands we make a change.

For me, the change came in the form of a car accident in which I sustained a brain injury. My memory was affected, my energy level was grossly diminished, and my filtering mechanisms and emotional control were totally skewed.

I was a mess. I could no longer work in the way I had previously, but I wasn't fully disabled and did not qualify for disability benefits. I still had to work to provide for myself, but I had to learn how to work differently.

Just to keep myself on an even keel, I had to place my well-being ahead of everything else. When it came to work, I needed to shape money-making opportunities around my personal health needs by working far fewer hours in quiet and calm environments. I needed work that supported all parts of me and was shaped around sustaining my health.

At first it looked like a tragedy, but now, many years later, I can look back and see that having a serious injury was the best thing that ever happened in my life. As recovery from injuries takes a long time and happens slowly over months and years, the recovery of my money-making ability also took years, and it happened slowly, one layer at a time.

Shape Work Around Your Life

I realized I needed to change how I worked and to learn to "put myself at the center" so that my basic needs were the primary consideration. With a brain injury, I needed to be able to sleep and rest at regular intervals; eat nutritious, regular meals that nourished me; and create quiet, low-stimulation environments at the center of my work life. I wasn't capable of eight-hour days or five-day weeks. I couldn't cope with noise, interruptions, or high demands.

I initially looked for a part-time job. Short shifts, occasionally. I had little stamina or long-term attention. I saw an ad for a job that entailed two three-and-a-half-hour shifts a week and would be done alone. It wasn't taxing emotionally, psychologically, or mentally. I applied for and got the job and discovered that it was relatively stress-free and that it allowed me tons of self-control at work. Twice a week, I drive a delivery route for the local library system. I move boxes of books from branch to branch between six rural library branches.

Ten years later, I still enjoy the quiet, contemplative practice of driving. I have happy, friendly interactions with library staff as I drop books off to them, and I stay fit, lifting and loading boxes of books. In addition to the hourly wage, I get a mileage amount, plus I'm paid in positive social interaction, physical fitness, and the peace that comes from quiet contemplation. And I am paid well.

We get hung up on the idea of a career and forget that there are lots of satisfying, low-stress, part-time jobs out there. We can find them if we transform our way of thinking about work and how we work. Look around in your community and see if there is something that might be a building block toward sustainability and the first step toward making money magically.

Get Paid to Do What You Love

Once I had been doing the job for a while, I read an article in the *Llewellyn's Herbal Almanac* and heard myself thinking, "I could have written that." I queried the editor and by luck was invited to submit some ideas for an article (as they had just had one author cancel and had an open spot). I had heard that you should "write about what you know," and with a small baby at home, I knew about making herbal remedies for the baby. I pitched the article and sold it before I even wrote it.

I love to write, and selling this first article opened up the possibility of getting paid to do what I love to do and what I was doing anyway. Now, years later, about one-fifth of my income comes from a wide variety of freelance writing. Not only am I paid to do what I love, but I can write off all kinds of costs associated with writing: books, paper, and pens; computer, printer, and Internet; office space, a portion of my household utilities and expenses, and even travel expenses, when they are related to an article that I can sell. I also have the payment of publication, author's copies, reader recognition and e-mails, and the joy of getting my name out there in the world.

Create Multiple Streams of Income

I wondered if other aspects of my life could turn into earning opportunities. Because I spent time daily doing the physiotherapy my healing body required, I wondered if I could somehow get paid to work out.

I undertook training that resulted in certification, and now I teach regular classes in the physical modalities that best benefit me: Pilates and functional fitness. The investment of time and money provided the know-how and certification. I qualified for professional insurance and now make about one-third of my income from teaching exercise classes.

Not only do I save all that money I'd been spending to take Pilates classes, now I am paid forty to fifty dollars per class to teach. I also benefit from increased fitness, positive social interaction,

and the satisfaction of helping build a caring social community. I write off the cost of my fitness equipment and workout wear; the cost of insurance, advertising, and accounting; and the registration fees to attend conferences and trainings.

Maybe you don't write or do physical workouts, but perhaps you have hobbies that you love that you can turn into streams of income—generating pottery or paintings to sell, repairing furniture or cars, or growing flowers or vegetables.

And remember, when you do what you love, it's not just money that you get paid. Look for all the other ways you benefit from your jobs and self-employment. There is so much more than mere dollars.

Earn with What You Already Own

Happy with my part-time job and my exercise classes, I realized from taking write-offs for both of these endeavors that I wanted to find more ways to write off my "hard" costs—the expenses I was going to incur in daily life anyway. The cost of carrying my home wasn't going away, so I wondered how I could further deduct property and utility costs as expenses come tax time.

My house required minor renovations to separate an apartment from the main house, but with the investment of money (which I was later able to write off against income) I now rent it. The tenant helps with house and yard maintenance in exchange for a moderately reduced rent, so I also benefit from the increased sense of community and collaboration. I have rental income on a monthly basis, and take write-offs against the hard expenses of owning a home. Based on the footage of the apartment, I write off 20 percent of my property and utility expenses against the rental income I earn.

With the rise of the digital economy, many people have started to rent rooms within their homes through AirBnB, and use their personal vehicles as taxis through Uber. With some safety and security systems built in for screening prospective clients, these websites can help you earn from what you already own, a self-sustaining practice.

Making Money Magically

These days, my life is blessed. My body and brain continue to recover, and my entire life is shaped around my deep need to care for myself. By engaging my power of choice and consciously changing my relationship with work, I used my power-from-within to enrich my life.

I work part-time, seven hours a week. I hold an elected office as a school board trustee, and I teach five exercise classes a week, both Pilates and seniors' functional fitness. I do a variety of freelance writing, model for local art classes, and earn rental income. I have seven different income streams from diversified sources, and enjoy a good economy of both time and money. I am able to determine what my work schedule will look like and have shaped it to support my fundamental human needs. I have lots of breaks between work activities, never work more than a few hours each day, and enjoy a lot of control over my work environments. I have learned to shape my money-making activities around my life.

Since that terrible accident, I've moved to the country, bought a house in a magical waterfront village, had a child, planted gardens, and begun to do what I love in many ways. I love my work. I'm rich with relationships, recreation, creativity, self-expression, joy, satisfaction, and health—all factors that were missing previously. And all of these things are made possible because I have learned how to make money magically.

Relax and Rejuvenate with Himalayan Salt

by Kerri Connor

Himalayan salt is not the same as your ordinary table salt. For starters, it's pink. It's also a far healthier alternative and comes with many great benefits. Himalayan salt contains eighty-four trace minerals that may benefit the human body and treat conditions such as asthma, eczema, psoriasis, acne, allergies, sinusitis, and bronchitis and other respiratory illnesses, all while boosting the immune system. Himalayan salt has also been used for anti-inflammatory and antibacterial purposes. It is believed it may even help prevent the common cold and the flu. Studies have shown that the inhalation of Himalayan salt particles has even helped patients suffering from cystic fibrosis. On the emotional and mental side of things, Himalayan salt produces negative ions, which combat positive ions and can help reduce stress and fatigue, leaving the user feeling relaxed and refreshed

In some parts of the world, people have benefitted from salt cave therapy for centuries. In 1843, Polish doctor Felix Boczkowski noted that the miners at the salt mines in Wieliczka had excellent health and didn't suffer from respiratory problems. Today the Wieliczka mine combines salt therapy with conventional medicine and is the largest underground treatment and rehabilitation center in the world.

Dr. Karl Herman Spannage noticed an improvement in his patients' health after they hid in the Kluterthöhle karst cave in Germany to evade bombing. Those who had respiratory issues showed significant improvement. For decades, "salt therapy" took place underground in the actual salt mines and caves. This type of therapy is called speleotherapy.

It wasn't until the late 1980s that a room was built for the purpose of salt therapy. This first man-made "salt cave" opened in Russia in 1987. Therapy in these above-ground, man-made caves (also known as halochambers) is called halotherapy.

These man-made caves are generally set up in a similar fashion. A large room is modeled to look like the inside of a cave. Some may put in fake stalagmites and stalactites, or perhaps a ceiling made to look like you are gazing up into a night time sky complete with stars (fiber-optic lighting). Half of the cave wall is generally Himalayan salt blocks, and then another material is used to create the cave the rest of the way up. Some of the blocks may have lighting behind them. This lighting serves two purposes. The first of course is to provide light that helps create a stress-free, peaceful environment. The second is to warm the salt to help produce negative ions. The cave is generally equipped with zero gravity chairs, blankets, additional salt lamps, and possibly headphones. Music lulls clients into a relaxed, meditative state.

One of the most important elements of the cave is the floor. The floor is covered in salt, generally a fine to medium-course grind, and is several inches deep. Many businesses require the removal of shoes and give you clean, white cotton socks to wear while in the cave room. This helps keep the salt floor clean, and as people walk through the salt, they kick the salt particles into the air. Pathogens such as bacteria and allergens are killed off by the salt, keeping it a clean environment. The salt molecules are made of a positive sodium ion and a negative chloride ion. When you breathe in the salt air, the molecules break down in the lungs and release the negative ions. These ions help clear up airways and clear mucus. People with a sodium chloride deficiency in their airway are able to correct it with this type of therapy. The salty air also works on the outside of the body to help clear up even chronic skin conditions.

While the popularity of salt caves is growing, they are still few and far between and generally only exist in large cities, making it difficult for people to try out this type of therapy.

Large salt caves are also expensive to build, considering they require literally tons of salt, design, construction, and upkeep. For ultimate benefits, man-made salts caves need to be climate controlled. Spas add to the experience by creating a relaxing atmosphere, with lights and sound systems as well. All these components add considerably to the cost of building a large-scale, multiperson salt cave, which can easily cost several hundred thousand dollars by the final price tag. Because the cost to build is so high, sessions are also generally expensive as well. Sessions usually last forty-five to sixty minutes and range in price from twenty to fifty dollars, depending on location.

Himalayan Salt Therapy at Home

There are some less expensive, alternative ways to bring Himalayan salt and its benefits into your life.

If you have the money and space is not a limiting factor, you can always build your own smaller-sized, personal cave. This is obviously not an option for everyone and could easily total in the thousands of dollars, depending on how elaborate you go. However, if you have the funds and space, it could pay for itself with use by yourself, family, and friends.

A recent option on the market is found in the infrared sauna business. Some companies are now including blocks of Himalayan salt with their sauna kits. These kits run from about $1,250 to $3,500, depending on the size of the sauna. While this will provide some of the benefits derived from salt caves, it doesn't give you the opportunity to kick up salt particles into the air to inhale, unless you add your own to the sauna floor.

Both of these alternatives, however, still require funds in the thousands and the dedicated space for a full-time salt cave or sauna. You can create a similar atmosphere right in your own bathtub for a fraction of the cost, though it will require setup and takedown time to use. You can start with the very basics and add to your collection as funds allow.

For starters you will need to find a bulk supplier of Himalayan salt. There are many online, and prices vary greatly. For this purpose you do not need food-grade salt. You will want a medium- to heavy-course grind. If you can only afford to buy ten pounds in bulk, start with that and add to it later on. If you can purchase twenty-five to fifty pounds, that would be ideal. Be sure to look for a company that offers free shipping. You will need five-gallon buckets with tight-fitting lids. (You may be able to get free ones from your local bakery—frosting comes in them.) This is where you will store your salt when it is not in use.

You will also want a queen-size sheet or comforter. (Do not use a knit blanket.) A comforter will hold its shape and stand up better than a sheet. Use this to line the bathtub after thoroughly drying the tub with a towel. If your tub is not enclosed, you can let the lining hang over the side to keep it from collapsing and falling in. If your tub and shower are combined, make sure your shower curtain is hanging the outside the tub so you be able to sit on the side of the tub with the curtain behind you. Standing inside the tub with clean white cotton socks on, close the shower curtain (or door) all the way and slowly start pouring the salt all over the bottom of the comforter or sheet lining the tub. As you pour, salt particles will float up into the air, and the shower curtain will help keep them confined to your area. Pour the salt slowly and evenly. After it's poured in, take a seat on the side of the tub, or use a pillow to sit on top of the salt, and relax. You can add music, actual salt lamps, and even a salt inhaler, if you feel you need more or to create a more relaxing environment.

Spend an hour or so relaxing. You can spend as much time as you want, but since the preparation and cleanup are time consuming, make sure you have enough time to make it worth the effort. When you are done, scoop the salt back into the bucket and store it in a cool, dry area. Be sure to wash your comforter or sheet, and, if you can, store it in a plastic bag for later use. If possible, have one dedicated just to this use.

If this is too much for you as well, you can start with simple salt lamps. These also vary greatly in price, from five dollars for tealight holders to more than a hundred for heavy-duty lamps. There are many different styles available, from natural-looking rocks to specially cut designs, such as pyramids, cubes, spheres, yin and yang symbols, and even flowers. Bowls cut from the salt and filled with salt chunks or wire baskets filled with salt chunks are also options. I have found many great ones with free shipping through eBay. If ordering online, take the time to find ones that come with free shipping, as the salt is often several pounds and shipping costs can add up quickly. It's ideal to keep a lamp or two in your bedroom and another one in rooms with electronics such as computers or TVs. These electronics give off a lot of positive ions, and the salt lamps help neutralize these with their own negative ions. If possible, keep computers, tablets, cell phones, and TVs out of your bedroom. Leave this room as a haven to relax, rest, and restore. While salt lamps give off negative ions, they don't offer the benefits that come with inhalation of the actual salt particles. You can get these benefits by using a salt inhaler. The Himalayan salt crystals fit into filters on the inhalation device. As you inhale, moisture from the air absorbs the salt particles, and then they enter your respiratory system.

Alterative Home Options

There are other ways you can add Himalayan salt to your life. If you have a hot tub, you can convert from a chlorine or bromine system to a saltwater system instead. Using salt is all-natural with no harsh chemicals. All it requires is salt, baking soda, white vinegar, and a special saltwater chlorinator. Instructions and measurements are provided with the devices.

You can add Himalayan salt to your bathwater as well. When ground finely, it will dissolve quickly and soften the water, leaving skin smooth, soft, and refreshed. Pink Himalayan salt soap and deodorant are also available to fill your hygienic needs. In the kitchen, of course, you can replace plain table salt with Himalayan salt, and you will be able to taste the difference with this alternative.

Finally, you can make a Himalayan salt sole to use each day as a natural way to detox, boost immunity, balance hormones, improve thyroid function, and more. To make a salt sole, use a glass jar with a plastic lid (an old mayonnaise jar is ideal). Fill the jar about one-fourth of the way with salt and top off with filtered water. Shake the jar. If all of the salt dissolves, add more. You want to fully saturate the water with salt. Once you have leftover salt at the bottom, it is ready. To use, each morning take one teaspoon of sole in a glass of room temperature water. Make sure to never use metal with the sole for long periods of time because it can oxidize.

Himalayan salt is a pure, natural resource that can help improve both physical and emotional health. It is truly a gift from Mother Earth.

Luminous Labyrinths

by Natalie Zaman

It's comforting not having to think about where you're going. The path is before you; you only need to trust it and follow. After the first turn or so, you might even be able to navigate it with your eyes closed. You can focus on a goal you want to accomplish or a person you wish to remember, or you can allow your mind to wander where it will. You have entered the labyrinth.

Walking the Magical Path

The concept of the labyrinth—as a pattern if not an actual pathway—is at least 4,000 years old. Labyrinths have been painted on pottery, carved on tombs, and minted into coins. They figure into a variety of cultures and spiritual practices: in India and ancient Rome, labyrinths were used as models of walled cities and therefore as protective symbols. Greek mythology saw the labyrinth as a means to trap the Minotaur. Labyrinths are ritual pathways; many Christian traditions see them as symbols of the soul's journey through life. Labyrinths were the sites of games and celebrations, the pathways used as racecourses or processional routes. Built of stone, tiles, or turf, they are elements of formal gardens, sometimes with trees planted at their centers. Unlike mazes, which are filled with dead ends and tricks, labyrinths are composed of a single path to a central goal, twisting and turning, but always steady and true.

There are permanent labyrinths with complex patterns to be found the world over, but you can create temporary versions wherever you are, indoors or out, with these few, easily obtainable supplies: chalk, masking tape, and strings of decorative lights. With a few additional materials, your meditative walk can become a ritual to ground, cleanse, and even create an altar. I've suggested specific spaces and materials for each of the following labyrinth rituals, but all are interchangeable and can be adapted according to your needs.

Will you walk the path?

Creating Movable Magical Paths

The spiral is a pattern found throughout nature in nautilus shells, spiders' webs, flower petals, and, perhaps most magnificently, the swirl of stars and planets in a galaxy. Spinning outwards, a spiral conveys a sense of expansion and growth, while circling inwards focuses on details. Both directions whirl into infinity; spirals are eternal.

Dancing with the Stars Labyrinth and Ritual

This ritual is a reminder that we are all divine creatures made of the same molecules and, contrary to whatever misconceptions may be thrown at us, important and necessary elements that light the night and day with our uniqueness. The walk inwards is a journey to the center of the universe, to be among the stars and rekindle this knowledge—and then come back to the world refreshed. This ritual can be performed during the day or night, but a more magical experience can be achieved in darkness.

Trace

For this labyrinth and ritual you'll need the following:

Access to a large space like a patio, driveway, playground area, an unused area of a parking lot, or any floor made of a material that you can draw on with chalk

Blue and white chalk

Tealights (battery operated are safest, especially if children will be participating)

Glitter in different colors representing the elements and five small bowls to hold it: copper for earth, white for air, gold for fire, blue for water, and silver for spirit

Glitter adds to the galaxy aesthetic of this pathway, but herbs can be substituted for glitter if you prefer. Use your favorite reference to select plants that correspond with each element.

Starting in the center of your ritual area, draw a large spiral. It is important to keep the space between the lines wide (at least two feet) to accommodate your walkers. Take your time, and use a ruler or yardstick to keep the pathway even. Make the spiral as large as your space will accommodate without cutting off any of the circuits. At the entrance to the spiral and working inward, write the following phrase based on a quote by astronomer Carl Sagan:

"We are all made of star stuff."

Next, place the bowls of glitter in the center of the spiral. Place the tea lights at random points on the lines of the spiral. Use as many tea lights as you want. The number can be symbolic: one for each person who will be walking; one for the number of years, months, etc., your group has been together; or any number that holds significance for you.

Track

Walk the spiral with a guided visualization. If you're doing this ritual as a group, send each walker into the spiral one at a time and have your participants take turns reading this for each other:

The air around you becomes darker and colder. You are walking in space. The lights above and below you grow brighter and sharper until all that is before you is blackness, save for the stars above and all around and the illuminated path at your feet. Slowly, carefully, look down. See the words that trace the path. These words are written in the stars and written on your heart. As you walk, you read, and as you read, you hear:

"We are all made of star stuff."

This is your mantra. Say it aloud or to yourself as you move towards the center. Feel the warmth of the words, the heat inside you, growing and glowing. See the light within yourself. See it ripple and shimmer outwards. Look at the stars around you. You love them, and they love you. They are a part of you, and you are a part of them. Know that you have come home.

When you reach the center, look down into its glittering core, the beautiful colors sparkling in the dark, reflected by the lights. Know that this is the star stuff that's in all of us.

Take a fingerful of the copper glitter in your right hand, place it in your left palm, and think or say aloud, "I am earth."

Take a fingerful of the white glitter in your right hand, place it in your left palm, and think or say aloud, "I am air."

Take a fingerful of the gold glitter in your right hand, place it in your left palm, and think or say aloud, "I am fire."

Take a fingerful of the blue glitter in your right hand, place it in your left palm, and think or say aloud, "I am water."

Take a fingerful of the silver glitter in your right hand, place it in your left palm, and think or say aloud, "I am the spirit that resides in all things."

Close your eyes for three breaths before you return to the world. As you walk back, sprinkle the glitter on the path, leaving a trail of light behind you. Remember, light is eternal, and that which you release will return to you infinitely.

Once you have completed the circuit, stand at the edge of the spiral and chant, *"We are all made of star stuff,"* over and over. Raise your voice with each repetition while at the same time raising your arms over your head to release the energy and send out love and acceptance for all beings. If you're doing the ritual as a group, form a circle around the labyrinth and join hands. Chant as a group and raise a cone of power to release the energy.

If possible, leave the labyrinth intact to be absorbed back into nature through wind and rain.

May Day Meander Labyrinth and Ritual

Not all labyrinths are symmetrical. The Snoopy Labyrinth at the Charles M. Schultz Museum in Santa Rosa, California, traces the shape of everyone's favorite beagle, but the Snoopy path's goal does not have a central end. Its overall shape and site are particularly special: according to creator Dr. Lea Goode-Harris, "Walking the Snoopy Labyrinth, your body aligns with the natural energy of the land." Among the places to stop and contemplate on the path is Snoopy's eye bench. Sit here and your gaze is focused on the direction of the summer solstice sunrise.

Meandering labyrinths planted with objects and experiences for reflection—music to listen to, objects to hold, words to read, or pictures and scents to trigger memories—are appropriate elements for life passage rituals, like initiation, handfasting, preparing for birth or death, grieving, healing, and entering adolescence. They can also be used as a means of celebrating birthdays, sabbats, and Moon cycles. Use this May Day meander as part of your Beltane celebrations or as inspiration to carve out your own unique path.

Trace

For this labyrinth and ritual you'll need the following:

Access to a large, grassy outdoor space like park, field, back garden, or the common area lawn of an apartment, condominium, or townhome complex (This ritual ends with a Maypole dance, which can also be done inside depending on your space and number of participants. Being indoors gives you the opportunity to have the path "meander" in and out of various rooms that can be decorated for ritual use.)

Several lengths of decorative light strings—how many will depend on the size of your space (Strings with many lights close together in a tube will work best for this ritual. If you don't have access to electricity, make sure you have battery-operated lights.)

Wire coat hangers cut into 6-inch pieces and bent into U-shaped pins (These will be tapped into the ground to hold the light tubes in place.)

Hammer

Pole or piece of wood at least 9 feet in length

Pots of marigolds, one for each participant (Healing and protective flowers are associated with Beltane.)

Masking tape

Red and white ribbons that are 2 to 3 times the length of your pole, one for each participant (The traditional Maypole is tied with red and white ribbons: red for the God and white for the Goddess. The red ribbons also symbolize energy, and the white symbolize purity. Dancers make a circle and spiral around the Maypole, weaving these energies together.)

Black permanent markers

Appropriate music for a Maypole dance and a means to play it

There are only two rules to follow when making the May Day meander: the path cannot cross over itself, and you need to leave a large enough area at the end to accommodate your Maypole and all of your walkers. Unlike the spiral where participants walked in the pathway between the chalk lines, walkers on the May Day path will follow the line of the light. Connect your strings of lights together and lay them out. Work with your landscape: allow the light to curve around rocks, trees, and structures. (Warn your walkers about changes in the terrain if there are any.) Use the hammer and coat hanger pins to secure the light tubes in place.

Next, prepare the marigolds and ribbons. Place a piece of masking tape around each marigold pot. Write a line from the song you've chosen for the Maypole dance on the masking tape with the marker, and then write the same message on one of the ribbons. (Alternatively, you can make up your own collection of affirmations to write on the pots and ribbons.) Make one set for each participant; each should have its own unique song line or affirmation. Place each ribbon and flower set at random points along the route.

Set up your Maypole in the center of the area at the end of the path. A Christmas tree stand can serve as a Maypole stand, but it should be weighed down with bricks or stones so

that it remains stable during the dance. As an extra precaution, a brave volunteer can be assigned the task of holding it steady during the dance—but give him fair warning that he might get a bit tangled up!

Track

Start the music and put it on a loop before sending your walkers into the labyrinth. As each walker enters, instruct her to silently ask the Goddess for a Beltane Blessing as she walks the path and to take one ribbon and flower set; tell her to take the set that calls to her. Stagger your walkers slightly so that they don't run into each other.

When participants reach the center, have them place their marigolds at the base of the Maypole, then have them read the song lines on the ribbons before tying them to the top of the Maypole. Tie the ribbons so that there is as much length as possible with which to dance.

If possible, alternate your dancers by gender and have them hold alternating color ribbons: female dancers hold white, and male dancers hold red. When the music starts, the female dancers will move clockwise around the Maypole. Clockwise is an invoking direction, and Beltane is the celebration of the beginning of the Goddess season. Male dancers will move counterclockwise, the direction used for closing. As the dancers move, they should also alternate passing their ribbons over and under each other—if done correctly, the ribbons will weave around the Maypole. (Good luck with that!)

At the end of the dance, have participants tie off their ribbon and take their marigold; the song line or affirmation is their blessing for the Goddess Season.

Tabletop Altar Labyrinth and Ritual

In Jim Henson's *Labyrinth*, the Goblin King (portrayed exquisitely by David Bowie) sends a young girl, Sarah, on a quest, seemingly to find her baby brother but really to discover her own strength. In the beginning of the film we get a view of Sarah's room which is filled with figures of mythical toys, books, and, as a bit of foreshadowing, a tabletop labyrinth. More like a maze, the object of the game—to navigate a steel ball around little wooden walls (while avoiding pitfalls) and hopefully reach the end—is mirrored in the labyrinth Sarah must traverse in the course of the story.

Labyrinths need not be walkable or complex to be effective meditation tools. Create a tabletop labyrinth that will turn, through ritual, into an altar to support your inner strength. This ritual can be done as a solitary or group activity, but unlike a walkable labyrinth, you won't need a lot of space to create it.

Trace

To create a tabletop labyrinth altar you'll need the following:

A table of any size (just be sure it's a table you can spare!)

Chalk and/or masking tape

A deck of tarot cards or some other oracle that speaks to you and a reference for interpretation, if you wish to use it

A collection of small crystals and a reference for meanings, if you wish to use it (The crystals should be in a pouch or box so they can be selected without participants looking at them.)

Brief mantras or affirmations that inspire you written on small pieces of paper (If you're doing a group ritual, make sure there is at least one for each participant.)

Place markers such as board game or chess pieces for everyone who will "walk" the labyrinth

Before you begin, clean your table of any debris or dust and smudge the space by lighting your favorite incense and carefully fanning the smoke over the table. Picture it sweeping away any cloudy energy. The size of your labyrinth will depend on the size of your table. Sketch it out in chalk before you draw it or lay it out in tape for ritual use.

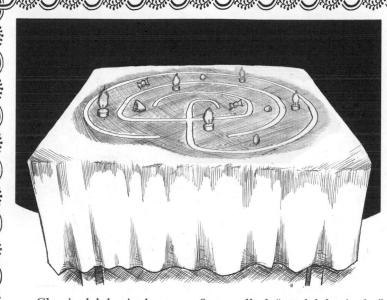

Classical labyrinths are often called "seed labyrinths" because you start with a "seed" design to guide you through laying out the pattern. In the center of the table, make the seed for the labyrinth. Draw a square, then place a dot at each corner. Next, make an equilateral cross in the center of the square so that four small squares are formed. Finally, erase the lines of the first square so that all you're left with is the cross and the four dots.

Make a series of arcs by drawing clockwise around the seed design. As you draw each subsequent arc, try to make the pathways between the lines as even as possible.

Connect the top of the vertical arm of the cross with the upper right dot. Draw over the top of the first arc by connecting the upper left dot to the right horizontal arm. Connect the left arm to the lower right dot. Finally, connect the lower left dot to the bottom of the vertical arm.

Once you have the labyrinth sketched out in chalk, you can darken the lines or use the sketch as a guide to lay out the labyrinth with masking tape. (Keep in mind that this will give you an angular, rather than rounded labyrinth.)

Track

Take a moment to ground and center before focusing on an issue for which you need help. You can also ask for general guidance for any upcoming challenges. Take the place marker that represents you and move it through the first circuit of the labyrinth. When you come to the first turning, stop and ask, *"What do I need to keep in mind as I walk this path?"*

Select a tarot card and take note of its meaning, then put it in the center of the labyrinth. When you're ready, move your marker over the second circuit. When you get to the second turning, stop and ask, *"What support do I need as I walk this path?"*

Close your eyes and select a stone from the pouch or box. Take note of the stone's meaning, then place it in the center on top of the tarot card. When you're ready, move your marker over the third and final circuit. When you reach the center, ask, *"What thought do I need to keep in mind during this journey?"* Select one of the affirmations and keep it with you so that you can refer to it when you need to draw strength.

Continue to grow the altar, placing tea lights, small stones, shells, pieces of candy, or other offerings on the path in gratitude as guidance is received. Leave the assemblage intact until your issue is resolved or for as long as you need.

Labyrinths in the Wild

There are labyrinths to be found all over the world—some may be closer than you think! Visit the Labyrinth Society's Labyrinth Locator at www.labyrinthlocator.com. Plug in your zip code to discover your neighborhood's magical pathways.

Shamanic Careers

by Lupa

So you wanna be a shaman for a living? Well, here's the deal: in the United States at least, the dominant culture doesn't have a shamanic niche. Indigenous cultures have their own sacred people (often lumped under the Siberian Evenk term *shaman*), but if you look in your average phone book you're not likely to see a heading for "Shamans, Medicine People, and Healers."

Moreover, the most common religion of the land, Christianity, isn't exactly a hotbed of overtly shamanic activity. Many adherents would be vehemently opposed to seeing a shaman on the grounds that it goes against their beliefs. Plenty of other folks would avoid seeing a shamanic practitioner because they simply don't believe that rituals and journeying will have any practical effect on their lives.

So what's a would-be shaman to do when the community you want to serve isn't automatically on board? Well, you can do what a lot of shamanic folk do and hang out your shingle as-is. You'll have to do a lot of explaining, and for the most part there's not a lot of money in it. You certainly won't be able to take anyone's insurance as payment. And you'll likely always have a pretty limited clientele.

For some people, that's perfectly acceptable. But what if you want to be able to help a broader spectrum of people in your community? Look at the specific role that shamanism plays in other cultures; then look at your own culture and see what vocations have similar roles. Here are some of the ways shamans interact with their communities:

Shamans act as intermediaries. They may bridge the spiritual and physical worlds or bridge humans and non-human nature. They can also mediate between their community and a neighboring community, though they may also take leadership roles in times of war. Shamans are generally pretty comfortable in the in-between places.

Shamans are often healers of the body, mind, and/or spirit. They may use herbs and other medicines, use sacred rites and charms, and even travel to the spirit world on behalf of their clients. This is probably the best-known shamanic role, but it is far from the only one: most shamans do not limit themselves to being only healers.[1]

Shamans may be the keepers of community lore and traditional practices. This most often presents as oral tradition, though sacred artwork and other records are common throughout indigenous communities worldwide, and in the twenty-first century, computer-based technology is a perfectly acceptable tool for furthering this knowledge base. Shamans also apply this lore in everyday life, such as for rites of passage.

Every community has its scapegoats, and even as important as a shaman may be to the people, in some cultures **shamans are outcasts**, living on the fringes and carrying the sins of everyone

---

1. To be very clear, shamanism and other such practices are not meant to be replacements for professional medical care, and this essay should not be seen as an excuse to stop going to your doctor, therapist, or other health care provider.

else. Their Otherness can also serve as a mediating force, questioning the community when it becomes too dogmatic in adhering to particular standards.

Matching Skills to Modern-Day Roles

You may have to get a little creative in your interpretations of the aforementioned roles, but if your goal is to serve as many people and as diverse a clientele as possible, here are some potential careers to look into:

Counselor: A counselor is someone who helps people mediate between themselves and their psychological health. Almost 20 percent of the American population has some form of mental illness in their lifetime, and unfortunately it often goes undertreated or even untreated. Yet even mentally healthy people sometimes have periods of great distress in which outside help may be sought, such as after the death of a loved one or after experiencing a traumatic accident. As a counselor, you can help people negotiate the sometimes perilous pathways of the mind. You're not "fixing" them; rather, you are their guide through their own emotions and thoughts. You also have recourse to a wide range of tools to help; depending on your training and credentials you can draw on everything from behavior-based therapies to rites of passage to (in certain circumstances) medications in order to help relieve symptoms.

Doctor/Nurse/Other Medical Professional: Western medicine often gets a bad rap in spiritual communities, yet most spiritual people will still go to the emergency room if their appendix bursts. As a medical professional, you have access to the vast body of knowledge and technology built up over decades of research and development. However, you also have the training to discern whether a given treatment will be good for your patient or not. The best doctors are those who treat their patients as though they are the experts on their own body's idiosyncracies; you partner with the patients to get them the most suitable treatment. Even if you can't go to medical school, just getting basic first aid training can help you be of greater service to your community in this capacity.

Clergy: When experiencing difficult times, many people turn to the clergy of their faith to find solace and answers. This

isn't limited to the big monotheist religions, either. Most spiritual paths have some sort of priest or other specialists who are particularly knowledgeable in lore and how to best care for their people. As a trained clergy person, you're able to leverage the hope and healing of your faith to support those in need and help them carry on until they're able to stand on their own again. And you're also able to enact sacred rites in your path; these may be crucial to the health of your community as a whole as well as the individuals who are a part of it. Some Pagan clergy particularly resonate with the role of shaman, though those of other faiths may also find it inspirational.

Artist/Writer/Musician: Faerie lore speaks of human musicians and other creatives being taken away into the fey realms and sometimes returning years later, much richer in talent and spiritual growth. There is something transformative about arts in general, both for the artist and the audience. As a creative, you're able to tap into emotions through expression, and if all goes well you can evoke a particular response. Sometimes this may be rallying the community around a given cause. Other times you can offer people a respite from their daily stresses by presenting a creation of great beauty. And all the while you may feel as though you are tapping into an alternate reality through your imagination—in some cases that may be exactly what's happening! Your creations don't have to be overtly shamanic in nature to be effective, though; any medium will work so long as it effectively conveys your intent.

Scientist: Science is another one of those things often shunned unfairly by spiritual people. Sure, physics may emphasize that you can't actually physically turn into another species of animal no matter how many rituals you perform. But particle physicists are discovering some of the most amazing realities in the tiniest bits of stuff in the universe, while astrophysicists are the closest to figuring out how the universe began in the first place. Whether your chosen vocation is chemistry, biology, botany, or any of a number of other sciences, you're able to travel into worlds most people only scratch the surface of and bring back great knowledge for the good of all. You may even explore uncharted territory and make new discoveries! That sounds pretty shamanic to me.

Comedian: The jester and the sacred fool are just two of the characters who have spent their lives questioning the communities they live in. Far from being useless and lazy bums, they serve a critical role by bringing up criticisms of the people, forces, and behaviors in power in a society, often using humor to make their point more digestible. There are very good reasons we want to know that the emperor has no clothes—he's only human, so his edicts can be questioned by the people, even the most humble jester. And even if the humor isn't pointedly political, the comedian offers a valuable gift to the people: laughter. In a world where we may feel overwhelmed by negative news and stress, a few moments of joy can mean everything.

~

These are just some of the roles in modern society that can serve similar functions to shamanism. With enough imagination, you may be able to combine your desire to serve as a shaman with just about any vocation you take on.

It is very important that if you're going into a more specialized path, such as being a doctor or counselor, that you get the proper training and credentials. Just because you practice shamanism doesn't mean you get to practice medicine without a license. Even herbs, for example, can be harmful if the wrong amount is taken or if an herb conflicts with another medication the client is taking. So make sure you research a potential career very carefully before embarking, and if a certain amount of training is required to use a particular title, don't call yourself that until you've gotten the proper credentials.

When you're in school or undergoing other training, don't make everything about shamanism, either. Immerse yourself in this world of learning, whether strictly academic or not. Don't let your agenda be the primary goal. If you're in art school, allow yourself to explore all the media that are presented to you, and play with a variety of themes in your work, not just spiritual ones. In fact, it's best to challenge yourself and break out of your comfort zone. That flexibility and breadth of experience will make you an even more effective shamanic practitioner, as you'll have more resources, internally and externally, to draw upon when helping your clients.

Finally, don't feel that you're stuck if you can't get into your chosen career. I always wanted to be a veterinarian, but my math skills are abysmal, which means there was no way I would make it through veterinary school. But I played to my strengths in the humanities and was still able to write about my spiritual work with animals. This also helped me expand my horizons beyond the critters and into the beauty of nature in general. There are always options, even if you just end up educating yourself through books and other resources.

Whatever path you choose, I wish you the best of luck!

Ten Essential Herbs

by Deborah Blake

Some tools and practices of the modern Witch are fairly new developments, like using different colored candles for the quarters or calling on deities from regions other than our own. Then there are the tools and practices that have come down to us through the centuries, utilized by virtually every culture in virtually every age, like the use of herbs in magical work.

The Egyptians used frankincense and myrrh, mistletoe and meadowsweet were said to be sacred to the Druids, and there are many references to herbs and plants in ancient Greek and Roman mythology. In Africa, magic and medicine were often entwined, and herbs played a part there as well.

Of course, this makes sense when you think about what herbs are; essentially, they are just plants, often growing wild in the areas where they were used or readily available from the garden. They are, in fact, one of the most powerful tools in the Witch's toolbox, as long as you choose them carefully. In this article, I'll share with you ten of my favorites, as well as some suggestions for easy ways to use them.

What Is an Herb?

What do we mean when we talk about herbs as a part of magical work? As always, it depends on whom you ask. Many folks, like Scott Cunningham, whose books are used as a reference source by many, include any and all plants. For instance, in his books *Magical Herbalism: The Secret Craft of the Wise* and *Cunningham's Encyclopedia of Magical Herbs,* Cunningham talks about everything from almonds (a nut) to yew (a tree).

Generally, herbs are plants used for seasoning or medicinal reasons, but for the purposes of Witchcraft, a more general and inclusive approach is usually accepted. If it is a plant, you can consider that it falls under the herbal umbrella.

Why Use Them? Why These Ten?

All growing things contain a certain energy. By using herbs in our magical work, we can tap into that energy and use it to boost or direct our intentions. Different energies are usually associated with specific plants, and you want to choose an herb that will work well with the spell or ritual you have in mind. For instance, certain herbs, like rose or lavender, are considered to be beneficial for love magic, while others, like rosemary and basil, are more likely to be used for protection magic. By becoming more familiar with the various herbs available to you, you will be better able to select the plant or plants that will best help you achieve your goals.

Some books on Witchcraft contain lists of many exotic and esoteric herbs, most of which are expensive and difficult to find. Mandrake, for instance, is a rare plant that has long been tied to magical work, in part because the root of the plant looks much like the body of a man and therefore lends itself well to sympathetic magic. But over my many years of practice, I have come to believe that common, inexpensive herbs do the job just as well. In fact, the majority of the herbs I use in my daily practice can be found in many people's kitchens or pantries or even growing on the windowsill. In fact, you will see that most of my favorites can serve double or even triple duty as culinary, medicinal, or cosmetic ingredients.

If you think about it, this is probably how most Witches in days past worked their magic—not hidden in dark woods around bonfires but bubbling in the pot on the stove, sprinkled on the floor by the entrance to the house, or mixed into a bath. There is, after all, nothing wrong with integrating your magic into everyday life, and if you can buy an herb that will serve multiple purposes, all the better.

Where Do We Get Them?

One of the most common questions I get is this: Where is the best place to get herbs for use in magic?

In a perfect world, the answer to that would be, "In your

own backyard." I grow many of my own herbs in my garden, and even if you don't have space for a garden (or a green thumb), most herbs are pretty sturdy and can be grown in a small pot on a windowsill or under a single grow light. But not everyone has the space or the inclination to grow their own plants, so luckily there are plenty of other options.

You can, if you are fortunate enough to have one near you, purchase your herbs at a Pagan or New Age shop. The advantage to this is that the folks who sell such things will probably have them labeled for magical use and will be able to save you a little research. You can also find these shops online. My favorite is one called AzureGreen. Such places often sell herbs in the form of essential oils or tinctures as well.

But in truth, I get most of my dried herbs from the local health food store. They have bulk bins filled with reasonably fresh herbs at a much cheaper price than you would find at the grocery store. In fact, I don't recommend grocery stores for dried herbs at all—they are often irradiated and over-priced. However, if you are looking for a fresh bunch of basil or dill, that's probably your best bet unless there is a farmers' market or organic farmer nearby.

Once you've brought your herbs home, you will have to decide whether you want to store them exclusively with your magical tools or simply in a kitchen cabinet. Personally, I tend to keep my herbs with my magical supplies; if I use them as part of cooking, then they are in the kitchen.

How Do We Use Them?

One of the qualities that makes herbs so intrinsic to a magical practice is their flexibility. Herbs can be combined with food or made into tea (though they should never be given to someone without his or her knowledge—not only does this go against the concept of free will, but you never know what someone is allergic to).

They can be added to baths or body products, tossed into a bonfire, or burned in a bundle (how sage is often used). You can make your own candles and mix herbs into the wax or soften a premade candle and roll it in dried herbs. In the form of magical oils, by utilizing essential oils herbs can be spread on the skin, dabbed on candles, or used to consecrate magical objects.

Herbs come in many forms, although not all plants are suitable for all uses. The most common forms are fresh, dried, in essential oils, and in incenses (make sure that these use the true plant and not an artificial scent, which won't hold the power of the actual herb). All the ones I list here are safe, but never assume that just because something is an herb that it is harmless. After all, deadly nightshade is an herb too!

My Ten Essential Herbs

These are the ten herbs I try never to be without and some of the ways you can use them in your magical work. It is no coincidence that most of them also have culinary and healing properties.

Basil: Basil is good for love, prosperity, protection, and purification. It can easily be used in the kitchen by tossing it fresh into a salad or sprinkling it dried into any Italian dish.

If you like pesto, dinner may suddenly be an opportunity for prosperity magic, since nuts are great for that too. You can also find basil as an essential oil, although it isn't as common as some of the others. I like to use dried basil in my yearly protection and purification mix that I sprinkle around my house.

Chamomile: This herb is used for love, meditation, protection, purification, and sleep. Chamomile is most known for its use as a medicinal tea to aid in sleep and calming both the stomach and the mind. Not surprisingly, its magical use reflects this, but it is also historically said to be useful in removing curses. For magical work, you can either use the pretty white and yellow flowers fresh, or use the dried flowers as a tea or infuse them into body lotions or creams. This herb is also available as a tincture and oil, although they tend to be more expensive than others.

Cinnamon: Derived from the bark of a tree, cinnamon's magical uses are broad and include healing, love, passion, increasing power, protection, and success. Cinnamon can be burned as an incense during ritual or added to food if doing Kitchen Witchery. I put a little in my hot chocolate every morning as a part of my own "kitchen alchemy," for prosperity and love. If doing a ritual outside, try sprinkling a bit of cinnamon around the periphery of your circle to boost the magical work done within.

Lavender: Another multipurpose herb, lavender is well known for its association with peace and sleep but is also useful magically for love, protection, purification, and general happiness spells. As a dried herb, lavender is often put into sachets or miniature pillows and tucked under the pillow. For love magic, try combining it with rose petals. It can also be readily found in essential oils and many bath and body products. Although not usually thought of as a culinary herb, lavender is sometimes used in cookies or other desserts. Traditionally, lavender is thrown into the Midsummer bonfire as a gift to the Goddess.

Marjoram: Often used interchangeably with oregano, the

Romans and Greeks used it as a symbol of happiness. It is used magically for protection and love, and, as a common culinary herb, it is easy to add to food for some delicious Kitchen Witchery. Add the dried herb to protection sachets or sprinkle around the edges of your property.

Peppermint: Another multipurpose herb, peppermint is probably best known for its use in healing and purification magic, but it also works for prosperity, love, and getting rid of negativity. Peppermint essential oil can be added to a house-cleaning wash; it smells wonderful, replaces negativity with healing energy, and keeps away pests as a bonus! Peppermint makes an energizing tea, using either the fresh or dried herbs, and the oil can be added to bath and body products. I have a spray that I use in the shower water every morning that combines peppermint, rosemary, and grapefruit essential oils; it smells wonderful and starts my day off on the right foot. Food-grade essential oil can be added to brownies or other goodies, too. Add dried peppermint to a prosperity sachet or put a few drops of the oil on a candle for prosperity, healing, or purification work.

Rose: The rose's main association is with love, of course, but it is also used for healing, fertility, clairvoyance, and luck. Rose comes as a fresh flower, as a dried whole flower or dried petals, or as rose hips (the fruit of the plant). It can also be found as an essential oil; it tends to be expensive, but a few drops go a long way. The rose hips are good for healing work, since they contain a large amount of vitamin C. Rose water can sometimes be found in specialty food stores or health food stores, and it can be used as a wash, added to cosmetics or body creams, and used in cooking. Add some dried rose petals or rose water to a bath for love or healing magic, or sprinkle the dried petals on your altar.

Rosemary: Rosemary is a powerful herb for both protection and mental powers, although it is also used for healing, purification, and love magic. Grow a small rosemary bush outside your door to ward off danger and thieves, or add it to a protection mixture you sprinkle around your home. Add it to a salad dressing or marinade if you do Kitchen Witchery, or bake it into a loaf of bread. Use the essential oil in a wash to purify body or house.

Sage: One of the most commonly used herbs in modern Witchcraft, sage is most often found as a white sage bundle or stick, bound together and burned to cleanse and purify sacred space or anyplace that needs it. Common sage, which is easy to grow in a garden or in a pot on the windowsill, can be used in cooking. Sage is also good for healing and prosperity.

Thyme: Another common kitchen herb, thyme is used magically for purification, protection, and clairvoyance. Thyme is another plant that is easy to grow, and the dried herb can be added to protection sachets or to food.

~

Herbs are one of the simplest, easiest, least expensive, and most flexible tools available to the modern Witch. Find a few to experiment with on your altar, in the kitchen, or anywhere else around the house, and I think you'll find yourself coming up with your own list of ten favorites without any trouble at all.

Balancing Technology and Nature

by Peg Aloi

Many of us depend on personal technology to get us through our day: we constantly interact with smartphones, computers, social media, and the Internet. But how much of this is really necessary, and how much of it may be negatively affecting our natural body rhythms and magical intuition? This article will explore the issue of technology addiction and suggest ways to effectively balance these modern tools with old school methods of working and socializing, to create renewed awareness and appreciation for nature and our connection to it.

One of the most significant problems with our current pervasive engagement with digital technology is that the ease of communication and the speed of data sharing has created an expectation of instant access and thereby instant gratification. We get impatient if we are unable to reach people by phone or text, if we have a slow Internet connection that makes it hard to download our favorite music or videos, or if we have to wait too long for a reply to an e-mail. This expectation of instant gratification then extends to other areas of our lives not necessarily connected to digital media: we get antsy waiting in line at the grocery store or irritable in slow-moving traffic.

We also expect instantaneous access to information. Before the age of the Internet, we searched through printed materials and resources found in libraries. The need to search in a thoughtful way for information led us to find more specific answers and perhaps helped widen our knowledge, as we had to absorb entire chapters or books to find the answers we sought. Now the Internet allows us to find information with rapid-fire ease, but it affects our critical thought and intuition.

Witches and Pagans often pride themselves on having good intuition or being able to follow "gut" feelings. Have you ever had an unbidden thought about someone you had not thought about in months and then suddenly received a phone call or e-mail from that person? It is said that our unconscious mind can sometimes pick up on things happening around us that we're unaware of. In magical workings, we often rely on our intuition to guide us, for example, in choosing which components to add to a spell or what words to use in an invocation. Magic is a creative and mercurial process, and if we are too distracted by technology, it can be hard to let this creativity flow. Recent studies have shown that creativity is most likely to occur in the brain when we are bored. Constant low-level stimulation experienced via personal technology means our brains never have that downtime when creative and inventive thoughts can blossom.

There is also evidence that our physical and emotional well-being are negatively impacted by our increased reliance on technology. Our sleep is affected, for one thing: using digital devices or social media before bedtime is shown to cause insomnia, bad dreams, and disturbed sleep. These devices can also cause stress. Many of us unconsciously may think we have to remain available 24/7 so that we don't miss important messages, news, or events. There's even a term given to the unusual anxiety some people feel when they're disconnected from social media—"FOMO" (fear of missing out). This stress can affect our health by lowering immune response, affecting our sleep cycle, and raising blood pressure.

Another consequence of overuse of technology is decreased time spent outdoors and exposure to nature. This is especially detrimental to children, whose play is taken up with video games and other technology-related activities. Children are remarkably sensitive to activities that help stimulate them mentally, and the increased emphasis on technology in schools sometimes means less emphasis on arts and music. Try helping your children engage with nature more directly. My friend's children help create an altar for every sabbat in the Wheel of the Year. They make pictures or sculptures, collect natural objects, write lists of words or poems specific to that holiday, and place food and drink on the altar as an offering. You might even have the kids use their tablets or computers to find information on what to put on the altar, but then make sure the gathering of materials and making of the altar is a tech-free experience! Your kids will soon learn to look forward to this creative activity, and it will strengthen their connection to nature and spirituality.

Solutions

What else can we do to help address our increasing reliance on these devices and applications? First of all, we'd do well to admit that we may have an actual addiction. As scary as that may sound, it can be helpful to understand how serious overuse of technology can be, and that in turn may help us to develop strategies to address the problem. Plans for decreasing this reliance may vary widely from individual to individual. But the other matter we're concerned with is the widespread disengagement from nature, which also causes some negative effects. It is possible to address both of these issues simultaneously by going outside.

This may sound ridiculously easy, but the fact is even if some of us use our smartphones, laptops, and e-readers while

we're outdoors, we may not actually be mindful of the fact that we're outside, surrounded by air, birds, trees, squirrels, bodies of water, flowers, etc. We tend to be so distracted by our gadgets and the functions we're involved with that we fail to experience nature even when it's all around us. But we can make a conscious effort to integrate more nature into our lives even as we strive to decrease our interaction with technology. Mindful interaction with nature while we use our gadgets is as simple as choosing a sidewalk café with free Wi-Fi and sitting as near to trees or gardens as we can. We can also choose to find a safe and unobstructed place, like a park or hiking path, to walk when we talk on our phones. Hands-free devices are helpful here too.

However, the main goal is to decrease our interaction with such distractions in the first place and replace this time and energy with exposure to nature in ways that help keep us healthy and productive (because after all, we tend to use all this technology because we think it's helping our productivity on some level). In addition to increasing our physical and mental well-being, being out in nature helps foster a connection to the natural world—and if we're serious about our spiritual engagement with nature, it's important to nourish it on a frequent basis. You may be surprised to realize how much less time you spend looking at nature than you did before technology became a big part of your life. For me, that attunement with nature is a big part of my magical identity as a Witch, and I start to feel disconnected from that identity if I don't spend time in nature.

Think of spending time in nature as a part of your daily routine, like brushing your teeth or hanging up your clothes. Taking a minute here or there to look at the Full Moon, to look at constellations in the night sky, to notice the deer grazing at sunset, or to observe a tree's changing colors in autumn. All of these things can resensitize us to the world around us and intensify our awareness. Plus, nature often makes us feel refreshed and alive, and that mindset and feeling are helpful when we're working on self-transformation or healing. It's all about awareness and being able to adapt.

For example, while it may be true that using an e-reader is lighter and more convenient, it can cause a bit more eyestrain than reading a paper book and is yet another electronic device that drains our vital energy and removes us from nature. Rediscover the beauty of physical books again. Revisiting your favorite used bookstore or finding a book-swap website with participants in your area can help you reintegrate your love of reading back to a place less dependent upon technology. Many Pagans and Witches have had intense experiences of discovering information and folklore in books that become part of their magical practice, and the tactile sensation of reading an actual book (the texture and smell of the paper) is a big part of that magic.

We can always go back to our earlier ways of doing things or try to balance them with new ways if it means improved quality of life. Finding creative new activities around foodways can help reconnect you to nature and the seasons. Go to a weekly farmers' market, have a picnic, or go out for ice cream after dinner to a place within walking distance. Winter food activities include bringing thermoses of hot chocolate with you to the local ice skating rink or getting bundled up for a nice, vigorous walk to a special destination, like the family's favorite restaurant. And don't forget to make foods specific to Pagan festivals you may celebrate: bake bread at Lammas, mix up some wassail at Yuletide, or color (then eat!) eggs at Ostara. Get the family involved in these ritual food preparations; they may prove to be a great tech-free source of fun and connection for everyone.

If you have teenage children, you may have noticed that it's very difficult to get them to reduce the time they spend texting or playing video games. Implement rules such as forbidding texting at the dinner table or enforce a mandatory number of hours spent outdoors per week. Create outdoor activities to get your younger children interested in nature: hiking, leaf peeping, collecting seasonal items like fallen acorns or nuts, identifying or counting migrating birds, identifying flowers, picking apples or berries—the list is endless. They might collect items in nature that can also be used for their own personal altars or collections or for holiday decorating.

You can even ease the technology to nature transition by using technology selectively to help coordinate your outdoor activities. Encourage the kids to learn how to check the weather online in preparation for outings so that they know how to dress for the temperature and possible changes. If you're planning a drive to a nearby town or neighborhood, the kids can check out restaurants or other destinations online before you get there or assist navigation while you drive.

Give It a Try

There are many ways that technology makes our lives easier and more enjoyable, but knowing when to limit our exposure can be hard when we're constantly using our devices. As people who value the ideas behind magic and intuition, it would benefit us to use our natural abilities and leave technology behind once in a while. Try going for a walk and leaving your phone turned off, and see what pleasure comes from interacting with nature unfettered by your smartphone. Try a whole week of not interacting with technology before bed and see if your dreams get more interesting. If you notice positive effects from lessened use of technology and increased time spent outside, be sure to remark about it to your loved ones and share your experiences with friends.

Your magical cohorts will surely find this an interesting discussion too! Ask them if overuse of technology interferes with their magical work, or if consciously lessening time spent on smartphones or tablets helps with being more attuned to spiritual or magical vibrations (however those may be defined for their practice). Invite others to share your activities without necessarily telling them that part of your motivation stems from wanting to decrease your reliance upon technology. The benefits to health, well-being, and personal happiness, as well as your magical or spiritual practices, will be their own reward, and you just may find an unexpected increase in productivity as well.

Drumming Up the Sun
by Najah Lightfoot

Oh darkness, I banish thee!
Bring on the light! Let it shine, let it glow!
Remake us, rebirth us, the time has come!
Blessed is the solstice. Bring on the Sun!

Long before the first humans graced the earth, dinosaurs roamed the area west of Denver, Colorado. After the dinosaurs were no more and the Earth turned with the passing of several more million years, Native Americans claimed the foothills of Denver as their summer home. The air was sacred and the Sun rose in its glory as Nature paused to honor the golden rays of light.

In the mid-1940s, an architect charged with creating a park for the city of Denver drew inspiration from his travels to Rome. The natural setting and glorious red rocks reminded him of ancient temples he had seen on his travels. From this vision he birthed into being Red Rocks Park and Amphitheater.

Musicians came. Legendary souls of music and sound graced the stages, filling the air with their magic. The people, young and old, blissful and ecstatic, reveled in their song.

While the park held the story of concerts and nights beneath the stars, it never forgot its role as a sacred place. And neither did the Pagan community of Denver, Colorado. Every winter solstice in the dark-dark of the winter morn, gatherers, practitioners, and Sun-worshippers Pagan and non-Pagan alike, make their pilgrimage to Red Rocks Amphitheater for our sacred ceremony called "Drumming Up the Sun."

Neither snow nor freezing temperatures will keep us from our blessed appointment with the golden Sun. Our soul music of drums, dancing, and chanting calls forth that which we remember in our hearts, the sacred honoring of the return of the light. We drum with intensity and intention until the first golden ray bursts across the horizon.

It is a glorious ritual to behold. In the blue-black of morning, ravens fly overhead. Drummers huddle under blankets (and yes, we have even gone when there were several inches of snow on the ground), children laugh, and dogs run. The steady drumbeat and shaking of rattles creates a ritual and trance unlike any other.

Blessed indeed is the winter solstice. We know in the duality that is the planet Earth that cold days and dark nights will carry on for months. But the solstice gives us hope and renewal, and in this we can rejoice.

I don't know how this Denver ritual came to be, only that it is and I am grateful for it. It's a secret hidden in plain sight. There's no one group that sponsors it, and many times you can't find confirmation of the event. Your only notice may be that your group, coven, or friends are going. If you search the Internet for the event, you may find confirmation of past drummings, and occasionally you will find information to not bother the drummers, that this is a sacred event, and to please use respect when taking pictures.

As the seats of the Amphitheater face east, drummers, dancers, and chanters are exquisitely poised to welcome the Sun. I've taken my drum many times, but I prefer to use my rattles. I have a pair of red and black rattles that are sacred to me. I find their sound mixed with the sacred heartbeat of the drums to be an

ecstatic experience. Plus, using rattles allows me to dance and move in trance as we furiously await the sunlight of a new day and a new beginning.

But what if you can't make Drumming Up the Sun or live where you can't participate in a winter solstice ritual? Not to worry! There have been plenty of winters I couldn't make Drumming Up the Sun and had to improvise. Always remember it's about intention. The Goddess appreciates the simple fact that we remember!

Here are a few ways to participate in ritual for the winter solstice other than in a mass group:

Light a yellow candle. Anoint it with olive oil and sprinkle it with gold glitter. Bless it with your prayers for the returning light.
Take your own drum outside and beat it softly at sunrise.
Burn frankincense and say a prayer of gratitude the dark days are now waning.

Create a winter solstice altar. Use a golden altar cloth, burn gold candles, and decorate the altar with anything that is a symbol of hope and renewal.

Rise before sunrise and take a walk. During your walk, meditate on the cycle of nature and how we believe in her promise to renew and regenerate life.

If you live where it snows, gather snow in a bowl and bring it inside. Watch the snow melt. As the snow melts, envision all your dark days and thoughts melting away. Return the melted water to the earth and know she is always with you.

Call a friend, text a message, or post a happy solstice greeting on social media. The possibilities are as limitless and boundless as your imagination.

Red Rocks Park

Red Rocks Park and Amphitheater is located in the town of Morrison, Colorado. The park is free and open to the public from dawn until dusk, except evenings when concerts are scheduled.

You can reach the park by taking Colorado Highway C470 to the Morrison exit. Follow the signs to the park. For more detailed information regarding Red Rocks Park and Amphitheater, be sure to visit the park's website, www.redrocksonline.com.

Air Magic

Absinthe: The Mystique of the Green Fairy

by Denise Dumars

No alcoholic beverage has been so whispered about, seemed so scandalous, and deemed so magical as absinthe. Now that absinthe is legal again in the United States and the European Union after having been illegal for over a century in some countries (but not the Czech Republic, Spain, Cuba, or Mexico) people are talking about it, imbibing, and expecting, well, interesting results.

A distillation process created spirits—called so because they came out of the alembics of the alchemists—but absinthe, invented in 1787, was a latecomer to the distillery. Before then, people drank *Artemisia absinthium*, also known as wormwood, by steeping the herb in wine. An anthelmintic, the name "wormwood" indicates that the herb was used in ancient times to expel worms from the digestive systems of people and animals. But that's not very magical—no, the real excitement came when writers, artists, musicians, actors, and other creative types declared absinthe to be their Green Muse and called that muse the Green Fairy.

Stoking the Muse

A Muse, in classical mythology, is one of nine goddesses who inspires a form of literature, science, or the arts. We attribute the Muses to the Greeks, and later the Romans, but they are far older. Debate continues over whether they originated in ancient cultures of Europe, such as Thracian, or in those of ancient African nations, such as Egypt and Ethiopia. It is certain, however, that by the time the Greeks adopted the idea, each Muse was given certain attributes. For example, Calliope was the Muse of epic poetry, and Terpsichore was the Muse of dance. This meant that poets, dancers, artists, and scientists each had their own deity to pray to for inspiration.

The idea of a muse never left, even when monotheism overtook the polytheistic faiths. After that, muses were often seen as individuals, places, or things that inspired the creative process. One's spouse, one's homeland, or even one's pet or a particular flower could act as a muse. The Green Muse, however, took creativity back to the days of gods and goddesses and magic. In much of Europe, folklore about fairies and similar spirits persisted, and so the spirit of absinthe was called the Green Fairy to honor its magical powers of inspiring creativity.

A Special Quaff

Just how does one differentiate an ordinary distilled liqueur—and there are many of them—from one that invokes a magical muse? For that, we have to learn the properties of the herbal formula that creates absinthe and also consider its history.

Grand wormwood—one of the *Artemisias*—is just the beginning. People obsess over the idea of the chemical thujone, found not only in wormwood but in closely related plants such as southernwood, mugwort, and all the salvias, as well as the six varieties of arborvitae trees of the genus *Thuja*. Many of the *Artemisias* are recommended as drought-resistant garden plants. So, what's the big deal about absinthe?

First of all, we must go back to the nineteenth century—the golden age of absinthe. For a time in France during a wine shortage, absinthe, which is normally a very expensive liqueur, became cheaper than wine. Most writers, artists, and creative types had very little money, so they began drinking absinthe. And it was most likely then that they discovered its special properties.

Interesting, but where does the magic come in? Well, for one thing, many writers, artists, and musicians of the Victorian Era belonged to the ever-more-popular occult lodges that were springing up in Europe and the United States at the time. For some it was a return to their Celtic heritage, while for others the newfound intellectual freedom had inspired curiosity about pre-Christian religious practices. Aleister Crowley was, of course, a fan of absinthe, but he came along afterward, when the Lost Generation (including Ernest Hemingway, James Joyce, Gertrude Stein, Isadora Duncan, and even Crowley himself) named themselves to express a sense of disoriented wandering during the time of World War I. Sounds like an idea that came out of absinthe imbibing to me!

It helps that absinthe is also associated with magical places that conjure up images of Gothic subculture and vampires, Voodoo and Santería, and libertine lifestyles: Paris, of course, but also Prague, New Orleans, Havana, Amsterdam, Barcelona, the Florida Keys, Martinique, and more.

But back to the Victorians. Charles Baudelaire, an ardent *absintheur*, was a major force in the Decadent movement of literature and loved to shock people with his interest in Satanism. Arthur Machen, Algernon Blackwood, W. B. Yeats, Arthur Conan Doyle, Bram Stoker, Maud Gonne, and A. E. Waite are just a few of the literary lights that belonged to the Golden Dawn, espoused Spiritualism, or practiced other occult arts, often under the inspiration of absinthe.

Only Oscar Wilde—probably the biggest absinthe booster of his day—denied a belief in any spiritual or

magical power. But he believed in the power of absinthe, as did Henri de Toulouse-Lautrec, Vincent van Gogh, Henri Matisse, Paul Gauguin, Guy de Maupassant, and Émile Zola, who comprised a large contingent of absintheurs who frequented the infamous Moulin Rouge during what was called the Belle Époque—also known as the Gilded Age—during the years 1871 to 1914. It is from these writers and artists that we know the most about the effects of absinthe.

When those well-known creative people and bohemian society in general began to get a bad rap, so did absinthe. Whether this truly happened or not, it was no surprise that the drink was seen as nefarious after a man in Switzerland supposedly killed his wife and family while under its influence. One after another, countries in Europe and the Western Hemisphere began to ban absinthe. There were only a few exceptions, such as Cuba, which is where Hemingway became acquainted with it.

Absinthe and Occultism

Back to our occultists. For them, the Green Fairy was a way to initiate themselves into the Mysteries. Divination, communing with the gods, creating ecstatic states of being, and many other mystical states and actions could be accessed through the use of absinthe. But what of the Green Muse? Well, this comes from absinthe's interesting effects, which are far different from most alcoholic beverages. Writers, musicians, and the like found that although absinthe certainly made them drunk, it appeared to leave the mind wide awake! Most people know that alcohol normally inhibits creativity, but with absinthe, the opposite seemed to be happening. Medically speaking, this is because wormwood is a stimulant, which obviously counteracted some of the soporific effects of the alcohol in absinthe. Medical literature lists many active ingredients in wormwood besides thujone, including antioxidants, and there are some proven medical uses.

Scientists list numerous chemicals that act on the brain and body. The well-documented article on wormwood on Drugs.com states that some of the major components of wormwood oil include chamazulene and nuciferol butanoate, among others. The article explains that its essential oils contain aromatic compounds and oxygenated monoterpenes, which contribute to a "pleasant-smelling volatile oil," as well as phellandrene, pinene, azulene, and more.

Wormwood is extremely bitter, so when it is made into a liqueur it is heavily flavored with sugar or honey, and a whole apothecary of sweeter herbs (such as anise, fennel, chamomile, hyssop, angelica, calamus, lemon balm, star anise, and spearmint), many of which contain medicinal properties themselves. Of course, wormwood relatives mugwort and southernwood are also sometimes added. It's a list that's starting to look a lot like a Witches' herbal if you ask me!

Nevertheless, the chemical that worries doctors is thujone, for in high doses it is a convulsant and does cause seizures. Wormwood essential oil should be strictly avoided, and absinthe should only be drunk in moderation under controlled circumstances, like in a ritual. Problems with absinthe in the past were sometimes due to added copper or antimony, which made the drink its expected shade of green, though normally the color is caused by steeping fresh herbs in the distilled liquor. Even worse, absinthe was sometimes served in "uranium glass" which, yes, was glassware made a glowing green from the uranium used in the manufacturing process!

Unless one has a seizure disorder, has kidney problems, or is pregnant (wormwood was once used as an abortifacient), the main thing to worry about with

absinthe is the alcohol. Most brands of absinthe are far stronger than the average distilled liquor. Absinthe should never be drunk neat, hence the ritual of preparing absinthe.

The Mystique of Preparing Absinthe

Part of the mystique of absinthe is in its preparation. Absinthe accoutrements like decorative slotted spoons, glasses with special reservoirs, water fountains, sugar cube dishes, and many other accessories added to the effect. However, the ritual of absinthe preparation can be performed with ordinary utensils, a sugar cube, ice water, and of course, absinthe.

Place one shot of absinthe in a glass. Some people like their absinthe on the rocks. Set the sugar cube on a spoon and the spoon atop the glass. *Do not light the sugar cube on fire!* This is done in some bars for entertainment value, but it makes the absinthe taste burnt and can easily set fire to something. Slowly pour the ice water over the sugar cube until it melts completely and the absinthe "louches" (grows cloudy). Add about four times as much water as absinthe.

Practitioners of magic who would like to invoke the Green Muse to help with creativity need only perform the absinthe preparation ritual above and observe the results. Intoxication is assured, but creative results may vary! For those who prefer a more spiritual or magical summoning, invoke the Green Fairy for divination, communing with Spirit, dream incubation, or other magical ritual. Then prepare the absinthe on an altar with a green cloth, two green candles, one black candle, and one white candle. Candles can be scented with a drop of fennel or anise essential oil if desired. Place a picture of a green fairy from a book or the Internet—for example, a still photo of Kylie Minogue's portrayal of the Green Fairy in the film *Moulin Rouge*. Keep your athame and any other forged iron away from the altar and outside of the circle. Cast a circle with a wand, light the candles, and prepare the absinthe.

Sit before the altar and take a sip of absinthe. Pour a bit into a glass or bowl for the gods if you wish. Ask the Green Fairy for what you wish to happen. Slowly imbibe, and see what happens next! May the blessings of the Green Fairy be upon you!

Here are some traditional absinthe cocktail recipes:

Absinthe Suissesse
1 jigger absinthe
½ shot orgeat syrup
1 egg white
¼ cup cream or half and half
Dash orange flower water
½ cup ice

Combine all ingredients in a cocktail shaker and shake vigorously for at least 20 seconds. Serve with the ice, or blend the drink to make an absinthe smoothie.

Death in the Afternoon

Ernest Hemingway created this drink for a 1935 celebrity cocktails book:

1 jigger absinthe
Champagne

Pour 1 jigger absinthe into a champagne glass. Top with champagne.

Hemingway recommended drinking "three to five of these slowly." I recommend one, if any!

Sazerac

¼ jigger absinthe
1½ jiggers rye whiskey
Peychaud's Bitters to taste
Strip of lemon peel

This is the official cocktail of New Orleans. Swirl the absinthe in a chilled Old Fashioned glass so it will stick to the sides. Place whiskey and several dashes of Peychaud's Bitters (never Angostura!) over ice in a cocktail shaker. Shake briefly, pour into glass, adjust bitters to taste, and garnish with lemon peel.

For Further Study

"Wormwood." *Drugs.com*. Last modified 2009. http://www.drugs.com/npp/wormwood.html.

Magic While Traveling

by Magenta Griffith

Being able to do magic when you are away from home has gotten more complicated over the years. It used to be limited mostly by how much you were willing to carry. Now, there are rules and regulations that everyone must follow, which can make matters more difficult for the Witch or the magician. Whether you travel monthly—or weekly—for your job, take an occasional vacation, or make a trip to Grandma's house, it can affect you. Practicing magic or Witchcraft on the road now presents many challenges.

For example, if you are flying, there are a number of items you can't take in carry-on luggage and a few things you can't take at all. Due to most airlines charging for checked bags, people often want to put everything in a carry-on for a short trip. But you can't take an athame in carry-on, and you can only take one book of matches. Only small amounts

of liquids are allowed, they have to be in containers that hold less than 3.4 ounces (100 milliliters), and security has to be allowed to inspect them if they want. Oils or other liquids that look "suspicious" can be confiscated, so labels should be innocuous but truthful. If asked, oils are "perfume oils," for example. Other common carriers, like trains, may have other rules. Laws vary from country to country, so if you are traveling internationally, it's an excellent idea to check each country's laws; there are usually websites for this purpose. Traveling by car gives you more flexibility, but you still want to be compact and efficient when packing.

Due to fire hazard, California and other places now ban candles and incense in hotel rooms; in any event, these can set off the smoke alarm. An oil infuser can substitute for incense, and electric tealights for candles. Many cities and towns have made it illegal to possess a knife over a certain size no matter where it is. There are at least two approaches— find substitutes or figure out ways to do without one's usual tools. For example, could you use a wooden wand to cast a circle instead of a metal athame? If an athame symbolizes air for you, could you substitute a feather? If you need a chalice, will a drinking glass be adequate, since most hotels have them? Which tools do you actually use every day, and which have become altar decoration?

Toolkits for Travel

If you are staying in an unfamiliar place, such as a hotel, I think it's a good idea to ward your room or area—that is, put up an astral or psychic barrier against hostile or unpleasant influences. Warding can be kept simple, which is good if you are short on time. If you are only staying a night or two, a quick warding can help you sleep better and feel more comfortable in an unfamiliar space. If you are staying longer, I would suggest a longer-lasting form. A simple warding my partner and I do anyplace we sleep that is not our own bedroom is a short version of our house wards. We cast a circle to purify the space, then put a very small amount

of essential oil (a blend my partner compounds himself)
on doors, windows, and mirrors. Many types of essentials
oils are available either as a single scent that feels right to
you or as a blend—there are several that are sold specifically for protection. Most are in a small enough container
to pass TSA requirements: less than 3.4 ounces in a one-
quart bag, along with things like toothpaste. I put our tiny
"imp"—a bottle that holds about an eighth of a dram—in
a tiny, ziplock bag, then in the larger bag so our toiletries
don't pick up the scent. At a Pagan festival or other event,
there is no need to hide what you are doing, but you still
may want to ward your tent or sleeping area. Festivals can
be very intense, and you may want to have a little space that
feels like yours alone.

If you travel by air frequently, it might be useful to
assemble a minitravel kit, ready to grab. It should have its
own case, perhaps an extra makeup bag or small toiletry kit.
Put in a scarf or other piece of cloth to use as an altar cloth,

a miniature tarot deck, a container of salt (I like kosher salt for ritual purposes), and a wooden (or other nonmetallic) letter opener for an athame. Salt and water combined can be used to bless yourself, your bath water, the bed, or even the whole room. You might include a postcard or other small picture or a very small deity statue. Since most hotel rooms include glasses, I don't bother with a chalice, but if you have one that's small and unbreakable, you can include that. Small stones that could symbolize the directions might be included: for example, an agate with shades of brown for north, a fire opal for south, turquoise for west, and citrine for east.

If most of your travel is by car, a small box kept in the trunk of your car could contain more tools—candles and candlesticks, incense and incense holder, or an extra-light robe (perhaps one that could go over clothing), as well as an athame, boline, wand, pentacle, and other tools you want to have with you. The box itself could be used as an altar and could even be decorated if you wish. In this case, you want salt and water dishes, and perhaps bottled water as well as a container of salt. Extra altar items like shells, rocks, or feathers and an extra tarot deck round out your supplies. If you can find a small bottle of wine and a small box of cookies or crackers, you have the ingredients for the "cakes and ale" at the end of many Witches' ritual. If you think you might be working magic, having food along in the form of granola bars or individual packages of cookies or crackers is important to use to ground afterwards. You'll have something you like to eat and not have to raid the overpriced minibar or hotel shop. In fact, packing snacks is an excellent idea for almost any trip.

After you do your working, be sure to clean up completely. Put everything away, wipe down any surfaces you have used with a damp washcloth or some tissue. Do a grounding and centering, if only something as simple as looking at yourself in the mirror and repeating your mundane name three times.

A tarot deck is especially useful to have along. Divination aside, aces can be used to represent the four major tools or the four directions. Various majors can be used as symbols of deities and principle of magic—the Priestess can represent the Goddess, for example. The Tower symbolizes sudden change—reversed it is stagnation, so if you want a situation to stay the same, the Tower reversed could be used to work magic.

Astrological Considerations

Take along a pocket astrological calendar or datebook if you can. Moon void-of-course, when the Moon has already had its last aspect with any sign but has not yet moved into another sign, and other times that are astrologically unfavorable should be avoided or warded against if you are engaged in business transactions or important events. Most Moon voids are brief. One technique to safeguard yourself is to cast a circle before you leave your room and shrink it to just around your body, keeping yourself in the time before the Moon went void until after an important event like a sales presentation or meeting your future in-laws. Knowing about difficult astrological events can often be enough to help avoid their worst effects.

Pay special attention to Mercury retrogrades, since these can interfere with travel and business. This influence is longer and trickier than a Moon void, lasting about three weeks. To make a Mercury talisman, obtain a small object such as a medallion with the astrological symbol of Mercury. Bead stores will sometimes have small charms of planetary symbols. You can even draw one on heavy cardboard. If you prefer a less obvious object, you might use a yellow agate or a yellow or orange topaz. If you can find an old United States Mercury dime (minted between 1916 and 1945) that would be excellent; they are often available at coin dealers. You need an object that resonates with you, that symbolizes the energy of the planet Mercury to you. Consecrate it in a circle at home, or wherever you usually practice, on a Wednesday if at all possible. Concentrate on the idea that this will be a shield, protection against adverse influences. Leave it in a safe place at home when not in use, not on your altar. When Mercury is about to go retrograde—consult an astrological calendar for the date—take it out and ask for protection from the effects of Mercury retrograde. Carry or wear it at all times during the retrograde; when it is over, do a short ritual to thank it and put it away again. If you are going to be traveling and Mercury has not gone retrograde yet, take it along in a small pouch so you can activate it at the proper time.

If you need to travel when there is a holiday or Moon you wish to celebrate, you can compile a list of must-have items to take. For a Full or New Moon, it might be as simple as the basic circle-casting equipment discussed earlier. For Pagan holidays, think of what is central to that holiday in your practice and what might be available at your destination. Flowers on the altar for Beltane can probably be bought almost anywhere. A skull could be used as a focus for Samhain; skulls are common Halloween decorations and easy to find. You could even take a picture of your altar set up for the holiday and use that to concentrate your attention.

Covert Ops

A different set of challenges is connected to visiting family or friends who are not aware of your Pagan or magical practices and when you want to be circumspect. This is a time when being able to work without tools comes in handy. A few things can be found and used in most cases—salt and water, for example. Don't take a tarot deck if it might upset people; learn the correspondences between a deck of playing cards and the tarot. The aces are in both decks and could still be used to symbolize the major tools and directions. Think of substitutions of ordinary household items, like a kitchen knife for an athame.

~

Ultimately, your mind is your first and best tool. An old friend of mine learned from his first teacher that "ritual is meditation with props." The props are useful, but learning to do more with less can be even better. You can direct energy with an athame, your finger, or just in your imagination. If you practice doing ritual without tools on a regular basis, you'll find it easier to cope with a situation where you have to do without. One way to do this is to build up an imaginary temple or circle in your mind. You can make sketches or even make a diorama to show your inner eye what your ideal ritual space looks like. Imagine yourself doing a ritual entirely in your head on a regular basis, in addition to your standard practice, and you will find yourself able to do ritual with whatever you have handy. Bringing those items you most need so they are available to you makes ritual on the road that much easier. As the Boy Scouts say, "Be prepared."

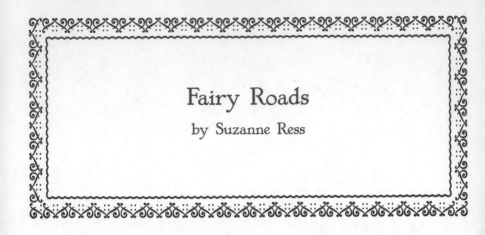

Fairy Roads

by Suzanne Ress

Some years ago, we were having a bathroom retiled on the uppermost floor in the old section of our house. The Sun had gone down, and the tile professional was staying late. I was in the other part of the house when he suddenly came rushing down the stairs and through the corridor, scared.

"I've seen a ghost," he said. "You didn't tell me you have a ghost up there."

Actually, both my daughter and I had heard a benign spiritual presence in that part of the house on several occasions, but it was not something I would normally bring up to an unknown handyman.

We talked, and he told me he was very sensitive to spiritual presences and ghosts and gave me a few examples of experiences he'd had in other people's houses. There was one story he told that opened my mind to the magical mystery of fairy, or spirit, roads.

He was working in an old house situated right beside a straight country road. The house was built at a lower level than the road, so the road passed very close to the second-story window in the room he was working. He had his back to the window, hunkered down, tiling the floor, when he heard the sound of a group of people passing by on the road on foot. There were a few murmuring sounds and some quiet crying, but otherwise these people did not speak. He turned to look and saw a procession of men and women dressed in dark clothes from about a hundred and fifty years ago, walking slowly along the road. None of them seemed to see him. He said all the hairs on his head and arms stood on end because he realized that what he was witnessing was a spirit, or fairy, funeral.

The ground we live on is not only what it appears to be! Below the surface is a wealth of artifact, and, quite possibly, some of the lingering spirits of those who were here before us.

Many people who live in populous areas can remember some place—an empty lot, a wooded area, a dirt road—where they spent happy moments playing and wandering as children. With time, a house was built in the empty lot, the woods were cleared to make a shopping center, and the dirt road was widened and paved for increasing traffic. Although the places may have been transformed physically, in our dreams and memories they live on as the magical places of childhood. To a newcomer, the previously empty lot is just another house, the former woods an abandoned mall, and the once-dirt lane is meaningless asphalt disappearing beneath car tires. If we tell the newcomer what those places used to be like, she might find it hard to believe.

Before your current dwelling existed, what was there? What was there before there were the roads you regularly use to go anywhere? I like to look at old photographs of places I've lived or visited and see how things have changed. Imagine stepping back one hundred, two hundred, or a thousand years but staying in exactly the same place. There would be something familiar about it, even if it were hardly recognizable.

We can look at old photographs and at even older drawings and paintings and maps to get an idea of how a place we think we know has transformed, but these visual aids can only take us back to a time when people were there and able to make a representation of a place on a flat surface. Before that, what was there?

Each autumn the leaves fall off the trees, and if no one rakes them up, by the following autumn they will decompose. With help from ants, fungi, and bacteria, the fallen leaves are turned into humus and, eventually, new soil. The new layer of soil will quickly bury any lost object, and you are unlikely to find it again. The earth will bury small items like rings and trinkets, but also larger ones such as dishes, shovels, and toys in just one season. As the years pass, roads, dilapidated sheds, and even abandoned houses are covered over completely with dirt. Entire towns can be buried and lost.

Hidden Histories

Friends around here involved in the field of building and construction tell stories of bulldozers mistakenly uncovering stashes of ancient metal objects, prehistoric pottery, and even crypts. Because obeying historical and cultural preservation laws and reporting these finds would halt construction work for years, such valuable finds are virtually never reported!

At the top of the hill where I live is an ancient chapel, dating to the early 1200s. Previous to being a church it was a Roman tower and fort, and it is believed that it was a Celtic sacred place in the Iron Age and earlier. About forty years ago several ancient stone tombs were found in an underground passageway beneath the church. When the first tomb was carelessly opened, remnants of a perfectly formed, long-dead man immediately turned to dust. Two more tombs were opened with more forethought, and now, under a thick layer of glass, the skeletons of what are believed to be Longobard priests entombed in about the year 600 are on display.

Near the bottom of my hill, in 1886, a farmer was ploughing his field when he came upon an enormous rock. With oxen power and much effort he was able to move it, uncovering, for the first time in two thousand years, the tombs of an Iron Age man and woman. The bodies had been cremated, but the tomb of the woman still contained an iron ring and chain. The tomb of the man contained a beautiful iron sword with a handmade bronze handle and an iron torque, showing he had been an impressive warrior. The items are on display in the archeological museum of Milan.

Throughout much of Europe, fortified dwelling sites that had their origins in the Iron Age used circular earthen works surrounded by a ditch or moat. They were usually on a hilltop and often on or near a natural spring or well. Straight, often invisible, lines connecting such a fort with another sacred dwelling place, such as a well, lake, or pool; an ancient oak grove; or massive erratic rock are known as fairy spirit roads.

An ancient yet ongoing belief is that disembodied spirits—whether those of the deceased, of fairies, or of live people traveling out of body—always move in straight lines and between sacred landmarks. This is a universal belief, similar to the timeless sensation of traveling down a dark, straight tunnel toward the light in a near-death experience.

Native American shamans travel spiritually by flying in straight lines. These spiritual paths are represented in many cases by physical roads. The Nazca lines of Peru are dozens of arrow-straight lines drawn into desert pampa. They crisscross at hillocks and other possible sacred places and are worn down by foot traffic. Similar spiritual path lines have been found in Chile, Bolivia, Colombia, Costa Rica, El Salvador, Honduras, Guatemala, Belize, and Mexico and in California, Colorado, Arizona, Nevada, and more.

In New Mexico, as part of the lost civilization of the Ancestral Puebloans, there are broad spiritual roads that continue

for hundreds of miles and never vary from dead straight—no matter whether they must cross over mountains or any other natural obstacle.

Peoples of the Hopewell tradition in Ohio also built straight spirit roads. The longest of these discovered so far travels sixty miles from geometric earthen works in Newark, Ohio, to the famous burial mounds in Chillecothe. It is now believed that these straight, sacred roads' primary use was symbolic and spiritual travel, although they were also used as regular roads if necessary.

Australian Aboriginal song lines, or dream tracks, are invisible roads connecting known landmarks. It is believed that Aboriginal shamans can send spiritual messages through the air along these song lines, something like wireless Internet!

In the Chinese feng shui tradition, dragon lines are straight veins of energy running through the earth on which spirits travel. It is considered extremely bad luck to build a house where a dragon line ends.

Out-of-body spiritual travel is pure freedom. All obstacles have been removed, so naturally, the chosen path is always straight!

Fairy Road Lore

From medieval times throughout Europe, special roads were used to transport coffins carrying the dead from the churchyard to the cemetery. The coffins were carried by pallbearers, and the roads between the two places often extended several miles in distance. Corpse roads were used only for carrying the body to burial, and it was considered bad luck to use them for any other purpose.

With the advent of horse-drawn hearses, and then motorcar hearses, the old corpse roads fell out of use. In some cases they came to be used as footpaths, bridleways, or shortcuts, and their original purpose was soon forgotten. In other cases the corpse roads became overgrown with weeds, grass, and trees, and were forgotten. Later on, other buildings may have been constructed right on the corpse way.

Nevertheless, even when the physical corpse road was no longer visible, local legend, passed from generation to generation, spoke of enchantment, haunting, and curses happening along these now-forgotten corpse roads.

Closely tied with corpse roads are fairy roads. Sometimes places where old corpse roads once were are now recognized as fairy paths, and other times fairy paths are not remembered as ever being anything but fairy roads.

In Irish tradition fairies are confused with, and often the same thing as, spirits. It is believed that fairies accompany corpses to burial and even that they held their own fairy funerals, which often foretold a real funeral for a specific person.

Traditionally, fairies were believed to be the lingering spirits of those who, for one reason or another, were barred from entering the afterworld. They were restless spirits, perhaps the spirits of those who committed suicide or murder. Fairies were not spirits to be fooled with.

Sometimes fairies tread on the ground, but more often they move by hovering just above the ground, and, as spirits, they prefer to travel in straight lines. Blocking a fairy path by building a house on it brings ill luck to those who dwell there.

Descriptions of fairies by people who have seen them vary widely, but there are a few traits that all fairy spirits have in common: they can travel invisibly, above ground, and in straight lines, and they can shape-shift. They demand respect, and a lack of it can cause them to retaliate by doing anything from playing harmless pranks to inflicting real hardship and even death.

Fairies are believed to inhabit prehistoric burial mounds. They might have a path going between a natural wellspring and a burial mound, for example. The sides of fairy roads are often marked by hawthorn trees.

Some visible fairy roads have been identified as ley lines. These were originally noticed by Alfred Watkins in the English countryside in 1920. They are straight lines connecting ancient sacred places, such as churches, burial mounds, tree groupings, marker stones, and wells. Watkins surmised that these mysterious straight tracks were designed by Neolithic ley men to help in finding their way over long distances. Later, enthusiastic ley hunters noted the similarities between fairy roads and ley lines and assigned ley lines a spiritual significance they may or may not have had initially.

Fairy paths, dragon lines, shamanic routes, dream tracks, and burial roads are all similar to one another, despite coming from cultures quite varied and distant. Much about all of them remains mysterious to modern humans, but what they all have in common is that they are straight, they connect two or more spiritually important landmarks, and obstacles should not block them. We can surmise that they were all meant primarily for spirit travel. Even when they are invisible, they are a real and important part of our magically human spiritual heritage.

The Journey to Yourself

by Justine Holubets

Desert. In this word there is a tale, an adventure, a mystery. Magnificent and vast, endless and simple. She reaches the heavens, touches the stars, and lets the wind of freedom wander swiftly through her body. She is frozen in eternal peace yet is always in motion. Speechless and calm, she is full of voices— secret, unknown, hardly heard—the voices of invisible genies who whisper old forgotten tales.

The Land of God, more commonly known as Morocco, was waiting for us—twenty enthusiasts from all over the world who arrived for the art volunteer camp. Due to efforts of local youth community and Berber artists, we learned the country and felt the depth of Desert spirit. We stayed in Zagora, a small town in the middle of Sahara. It hides in the southwest of the country in the valley of the river Draa. The mountains that surround it seem to be magic gates reliably guarding the peace of the inhabitants. Surprisingly, there are rich souvenir shops, which resemble Ali

Baba's caves with the heaps of unique Arabian treasures—true pieces of art.

Kasbah: A Secret Doorway

Our home for all those magic days was an outstanding place—Kasbah. Once a fortress and a dwelling for rich local families, it possessed truly medieval spirit: severe, majestic, and mysterious. Thick walls evoked the thoughts of powerful, invincible royal guards; spacious halls made us feel like part of the Arabian elite; the long spacious passages seemed to hide invisible ghosts; and high ceilings echoed each word, giving it importance and weight. An open-air, square inner yard in the middle of the castle was an axis of Kasbah and became the center of house life. During the day bright sunlight flooded in, and after sunset the sky above turned into a dark blue blanket embroidered with shining silver stars. While in the yard talking, meditating, and catching shooting stars, we felt ourselves revived heroes of old moresque paintings. With its keyhole-shaped arch doors, Kasbah itself seemed a huge portal to the mysteries of Desert, and I felt myself Alice in Wonderland when she diminished in size and desperately tried to reach for the key to open the cherished door.

Each day brought keys to us: playing chess, reading books, learning Arabic, listening to Moroccan stories, sharing simple meals, washing dishes in a bucket with heated water, hanging clothes on the rope just in the courtyard, taking showers in the common bathroom, meanwhile philosophizing over the days' impressions and sense of life. And each day was full of events: pottery practice in a neighboring oasis, visits to local schools, long walks around Draa and mountains. Every day was an adventure, but Kasbah remained the home: secure, warm, and native. We ate from chipped clay tableware, but we felt richer than in any luxury resort! The drafts whirled dust and dirt around our ankles yet we felt more clean than in any luxury spa. We didn't have private rooms and white linen sheets but felt privileged covering ourselves with thick, camel wool blankets. We had history. Kasbah put us back in time and connected us to some source that granted us with an inexpressible feeling of freedom. We were ready for the main and core event of the trip, most exciting, thrilling and wonderful—the New Year's Night in the desert.

Camel Sailing

No longer there were locals and foreigners. We were Zagorians, pilgrims to Sahara. In a small outpost in the desert, the camels for a long trip had been already prepared. After childish bustle around the animals, guys' jokes and laughter, and girls' delighted cries, all of us were at last seated by patient and hospitable Berbers, and the caravan set off. Our large group was divided into bunches, each led by a local.

Only blind people can call the desert empty, dull, and lifeless. In the outlines of the dunes, you can find thousands of images, looking in its endless horizons you can feel thousands of emotions. We turned into kids: everyone wanted to feel like a main hero from a favorite movie or book. We were treasure hunters from *The Mummy*, brave Tuaregs from *Il principe del deserto*, the exceptional hero Lawrence of Arabia, charming Angélique captured by Berbers . . . In the twilight, laughter and talking ceased, and everyone was plunged in his or her own thoughts. Merry emotions faded, and Desert touched some deeper strings of our hearts. The lengthened shadows of camels gained fanciful forms. We were in a dream. The rhythmic pace of grand animals possessed strange power: it put us in a trance, caused a weird feeling of being on a boat. Hoping to notice a mirage in the distance, we didn't realize that here, among those shifting dunes, we ourselves were a mirage. We were just a dream of Desert. She slept, and in the depth of herself she was dreaming of us.

New Year's Night: Phoenix's Fire

New Year's is a threshold between times, a symbol of end and beginning. We managed to rediscover and feel its magic again, in a Berber camp inside the heart of the desert. We even didn't know if we were in Morocco or in Algeria. Borders appeared to be senseless human inventions—it was Sahara, nothing more, and we had no connection to the outer world. To celebrate, we had no alcohol, no tonics, no entertainment, and no DJs. Our restaurant was a few tents in the middle of nowhere, our illumination was

a few candles in clay plates with sand instead of candleholders, and our disco was Arabic drums and hoarse Berber voices singing their desert tunes to us, their guests.

The desert collected people with shared values as well as open minds and hearts: they supported my offer to hold a ritual with enthusiasm. My traditional yearly ritual, Magic Sacks, has a simple theme—getting rid of bad things to visualize new dreams. On three pieces of paper, draw the outline of three sacks. On the first one, with a black pen you write all negative events you want to get rid of, and on the second, list all your pleasant lessons and successful experiences in the appropriate color (pink for romance, yellow for career achievement, deep red for passion, blue for creative work, and green for money). The third sack should use the same colors and be filled with big dreams. The first one should be burned and the last two kept in a secret place throughout the year.

After a modest dinner, there was silence in the camp as all of us were knitting brows and gnawing pencils, bowing over the "sacks." I guess the Bedouins, who were wandering among us as if doing household business, enjoyed our funny, concentrated, and dreamy looks. When "dark" sacks were over, one of our provident hosts collected them into a big copper plate to burn. Before midnight, the Berbers made a fire, and its crackle cheered us more than any other sound. The night's chill was not hostile; still it pushed us closer to the only source of light and warmth, which seemed the initial fire of creation. First of all, the dark sacks went into the flame as a peculiar feast sacrifice. We stayed silent for a while, watching how our negativity turned into ashes and feeling how burdens were leaving us forever. And from those ashes something new was being born. We were standing around fire in a circle, this initial symbol of community, spirituality, and wholeness. Joined emotions, joined spirit, joined inspiration. Indeed divine power. Desert enveloped us with her magic. She was in the dancing bonfire; she was in the ebonite eyes of her sons—mysterious Berbers—in their hardened hands, in their imperturbable moves, in their wrapped turbans and veils. She was in the darbuka's strokes; its rhythms were her breath; they echoed in our chests and merged with our heartbeat.

After completing our wish ritual by burning our negative experience list and meditating upon the bonfire within the circle, we greeted each other. Hugs and a short but sincere "Happy New Year" seemed to mark the threshold between the years more appropriately than the usual parties and speeches. We laughed at such an original and weird way of our celebration. We didn't have even a good watch to synchronize the time, but did time matter in the desert? Without any concern about what others would think, some moved a bit away and stared up into the sky, probably making wishes; others stayed around the bonfire and addressed its spirits with requests to fulfill cherished dreams. The tongues of flame whirled passionately, as if genies gathered for dance and were throwing generously the heaps of sparkling precious gems around. We drew the fire streams into our palms and were inspired by its charm.

A Golden Dawn

The next morning we witnessed a bright scene of birth when Desert granted a newborn Sun to the world, pushing it softly out of her womb. I was awoken by a shining beam of the light. Smiling, I got out of the tent and noticed I was not the first. Nearly all of the foreign volunteers were standing on the dunes among the still-sleeping locals, and our eyes were directed at the golden sphere slowly appearing over the barchans. We stiffened with astonishment, afraid to break the wonder with a fidgety move. Feeling the warmth of the awakening desert, we greeted a new day, new year, new life, new start, and we felt as if we had just received communion in one of the most majestic temples on earth. As a careful goldsmith, with its dazzling beams the rising Sun was carving new letters in our hearts, purified by night flame. And the golden sand we held in our palms with thrill of joy filled all the body with the power and strength of Mother Earth. Desert became a part of soul. It was an experience, life, breath. There, each paradox which puzzled our mind in common life became clear and gained sense. Kasbah was a portal, each day was preparation, and the magic night was a full initiation.

Depriving of all "goods of civilization" which have such a great power over us, Desert gives something more instead. She changes personality, cleanses the mind from mental dirt, purifies the soul from burdens and vanity, and charges with power of wisdom and passion. She teaches how to see deeper, to feel intensely, to live at full blast. And though it was difficult to get back to our usual life at home, her power supported us and helped us cope successfully with any difficulties. Someone would tell we were lucky, but only we know what a job we did with our spirit and mind and what treasures we gained.

People are obsessed with *One Thousand and One Nights*. We lived just one in the Sahara, but it contained the magic and wonders of all the rest. This magic is alive and is always with me.

The Magic of Dolls

by Charlie Rainbow Wolf

No one knows exactly when the first doll was created, but there is evidence that they have been part of the human experience since prehistoric times. Sometimes they were religious items, dedicated to gods and goddesses; other times, they were simple playthings. The earliest dolls were made from primitive materials. You might think that as humankind advanced the dolls would grow to be more sophisticated, and to an extent you'd be right. However, even today, dolls are made from corn, wood, and other natural fibers, as well as manufactured as brightly colored, plastic toys seen in the aisles of department stores.

Initially, dolls were quite crude, but in an attempt to make them more lifelike, they evolved to have moveable arms and legs and also their own garments. In Egypt, Greece, and Rome, there's evidence of dolls being placed in tombs of the wealthy. It's thought, because of this reverence, that dolls were cherished and important. Most of these were very simple creations, but some were more elaborate and made from pottery or even alabaster.

Some of the traditions have endured through time. There are many ritual and spiritual uses for dolls today that can be traced back through the ages. Whether to heal, to help with divination, to assist with magic, or to honor deities or deceased loved ones, dolls are as much a part of spiritual practice in the modern world as they were during the times of our ancestors.

Poppets

Mention poppets to people, and they usually think of Voodoo. The truth is that these dolls—sometimes called handkerchief dolls, church dolls, or pew dolls—have been used in sympathetic magic for millennia. Wax images were popular

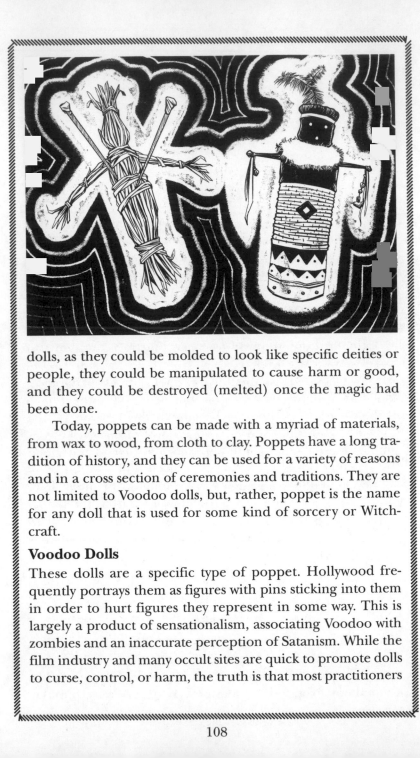

dolls, as they could be molded to look like specific deities or people, they could be manipulated to cause harm or good, and they could be destroyed (melted) once the magic had been done.

Today, poppets can be made with a myriad of materials, from wax to wood, from cloth to clay. Poppets have a long tradition of history, and they can be used for a variety of reasons and in a cross section of ceremonies and traditions. They are not limited to Voodoo dolls, but, rather, poppet is the name for any doll that is used for some kind of sorcery or Witchcraft.

Voodoo Dolls

These dolls are a specific type of poppet. Hollywood frequently portrays them as figures with pins sticking into them in order to hurt figures they represent in some way. This is largely a product of sensationalism, associating Voodoo with zombies and an inaccurate perception of Satanism. While the film industry and many occult sites are quick to promote dolls to curse, control, or harm, the truth is that most practitioners of Voodoo use pins to focus energy rather than to do evil! The media has a lot to answer for.

Voodoo dolls are often depicted as having some kind of supernatural power over the person to whom they're attached. The dolls themselves have no power. What gives them any importance at all is the vibration and intent that the maker and user apply to them. The movies show us that a Voodoo doll can control what we do, but the truth is that we alone determine what controls us—although in sympathetic magic there can be a lot of subtle influence.

Muñequitas

These are dolls that are associated with the religions of Espiritismo and Santería. Here, the dolls can represent deceased loved ones, saints, and ancestors. They are part of the household, and stories are told about them—and to them. The dolls are not placed upon the home altar, but rather they have their own honored place in the house, where they can still be among the family.

The dolls are not just for decoration. They are believed to be able to communicate to those who live there. Some represent spirit guides. Others are said to represent deceased family, and when the dolls are dressed, they are done so to honor that family member. Sometimes the dolls are handmade, but it is not unusual to see a mass-produced doll that has been clothed and adorned to represent the family member. Like the spirits of the deceased, the dolls are a part of the family to their owners and reverently passed down from parent to child.

Spirit Dolls

Similar to the muñequitas are the spirit dolls (sometimes called altar dolls) that Wiccans and other Pagans use. They are used as a focus for energy or as a means for communications with the spirits. Usually there's one doll per energy or entity, so if more than one deity or being is being invited, more than one doll should be used. The purpose of a spirit doll is to give the helper spirits a place to stay while they are assisting you.

Once the spirit doll has been activated, it has to be cared for. Offerings of food, drink, incense, or candles can sweeten the doll's energies. Usually with magic or ritual, the more you put into it the more you get out of it, so the more you care for your doll, the more harmonious and helpful the energies between you and it are going to be. An altar doll may not always stay with you, though. The spirit may need to leave the doll because it has fulfilled its role or helped you as much as it can. It could also be that it is time for the spirit and the doll to move on to someone else, in which case the owner of the doll often gives it to that person, so that the spirit in the doll can continue the work it is called to do.

Fetishes

A fetish is another kind of doll, similar to a poppet, but instead of representing a particular person or energy, this doll possesses spirits that connect it with its owner. It's used as a charm: sometimes worn, sometimes carried. It is said to

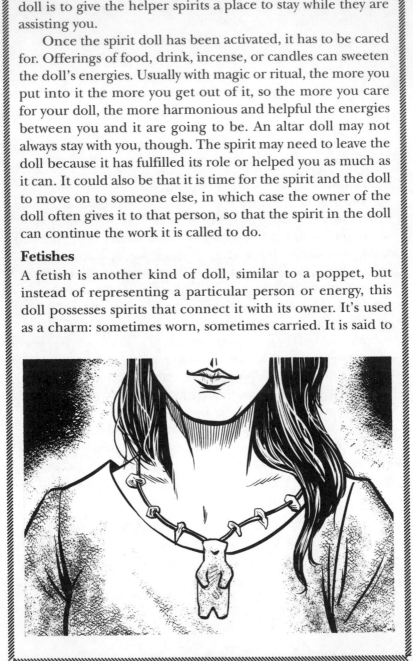

contain a lot of power, and at one time, a slave could be killed for being found with a fetish doll on his or her person.

It wasn't just slaves who carried fetishes, though. Native Americans also worked with fetishes. The most well known of these is probably the Zuni fetish animal necklaces, which are made of stones carved into the shapes of animals. These carvings give the spirits of animals a place to live while they are helping the wearer of the fetish. Fetishes may also be made out of wood, shell, or bone, and can represent nature spirits as well as animals. Nearly anything can be carried or worn as a fetish once the owner infuses it with that power.

Corn Dollies

These are just what they sound like they are: dolls made out of corn. In this case, the corn was the last wheat of the season. Here the spirit of the corn resided until the next year, kept safe and given a revered place in the home. Often the corn dollies didn't resemble a figure but rather a sacred geometrical shape. They were decorated with ribbons and flowers and sometimes given to sweethearts as a token of affection. These corn dollies originated in Europe but have spread throughout the world.

Native Americans had their own version of the corn dollies, the corn husk doll. It's said that it originated with the Oneida or other Iroquois nations, but all nations who grew corn would have had a version. As well as being toys for children, corn husk dolls are also used in healing ceremonies and other practices. The Iroquois nations used them to help purge nightmares. A doll was made to absorb the dream, and then it was buried so that the negative energy returned to the earth. The dolls are usually made without faces because of an Oneida legend. The story goes that a beautiful corn husk doll became so enamored with her appearance that she forgot to tend to the children. Making the dolls without faces teaches us to be humble and to take care of our responsibilities.

Make a Poppet

It's easy to make your own poppet. It can be as simple or elaborate as you desire. Just remember that it is a representational object; it needs to represent a person, a deity, or an energy. You also need to determine the purpose for the poppet; it can be for protection, to stop gossip, for safe travel—pretty much anything can be embodied in a poppet. Just get your idea firmly in your head so that you don't have to start over! Making the poppet is as magical as the actual poppet itself.

Next, you will want to choose your fabric. Take some time with this. For example, if you want to draw love, you might choose pink. Blue would be good for health, while green might be chosen for money spells. If you can use fabric that in some way links you with the person or the energy that you want to use, so much the better. For example, if you want to draw a lover into your bed, you might want to use fabric from your pajamas or the bed sheets. See how it connects?

Cut the fabric in the shape of a human. If you're making this with a specific person in mind, try to emulate him or her.

If the person is chubby, make the poppet chubby—that sort of thing. Sew the shapes together using your favorite method; hand or machine, it doesn't matter. Remember to put the outsides of the fabric together when you sew the seams so that they are on the inside when you turn it inside out. Leave an opening for the stuffing.

What goes in your poppet? Well, you'll want some old rags or even some polyester stuffing material that you can buy at craft shops. This doesn't have to be anything fancy, but you do want to consider adding things to your poppet to help give it power. If you're making a poppet for love, add rose petals, because roses are the symbol of love for many people. If you're making the poppet for money, add a coin. Get the idea? If this poppet is to connect you with another person, you could add a taglock. This is something belonging to that person: a lock of hair, a fingernail clipping, a piece of their handwriting, or even a photograph.

Decorate the poppet however you want, but if it is going to represent that person, then put that person's likeness onto it. For example, give it the same color hair, draw on any birthmarks or tattoos, or add a beard. Don't forget to name your poppet, too! You don't have to give it a person's name, but you want to tell the poppet why it was created. If you made the poppet to serve as a token for someone in your life, then call it by that person's name. Remember, the more you put into the doll, the more it will assist you in your ceremony, ritual, or magic. Intent is everything!

Good Advice or Static Law?: When Magical Knowledge Is Passed Down

by Michael Furie

Since magic and Witchcraft were secret (and illegal) practices for so many centuries, information was passed down from person to person; it's not as though guidebooks on Witchcraft could be openly published during the burning times. Most magical lore was shared orally, which had the advantage of being safer but had the drawback of occasionally being incomplete. Anyone who has played the telephone game—wherein a group of people sit together whispering a message from person to person until the last one announces what the message is to the group—can attest that messages can be misheard or remembered incorrectly. When miscommunication or an incomplete message is repeated, this confusion is reinforced; if continued long enough, the original statement, message, or teaching can become completely distorted or entirely lost. In the case of magical teachings, a great deal of wisdom has been compacted down into various adages and "laws" as an unfortunate result of orally passing down knowledge. Many of these laws are presented without their proper context, resulting in fragmented knowledge.

On the positive side, this lack of context isn't necessarily harmful because these rules are designed to prevent or avoid magical mishaps. The only negatives are that when rules are presented as absolutes, they can curtail free expression and experimentation in those who choose to follow them, or paradoxically, they can engender disbelief in those who realize absolutes cannot be effectively applied to every situation. A critical mass of people losing faith in the "laws" could lead to a total rejection of rules and structure, which could be potentially dangerous. That is why I feel so strongly about the importance of thorough training. Magical adages and laws are fantastic to learn, study, and meditate upon in order to gain greater insight into the workings of spiritual forces, but they shouldn't really be taken as unwavering universal laws. Most practitioners have heard all of these at least once, but so few of us have heard their origins or their full meanings.

Threefold Law

Of all the magical advice we're given, one of the most often stated is known as the threefold law. As it is usually given, the threefold law says that whatever you send out returns to you with three times greater force—in other words, if you do positive actions and magic, then what returns to you will be positive. Conversely, if you do negative things, negative things will return. This is a nice guideline for the working of positive magic, but it doesn't really explain how this law works or why things would return "times three." In the *The*

Kybalion: Hermetic Philosophy, the book detailing Hermetic philosophy, there are listed seven "universal" principles, one of which is the principle of cause and effect. It states in part that "every cause has its effect; every effect has its cause; everything happens according to law; there are many planes of causation but nothing escapes the law." This principle is similar to Newton's third law of motion: for every action there is an equal and opposite reaction. Neither example gives a threefold value to the forces of action and reaction, though Newton spoke of equal force and *The Kybalion* hints at multitiered causation.

In some older traditions of Witchcraft, the threefold idea and the notion of energy return are two separate concepts. The law of return seems to agree more with the Newtonian law in the belief that what goes around comes back around, generally in equal measure. The old notion of threefold appears to have been that when an act is committed, it reaches through at least three levels (physical, mental, and spiritual). If the act is harmful, in order to rebalance the energy three positive acts must be performed to make things right: one to stop the harm, one to fix the damage, and one to tip the scales back to good. This concept seems to be more in line with the Hermetic cause and effect. At some point, these two ideas were conflated into one overriding principle, which is the law of threefold return.

Some philosophies other than Witchcraft believe that consequences return sevenfold, tenfold, or even one hundredfold, but a basic notion to keep in mind is that what you send out (magically and also through mundane actions) returns to you. The nature or volume of this return is really a secondary concern to the fact that it does indeed come back to its point of origin. Armed with this knowledge, all magical practitioners must carefully consider their actions and the type of spells they wish to cast, since they become responsible not only for what they release into the world but also what they receive as a consequence.

Harm None

It is, however, not a wise idea to become overly obsessed with trying to avoid anything that could be classified as harmful or negative. Another apparent magical law that has come to be known as "the Wiccan Rede" would, on the surface, appear to disagree with me on this point.

Anyone who has studied or practiced magic for even a short time has heard the statement, "An it harm none, do as you will"—but is that even possible? Judging by what I have seen and read, most of us try to live by this guideline as best we can, seeking to avoid perpetuating harm while at the same time not being afraid to take action as needed. Some magically minded folk see the harm none concept as either an immutable law restricting even the most basic of magical efforts, or, since it is essentially impossible to live a life free from causing some form of harm (stepping on grass, swatting a mosquito, etc.), they believe that the concept itself must be faulty and should therefore be discarded. Whether the law is accepted or rejected seems to be based on whatever perception the practitioner carries regarding the law rather than the original nature of the concept itself.

Though the origins of the law are somewhat uncertain, it is believed to be an alternative version of a teaching given by occultist Aleister Crowley, found in his *Book of the Law.* "Do what thou wilt shall be the whole of the law; love is the law, love under will." If this is to be accepted as the inspiration for the Wiccan Rede, it modifies the meaning of the rede to one being specifically guided by the intent of love regulated by a disciplined willpower. Basically, though it may indeed be impossible to live freely without occasionally causing harm (depending on how strict you believe the definition of harm to be), the rede guides us to "do as we will" as long as our actions are done consciously and with loving intent. Reckless actions without regard to potential consequences are the type to be avoided. If a spell is cast with the intent that it be "for the highest good," "with harm to none," and/or "for the good of all," then we can safely use virtually any type of magic while still adhering to the rede. The idea of harm none was never meant to curtail magical or personal freedom but rather to advise us to work with disciplined awareness and always from a place of love.

Only Move Sunwise in the Circle

Another teaching that has received a great deal of attention is the notion of directional movements while inside a magic circle. The belief is that any movement in the circle should be done "sunwise," as in the direction the Sun appears to travel in the sky (circling clockwise in the Northern Hemisphere and counterclockwise in the Southern Hemisphere) for positive magical purposes or "moonwise" (the reversed directions) for negative magical purposes. Though this is a sound metaphysical teaching, a lack of proper context for what constitutes "positive" and "negative" magical purposes can leave some practitioners fearful of making a harmful mistake.

The idea of positive and negative should really be taken with a grain of salt. Though harmful magic does frequently utilize moonwise movement as part of the spell, that doesn't mean the direction itself is inherently evil. Rather than "posi-

tive and negative," clearer descriptive terms would be "winding and unwinding," "building and dissolving," or "forming and releasing" for the effects generated by sunwise and moonwise motions respectively. Some sabbat rituals call for dancing in one direction and then reversing to the opposite direction at some point in order to emulate the energy shifts taking place at that time. Also, some coven dances have two circles of dancers, one going clockwise and the other moving counterclockwise, and this is in no way harmful. Some unhexing or releasing magic utilizes moonwise motion to break down the troublesome energy and cast it away. Much like the concept of yin and yang, positive and negative are inextricably linked and not intrinsically good or evil; those are intentions held by the individual.

~

I hope that examining these guidelines and their meanings shows that our predecessors did indeed pass down powerful knowledge of magical forces. There is flexibility contained within these teachings, as opposed to them being "commandments" or proclamations to which we must adhere under threat of some unnamed danger. That would be forfeit of personal strength. Keeping an open but questioning mind is the key to continued progression and spiritual growth; blind acceptance is not advised. It is far more empowering to work with these concepts if they are viewed as helpful advice and important facets of our shared magical heritage.

The Magick of Social Media

by Emily Carlin

We live in a world that is more interconnected than ever. In the blink of an eye we can talk to people across the globe via social media in real time—as if they were in the next room. Of course, we often use this amazing technology to send each other videos of synchronized dancing and pictures of cats. (Not that there's anything wrong with that.) However, as magickal people we could be doing so much more with social media. The same technologies that create viral videos and trending tags can be used to both gather and send out energy in order to manifest your magick in the world.

One of the fundamental concepts in pop culture magick is that popular things have their own energy reservoir that can be tapped into by a knowledgeable practitioner. The idea is that things that are experienced and enjoyed by the masses are given energy through those interactions. In other words, you can work with a character or concept you like from a popular television show or book and take advantage of the energies poured into it by other fans. Similarly, in ceremonial magic a ritual is considered more potent for the energies of the many practitioners who have performed it in the past. It's about boosting a magickal working with not only the energy of the practitioner performing it, but also with the energies of those connected via emotional or metaphysical links. What does this have to do with doing magick on social media? *Everything*.

The purpose of social media is to allow people to create and share information, ideas, images, and videos in virtual communities. Through tags, trends, and sharing, we can see thoughts and images spread around the world, experienced by countless individuals. Each person that experiences a piece of media online imparts his or her own bit of energy to it as

it passes through his or her mind. How much energy do you think a meme gathers as it spreads across the Internet? We can take advantage of this natural energy accumulation by creating and sharing magickal media. Imagine creating an image deliberately infused with your magickal will that goes viral; how much energy would that raise in the service of your intent?

Selecting a Social Network

There are many social networks that can be used to share your magickal works, and each one has particular strengths and weaknesses. Some social networks are primarily focused on networking, creating interest groups, or staying connected with friends and family—think Facebook, Google+, or LinkedIn. Other networks are focused on sharing art, articles, hobbies, and commentary—like Tumblr, Instagram, or DeviantArt. Still others focus on sharing news, opinions, and information—like Twitter or Reddit. It's important to choose the right network for your magickal style. If you want to pull energy from a particular kind of person be sure to share your crafted content in a group that you know comprises those people. If you want to inspire others to create something based on your media, then share it on a network that is composed of largely of artists. If you want to spread your spell as far and wide as possible, be sure to tag it with the most popular and appropriate tags and post it everywhere you can. Rather than explore the many social media options out there, for brevity's sake we'll look at three in detail: Facebook, Tumblr, and Twitter.

Facebook: Connections

Facebook is one of the most popular social networks in the world. Everyone and their mom are on Facebook; *my* mom is on Facebook. This means that there are also a lot of magickal folk on Facebook. A quick search will show you thousands of different groups for magickal practitioners of every flavor. Not only are these groups an excellent place to get advice and feedback on your practices, they're a great place to gather energy and appreciation. One of the most common bits of social media magick I've seen on Facebook is devotions. When practitioners call upon external entities (deities, fae, Goetics, spirits, etc.) in the course of a magickal work, the deities often ask some kind of special recognition in exchange for their aid. It's not always practical to perform a chant extolling the kindness and virtues of Maman Bridgette on the street, but it is absolutely appropriate to do so in a Facebook group devoted to the Loa. I would argue that it is better to post such thanks in a smaller but focused social media group than in a less restricted but targetless place because the folks in a magickal group will understand the significance of your devotions and appreciate them more fully. There are many ways to do magick on Facebook, but sharing devotions in the appropriate group is one of the best.

Tumblr: Visuals

Tumblr and other visual-heavy social networks are the places par excellence for sharing magickally charged images. There are many ways to charge an image with magickal intent. One of the easiest is to add a sigil that you've created to the image. For example, to do a spell for finding a new job, create a digital sigil that embodies your full intent in a program like Microsoft Paint or Adobe Photoshop and then paste it into an image of someone doing your dream job. Then you can share that image with tags like #ProsperitySpell, #NewJobForMe, or #Prosperity-AndAPromotion. If you're more creatively minded you might compose an altar photo that contains all the elements of a traditional prosperity spell and then share that image. If you're an artist you can create an original piece of art that incorporates your intent and then share it. Some great examples of blogs focused on just this are http://problemglyphs.org and http://everydaysigils.tumblr.com. Be sure to take advantage of your chosen network's tagging and captioning systems so that others can find your work if they don't follow you. Captions are also important for making sure the visually impaired aren't excluded from your working. These techniques can also be used for charging audio or video files. Creating interesting, bespelled images that grab people's attention and get shared is a great way to harness the power of art-heavy social networks.

Twitter: Words

For the more verbally inclined there are networks like Twitter. While you certainly can post images and links in Twitter, the very best posts are 140 characters of just the right words. The most obvious magickal use of Twitter is to write a 140-character spell—which is more difficult than you might imagine. A lot of times, trying to reduce a full spell into 140 characters or less will just create a semimagickal haiku that doesn't make much sense. This is a good medium for simple, active spells and for prayers and petitions. For example, "Athena, guide me this day so that I act with insight, consideration, and grace #Wisdom #GuideMe." A good Twitter spell requires time and effort to get just right, but that very effort will infuse your words with your intent and make their impact on those who read them that much more potent. Add a good hashtag or two and your spell will be seen and shared by the masses, lending your words far more energy than if you'd simply spoken them aloud. Twitter is the network of bon mots rather than drawn out discourse, so keep your workings straightforward and you might just be a trending tag.

~

Social media has the power to spread your magick around your community and the world at large. By intentionally posting words, images, videos, and other material that contain your magickal will, you can take advantage of the energy that the people who experience it put forth. Find the medium that most appeals to you, be it art, words, music, video, or something else entirely. Find the right network on which to share it, and then send it out into the world to gather what it will. Most of us already belong to at least one social network, so why not take advantage of it? Unleash your creativity online and see where it takes your magick.

Get in Touch with Psychometry

by James Kambos

Several years ago a friend of mine who is a visual artist decided to take an art workshop. For the first activity, the instructor of the workshop passed around a box containing tubes of different colored paints. The box was closed except for a hand-sized hole on the top so that the artists were unable to see the tubes of paint. As the box was passed around the room, the instructor told everyone to reach into the box and, when they thought a tube of paint "felt right," to pull it out. Amazingly, almost every individual pulled out his or her favorite color!

Whether or not they realized it, the artists in this workshop were practicing a psychic skill known as psychometry.

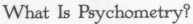

What Is Psychometry?

Psychometry is the psychic ability to "read" or to obtain some type of information about an object by touching or feeling it. This reading can give a psychic clues about an item's history, about its origin, and about its owner or owners. It's similar to a reading done by scrying with a crystal ball or a magic mirror, but in psychometry the reading is done by touching a particular object. Think of psychometry as scrying by touch.

The term "psychometry" was created by American physiologist Joseph Buchanan. It's a combination of the Greek words *psyche,* or "soul," and *metron,* which means "measure" or "meter." Professor Buchanan experimented with psychometry in the 1840s. His original belief is that all objects possess a soul or memory.

Some psychometrists today still hold onto the belief that objects have a soul that can be sensed or measured. Other psychics believe that objects don't have a soul but are imbued with an energy left by someone that can be felt.

How It Works

In the opening example, artists were able to sense some type of connection with the tubes of paint by touching them. This connection enabled them to unknowingly select their favorite color in most cases. This is indeed a form of psychometry. However, psychometry is usually used to form a contact with a person—living or dead.

To do this the psychometrist is given an item or items that have a long history associated with a particular individual. These objects could be clothing, keys, jewelry, a hairbrush, even a photograph. And if the person in question is lost, it's not unusual to include a map.

The psychometrist will then handle the items, perhaps breathing on them or holding them to his or her forehead.

Now the natural abilities of the psychic will take over. Some will feel emotions coming from an object—love, joy, fear, anger. Anything is possible. Others will actually see or hear an entire scene, like watching a film.

If you're trying to establish a link with a specific person, whether deceased or alive, the objects used must have a history with that individual. The age of an item doesn't matter. Psychometrists have been known to give accurate readings after touching objects thousands of years old.

I'd like to add that many experts in the field of psychometry feel that metal objects are the best items to use for a reading. The belief is that metal has the ability to "hold" a memory or an impression better. This idea isn't as widespread as it once was. I think as long as an object has an attachment to the person who's the subject of the reading, that is what's important.

If you choose to use psychometry to connect with the spirit of a deceased individual, you won't need to establish a contact with a spirit or a spirit guide. The object you use will be the only contact you need. This is one of the advantages of psychometry.

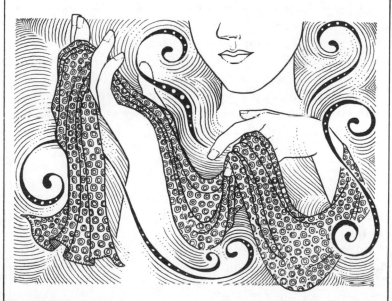

Here's my experience with psychometry: My mother had a favorite scarf, and she had it for years. For about a month before she died unexpectedly, it seemed that every time she wore it she'd receive many positive comments about it. I thought it was slightly unusual but forgot about it. Then several months after her death, I went to a meeting of psychics. Something told me to take that scarf with me. While there I met a woman who practiced psychometry. After speaking to her she said she'd be glad to "read" the scarf. She wrapped it around her fingers and gently pulled it through her hands. Then she began to give me accurate details about my mother's life. I was amazed.

But psychometry can be used for more than connecting us with our departed loved ones. A highly skilled psychometrist can be used to solve crimes. Given items from a crime scene, a psychometrist who is talented at receiving visual images would be able to describe a crime as it happened. They could give details on the number of people involved, the weapon used, or where the weapon might be hidden. And psychometrists can be very valuable in helping track down a runaway.

Humans aren't the only ones psychometry can help. Pet owners have been known to provide a psychometrist with their pet's photo or an item such as a collar when they needed help finding a lost pet. Psychometry has also helped pet owners find out what is on their pets' minds, which can help solve some behavior issues.

Do It Yourself

Don't be afraid to give psychometry a try. You don't need to be a wizard. And most psychics agree that the objects you touch aren't controlled by some spirit. Your mind is in control. Here is an exercise to get you started:

First, gather with some like-minded magical friends. It would be best if there were several of you. Discuss the idea

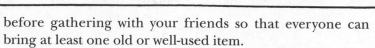

before gathering with your friends so that everyone can bring at least one old or well-used item.

Make sure you won't be disturbed. Being quiet is a must—no cell phones, please. Whoever wants to try reading an item should sit quietly with their eyes closed. Palms should be up and feet flat on the floor. Ground and center while breathing calmly. Release all cares and thoughts.

When you feel ready, you should say that you're prepared to accept an object. Keep your eyes closed, and someone should silently place an object in your hands.

Feel the item. You may simply hold the object or raise it to your heart or forehead. You'll probably feel some emotions coming from the object. If you can, "see" the feelings you're receiving.

Begin to say what you're feeling and seeing. Don't analyze anything, just keep talking as long as you're getting messages. Something you think is crazy may make total sense to the person you're reading for. Keep your first sessions short, perhaps about five minutes.

In the beginning don't worry about accuracy. Just keep talking about the images or feelings as they come to you.

The more you practice the better you'll become. Soon, you'll begin to master the incredible psychic skill known as psychometry.

Something in the Wind

by Monica Crosson

There are nights the wind asserts its surly howl, blowing wildly in mad swirls around my house. It seeps through cracks in my panes and breathes desperately in my ear as I try to sleep, reminding me of my insecurities, lost dreams never to materialize, projects left unfinished, and plans forgotten. I wake tired and weary with the knowledge that my life is somehow escaping me.

But there are other times, when I am worried or upset and feel the need to be wrapped by the Goddess's soothing embrace, that I will walk the two-mile stretch of road that leads to a single-lane bridge that spans the Sauk River before meeting the highway. There, under the cover of magickal big-leaf maples, towering conifers, and the ever-present shushing of the river, a soothing breath envelopes me. It dances around me and plays in my hair, intoxicating me with the scent of fresh earth. Carried on this breeze is reassurance and hope for a better tomorrow, promises of greener days, and a message that with each new dawn there is joy.

"There is something in the wind," my grandfather always said. His face was drawn upwards, toward the sky, and gray tufts of hair were caught up in the wind's play.

"What do you mean, Grandpa?"

"Well, if you listen, sweetheart, the air speaks. But you have to listen very close." He paused. "Can you hear it—the words?"

I leaned into the breeze and perked my ears, trying desperately to receive the message I knew rode on the breeze. But all I heard was the scuttle of dry leaves as they tumbled in the wind's wake and the quiet murmuring of branches that trembled in the tall trees above me. "I think I hear it, Grandpa," I said, unsure.

"Don't worry. It doesn't work if you try too hard." He pulled at my braid. "But it will happen."

~

My grandfather (or rather, step-grandfather—my mom's real dad died when she was two) was an old southern farmer. He was a stern Baptist whose strict religious upbringing blended smoothly with the old folkways that had been passed down through generations of his family. He gardened by the phases of the Moon and told stories of haints that haunted my grandparents' barn. He believed in the power of mojo bags and made poultices from plants he gathered from the surrounding woods. But, on the other hand, he never missed church, had a Bible quote for every scolding, and when excited used "praise the Lord!" like a comma.

Of all the things I gleaned from my grandfather, his message of "something in the wind," fascinated me most. It wasn't until years later that I realized he was talking about the element of air.

The Element of Air

The Greek philosopher Anaximenes said that air is the "stuff of breath and soul, and therefore the principle of life, sensation, and reaction." We all live by breathing air. And though it is invisible, it is always present. Air moves us. It surrounds us.

Air transforms us. In the form of wind, we witness its power of transformation in nature every day—from the delicate stirring breeze that ruffles our senses to the devastating power of storms, such as tornados or hurricanes.

Air can be used to help guide us with knowledge of new life and possibilities. Magick involving air includes travel, divination, new possibilities, recovering lost objects, and transformation. Air represents the intellect and freedom. It's a masculine element and governs the magick of the four winds. Its direction is east and time is dawn. Its season is spring.

To experience the breezy power of this element all you need to do is walk outside and lift your face to the clouds. Stand on a sandy beach and open your arms, facing the wind. Climb to the highest point you can find and yell out your intentions. Sing a song or play a musical instrument, inhale the scent of a fragrant blossom, or feel the sensation of a feather brushed delicately across your skin.

People born under the signs of Libra, Aquarius, and Gemini are all air signs. They tend to be perceptive, curious, intelligent, and analytical. They see all sides of an equation, and balance is important to them. There is no prejudice with airy people. They are idealists who can accomplish much.

Goddesses Connected to the Element of Air

Arianrhod: A Celtic mother goddess and keeper of the circling, silver wheel of stars, she is sometimes depicted as a weaver. She presides over the fates of departed souls and nurtures their journey between lives. Her symbols include the owl, wolf, and birch tree. Invoke her for spells regarding beauty, past lives, fertility, reincarnation, and feminine powers.

Aradia: Goddess of the Witches, she is daughter to Diana and Lucifer and was instructed by her mother to become a teacher of the "Old Religion." She was honored by the Witches of the Tuscany region and was not well known outside of Italy until the publication of *Aradia, or the Gospel of the Witches* in 1899. Her symbols are the Sun, the Moon, and the red garter. Invoke her power in matters of freedom, knowledge, new projects, or beginning a new spiritual path.

Nut: Egyptian goddess of the sky and one of the oldest known deities, Nut helped Ra escape earth by transforming into a huge cow and lifting him to heaven. Her efforts made her dizzy, and it was the four winds who came to her rescue. Her symbols include stars, wind, and pot and cow images. Invoke this goddess in matters of health, motherhood, sexuality, and fertility.

Cardea: Roman goddess of the hinge and keeper of the four winds, she looks both forward and backward. Honored at Beltane, she was originally the hinge on the Wheel of the Year. She resides at the hinge of the universe behind the north wind. Hawthorn is her sacred tree. Invoke her power in matters of the home and of children.

Magick on a Breeze

Words are a powerful tool that when released can bring about compelling results. Remember the Wiccan Rede and be careful what you wish for, for it might just come true. We will invoke Arianrhod for her feminine strength. This is a great activity for mothers and daughters to do together on the night of a Full Moon.

Empowerment Wind Catcher

You will need the following:

An interesting piece of driftwood or a small branch about 6 to 8 inches long (remember to be responsible when gathering—take from the ground, not from the tree)

Silver ribbon or embroidery floss

Parchment paper

Pen

Hole punch

After you have gathered your materials, sit down with your parchment and pen and thoughtfully write down words that empower or heal, new skills to acquire, or endeavors to accomplish. For each wish to set upon the wind, write on a separate piece of parchment. When finished, roll up each paper into a scroll and tie with a bit of the silver ribbon so it won't unroll. Use your hole punch to punch the top of each scroll. Now take your ribbon and cut 12-inch pieces for as many scrolls you have to hang. Tie one end through the punched hole and wrap the other end around the branch so they hang freely and evenly. When finished, say this:

> *Arianrhod of the silver wheel,*
> *I invoke your power with words that heal.*
> *So with the power of three times three,*
> *Help guide my wishes.*
> *So mote it be.*

Hang in the branches of a tree where the wind blows freely. Meditate under the tree, focusing on your healing thoughts, empowering words, new life goals, and endeavors as your words ride the breeze.

Visualize Your Potential

Air, for me, signifies transformation. It is something I both desire and fear. For one to transform, one has to change, like a caterpillar to a butterfly. And though I know that through change one grows, learns, and finds true empowerment, for a watery soul like myself (I am a Cancer), stepping out of my comfort zone has been a bit of an ordeal. Using the element of air as a guide through visualization has helped.

Visualization is a tool that helps to enhance consciousness and self-awareness and to focus the mind. Through this process you can harness the power of air to help clear away the clutter and see your true potential. You can either do this on your own or use a guided meditative journey to help you stay focused. I have included this breezy journey to help chase away the angry clouds of contentment and forgotten dreams.

If you have ever dreamed of riding the wind with leaves flying before you and stars at your back, this is your opportunity. This meditative journey was created by my colleague Mardi McLaskey for her *Faery Wheel of the Year* series.

Record yourself reading the following journey aloud. Speak slowly and carefully and add the pauses where indicated. Make yourself comfortable, reclining if possible. It is very important that you use headphones to listen to this. Close your eyes and breathe deeply and slowly five times. Turn on your recording device and ride the Wild Hunt . . .

Wind Horse Dreams: Riding the Wild Hunt

And now, in that wonderful imagination of yours, I want you to notice that you have entered into a time outside of time, of light and the wild air.

And, because this is an enchanted place, I want you to bring your attention to a beautiful path that leads deep into the forest. It is crisp autumn. The trees drop their golden leaves, one after the next, to the mossy ground. Around you swirls a golden dazzle of falling leaves as they enjoy their last dance with the wind. (Pause)

On you walk deep into the thick forest. An owl calls to you from a sleepy tree. High above you an eagle, that lord of the air, rises in wide spirals until he is lost in the violet dusk.

The path narrows, and water shows as a gleam of silver through the ferns. And then you step into a hidden meadow, where the sunlight dances, and a sweet wind teases your hair. The ground at your feet is starred with blossoms. (Pause)

You notice that at the exact center of this meadow is a silvery lake. The water of this lake moves among the reedy places at the shore's edge. Amidst the cattails, willow, and waving rushes, the water swirls in shimmering song, and you can see the spirit of the water glitter like jewels in the fading Sun. (Pause)

Twilight fades to purple, and the night sky is filled with pools of brilliant stars. As you gaze upon this lake, you find you are longing for a wild adventure. Hearing the cry of voices in the wind-swept sky above you, you look up, thinking they are geese, but instead you are amazed to see fierce Riders of the Sky. From the time of legends, the Wild Hunt has been handed down through the wind. Now their leader, the Lady of the Wild Hunt, blowing a breath of wind, calls out to you, "Come ride with us this starbright night! Across the sky 'til dawn's pale light. Come ride with us this wind-swept night!"

Anxious to join the Wild Hunt, you watch in amazement as an enchanted horse, proud and untamable, prances from the forest and crosses the meadow. You realize this is Liath Macha (LEE-ah MAH-ka), the Gray Mare of Macha. She stands before you, tossing her long, silvered mane. The Gray of Macha is your air spirit, your wind horse, your faithful steed, willing to serve you all the days of your life. Her beauty and power capture your heart and your mind. The air around you trembles.

With joy, you spring aboard her back, and a mighty wind lifts you up and takes you along a hallowed, windy way. Together, you ride the bright wind that sweeps across the star-spread sky. Fiercely elegant, you become a rider of the wind and the night. (Pause)

The Gray of Macha, with her gleaming, silvered head and golden hooves, looks magnificent galloping over the clouds. Outfitted with the finest brass trapping, inlaid with rare stones and delicate enamel, she is a fearsome, swift, flashing steed. Her bridle is gold with tiny sliver bells on the rim.

Dark, foreboding clouds scud across the face of a Full Moon as you ride the wind, following the Wild Hunt. You and your wild horse are one, as over the clouds you jump, riding on the breath of the wind, wild and free. (Pause)

Galloping hard now, you and your wind horse chase all of the dark, angry clouds away. Powerful now, you ride among the tangled stars and chase the clouds away, until the sky is swept clean. (Pause)

The sky is now clear and ablaze with frosted stars. The Moon ceases her wandering across the purple night. You are now the Shepherd of the Starflock. Proudly ride your wind horse among the stars. (Pause)

And now, the Gray of Macha returns to the flowery meadow and brings you down softly to the shore of Silvery Lake. You dismount and hold her elegant head in your hands, and she says, "My heart makes a song, a song of peace." After nuzzling you gently, she returns to the depths of the forest, where she awaits your next Wild Hunt.

Above you, in the star-strewn sky, the Lady of the Wild Hunt calls to you in a sweet, silvery voice, "You are a child of the universe. You were created from light and the wild air. You have a right to be here. You are a perfect child of light. You deserve all the wonders this universe has to offer."

She raises high her sword and salutes you for your courage, then races away on the wind.

You now feel as clear and free as the wind-swept sky. The stars blink and sing a dream of beauty in their heaven as you drift off to sleep . . . and dream your dreams of beauty.

~

I have to admit of all the elements, it is air that stirs my soul. Sitting on a tree-shrouded rise as the wind tangles my hair, I am no longer the home-schooling mom who lives a simple life on the banks of the Sauk River. I am the Lady of the Hunt who travels the wind! Yes, there are still times late at night when the window creaks open and the wind begins to stir that I'm not sure I want to hear what it has to say. But I will listen. I have to! I know for transformation to happen I must set myself free. And that is my advice for you, dear reader: spring forth and ride the wind. Let your hair blow wild and free and listen—there is something in the wind.

For Further Study

McLaskey, Mardi. *Faery Wheel of the Year.* Pony Wings Press, 1990.

Opsopaus, John. "The Ancient Greek Esoteric Doctrine of the Elements: Air." Biblioteca Arcana. Last modified 1998. https://web.eecs.utk.edu/~mclennan/BA/AGEDE/Air.html#H.

Almanac Section

Calendar

Time Zones

Lunar Phases

Moon Signs

Full Moons

Sabbats

World Holidays

Incense of the Day

Color of the Day

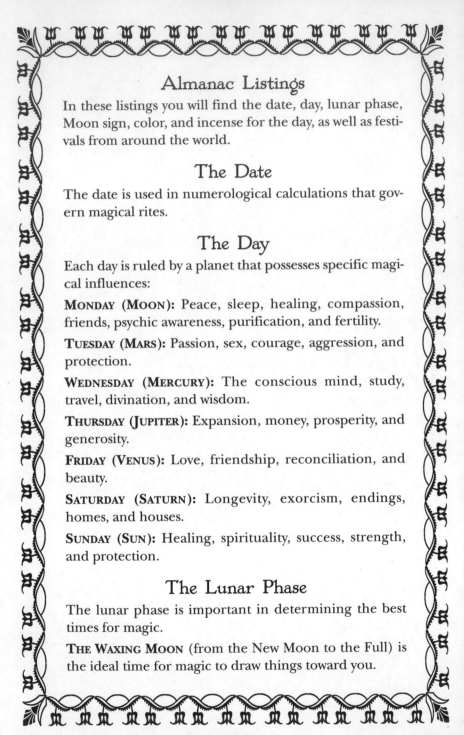

Almanac Listings

In these listings you will find the date, day, lunar phase, Moon sign, color, and incense for the day, as well as festivals from around the world.

The Date

The date is used in numerological calculations that govern magical rites.

The Day

Each day is ruled by a planet that possesses specific magical influences:

MONDAY (MOON): Peace, sleep, healing, compassion, friends, psychic awareness, purification, and fertility.

TUESDAY (MARS): Passion, sex, courage, aggression, and protection.

WEDNESDAY (MERCURY): The conscious mind, study, travel, divination, and wisdom.

THURSDAY (JUPITER): Expansion, money, prosperity, and generosity.

FRIDAY (VENUS): Love, friendship, reconciliation, and beauty.

SATURDAY (SATURN): Longevity, exorcism, endings, homes, and houses.

SUNDAY (SUN): Healing, spirituality, success, strength, and protection.

The Lunar Phase

The lunar phase is important in determining the best times for magic.

THE WAXING MOON (from the New Moon to the Full) is the ideal time for magic to draw things toward you.

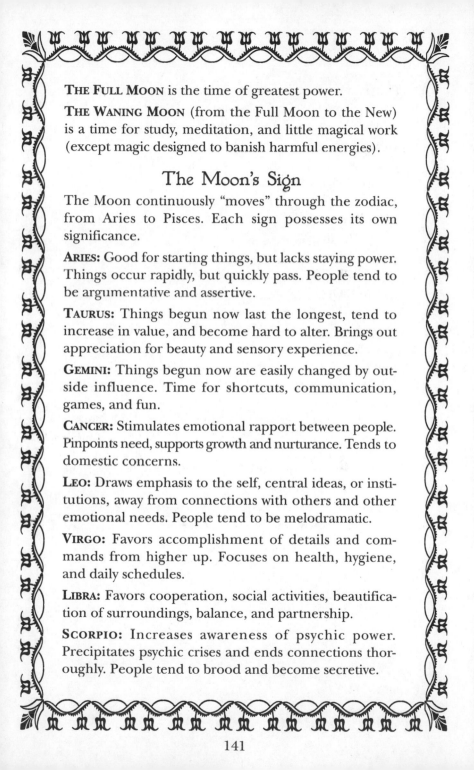

THE FULL MOON is the time of greatest power.

THE WANING MOON (from the Full Moon to the New) is a time for study, meditation, and little magical work (except magic designed to banish harmful energies).

The Moon's Sign

The Moon continuously "moves" through the zodiac, from Aries to Pisces. Each sign possesses its own significance.

ARIES: Good for starting things, but lacks staying power. Things occur rapidly, but quickly pass. People tend to be argumentative and assertive.

TAURUS: Things begun now last the longest, tend to increase in value, and become hard to alter. Brings out appreciation for beauty and sensory experience.

GEMINI: Things begun now are easily changed by outside influence. Time for shortcuts, communication, games, and fun.

CANCER: Stimulates emotional rapport between people. Pinpoints need, supports growth and nurturance. Tends to domestic concerns.

LEO: Draws emphasis to the self, central ideas, or institutions, away from connections with others and other emotional needs. People tend to be melodramatic.

VIRGO: Favors accomplishment of details and commands from higher up. Focuses on health, hygiene, and daily schedules.

LIBRA: Favors cooperation, social activities, beautification of surroundings, balance, and partnership.

SCORPIO: Increases awareness of psychic power. Precipitates psychic crises and ends connections thoroughly. People tend to brood and become secretive.

Sagittarius: Encourages flights of imagination and confidence. This is an adventurous, philosophical, and athletic Moon sign. Favors expansion and growth.

Capricorn: Develops strong structure. Focus on traditions, responsibilities, and obligations. A good time to set boundaries and rules.

Aquarius: Rebellious energy. Time to break habits and make abrupt changes. Personal freedom and individuality is the focus.

Pisces: The focus is on dreaming, nostalgia, intuition, and psychic impressions. A good time for spiritual or philanthropic activities.

Color and Incense

The color and incense for the day are based on information from *Personal Alchemy* by Amber Wolfe, and relate to the planet that rules each day. This information can be taken into consideration along with other factors when planning works of magic or when blending magic into mundane life. Please note that the incense selections listed are not hard and fast. If you cannot find or do not like the incense listed for the day, choose a similar scent that appeals to you.

Festivals and Holidays

Festivals and holidays of many cultures and nations are listed throughout the year. The exact dates of many ancient festivals are difficult to determine; prevailing data has been used.

Time Zones

The times and dates of all astrological phenomena in this almanac are based on **Eastern Standard Time (EST)**. If you live outside of the Eastern time zone, you will need to make the following adjustments:

PACIFIC STANDARD TIME: Subtract three hours.

MOUNTAIN STANDARD TIME: Subtract two hours.

CENTRAL STANDARD TIME: Subtract one hour.

ALASKA: Subtract four hours.

HAWAII: Subtract five hours.

DAYLIGHT SAVING TIME (ALL ZONES): Add one hour.

Daylight Saving Time begins at 2 am on March 12, 2017, and ends at 2 am on November 5, 2017.

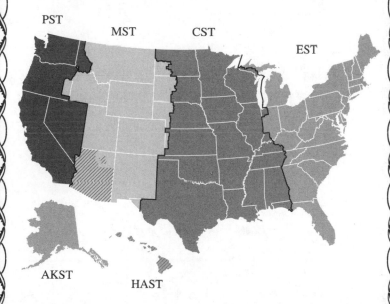

Please refer to a world time zone resource for time adjustments for locations outside the United States.

2017 Sabbats
and Full Moons

January 12	Cancer Full Moon 6:34 am
February 2	Imbolc
February 10	Leo Full Moon 7:33 pm
March 12	Virgo Full Moon 10:54 am
March 20	Ostara (Spring Equinox)
April 11	Libra Full Moon 2:08 am
May 1	Beltane
May 10	Scorpio Full Moon 5:42 pm
June 9	Sagittarius Full Moon 9:10 am
June 21	Midsummer (Summer Solstice)
July 9	Capricorn Full Moon 12:07 am
August 1	Lammas
August 7	Aquarius Full Moon 2:11 pm
September 6	Pisces Full Moon 3:03 am
September 22	Mabon (Fall Equinox)
October 5	Aries Full Moon 2:40 pm
October 31	Samhain
November 4	Taurus Full Moon 1:23 am
December 3	Gemini Full Moon 10:47 am
December 21	Yule (Winter Solstice)

All times are Eastern Standard Time (EST)
or Eastern Daylight Time (EDT)

2017 Sabbats in the Southern Hemisphere

Because Earth's Northern and Southern Hemispheres experience opposite seasons at any given time, the season-based sabbats listed on the previous page and in this almanac section are not correct for those residing south of the equator. Listed here are the Southern Hemisphere sabbat dates for 2017:

February 2	Lammas
March 20	Mabon (Fall Equinox)
May 1	Samhain
June 21	Yule (Winter Solstice)
August 1	Imbolc
September 22	Ostara (Spring Equinox)
November 1	Beltane
December 21	Midsummer (Summer Solstice)

Birthstone poetry reprinted from
The Occult and Curative Powers of Precious Stones
by William T. Fernie, M.D.
Harper & Row (1981)

Originally printed in 1907 as
Precious Stones:
For Curative Wear; and Other Remedial Uses;
Likewise the Nobler Metals

January

1 Sunday
New Year's Day • Kwanzaa and Hanukkah end
Waxing Moon
Moon phase: First Quarter
Color: Orange

Moon Sign: Aquarius
Incense: Almond

2 Monday
First Writing Day (Japanese)
Waxing Moon
Moon phase: First Quarter
Color: Lavender

Moon Sign: Aquarius
Moon enters Pisces 4:57 am
Incense: Narcissus

3 Tuesday
St. Genevieve's Day
Waxing Moon
Moon phase: First Quarter
Color: White

Moon Sign: Pisces
Incense: Ginger

4 Wednesday
Kamakura Workers' Festival (Japanese)
Waxing Moon
Moon phase: First Quarter
Color: Brown

Moon Sign: Pisces
Moon enters Aries 11:20 am
Incense: Lilac

☽ Thursday
Bird Day
Waxing Moon
Second Quarter 2:47 pm
Color: Purple

Moon Sign: Aries
Incense: Clove

6 Friday
Epiphany
Waxing Moon
Moon phase: Second Quarter
Color: Pink

Moon Sign: Aries
Moon enters Taurus 3:18 pm
Incense: Rose

7 Saturday
Tricolor Day (Italian)
Waxing Moon
Moon phase: Second Quarter
Color: Indigo

Moon Sign: Taurus
Incense: Sage

January

8 Sunday
Midwives' Day (Bulgarian)
Waxing Moon
Moon phase: Second Quarter
Color: Amber

Moon Sign: Taurus
Moon enters Gemini 5:06 pm
Incense: Eucalyptus

9 Monday
Feast of the Black Nazarene (Filipino)
Waxing Moon
Moon phase: Second Quarter
Color: Gray

Moon Sign: Gemini
Incense: Hyssop

10 Tuesday
Feast of St. Leonie Aviat
Waxing Moon
Moon phase: Second Quarter
Color: Black

Moon Sign: Gemini
Moon enters Cancer 5:49 pm
Incense: Bayberry

11 Wednesday
Carmentalia (Roman)
Waxing Moon
Moon phase: Second Quarter
Color: Yellow

Moon Sign: Cancer
Incense: Lavender

☺ Thursday
Revolution Day (Tanzanian)
Waxing Moon
Full Moon 6:34 am
Color: Crimson

Moon Sign: Cancer
Moon enters Leo 7:08 pm
Incense: Jasmine

13 Friday
Twentieth Day (Norwegian)
Waning Moon
Moon phase: Third Quarter
Color: Rose

Moon Sign: Leo
Incense: Thyme

14 Saturday
Feast of the Ass (French)
Waning Moon
Moon phase: Third Quarter
Color: Brown

Moon Sign: Leo
Moon enters Virgo 10:52 pm
Incense: Pine

January

15 Sunday
Korean Alphabet Day
Waning Moon
Moon phase: Third Quarter
Color: Gold

Moon Sign: Virgo
Incense: Juniper

16 Monday
Martin Luther King Jr. Day
Waning Moon
Moon phase: Third Quarter
Color: Silver

Moon Sign: Virgo
Incense: Lily

17 Tuesday
St. Anthony's Day (Mexican)
Waning Moon
Moon phase: Third Quarter
Color: Maroon

Moon Sign: Virgo
Moon enters Libra 6:16 am
Incense: Cinnamon

18 Wednesday
Feast of St. Athanasius
Waning Moon
Moon phase: Third Quarter
Color: White

Moon Sign: Libra
Incense: Honeysuckle

◐ Thursday
Edgar Allen Poe's birthday
Waning Moon
Fourth Quarter 5:13 pm
Color: Turquoise

Moon Sign: Libra
Moon enters Scorpio 5:09 pm
Sun enters Aquarius 4:24 pm
Incense: Myrrh

20 Friday
Inauguration Day
Waning Moon
Moon phase: Fourth Quarter
Color: Coral

Moon Sign: Scorpio
Incense: Vanilla

21 Saturday
St. Agnes's Day
Waning Moon
Moon phase: Fourth Quarter
Color: Blue

Moon Sign: Scorpio
Incense: Ivy

January

22 Sunday
St. Vincent's Day (French)
Waning Moon
Moon phase: Fourth Quarter
Color: Yellow

Moon Sign: Scorpio
Moon enters Sagittarius 5:45 am
Incense: Marigold

---

23 Monday
Feast of St. Ildefonsus
Waning Moon
Moon phase: Fourth Quarter
Color: Ivory

Moon Sign: Sagittarius
Incense: Clary sage

---

24 Tuesday
Alasitas Fair (Bolivian)
Waning Moon
Moon phase: Fourth Quarter
Color: Gray

Moon Sign: Sagittarius
Moon enters Capricorn 5:43 pm
Incense: Geranium

---

25 Wednesday
Burns Night (Scottish)
Waning Moon
Moon phase: Fourth Quarter
Color: Topaz

Moon Sign: Capricorn
Incense: Bay laurel

---

26 Thursday
Australia Day
Waning Moon
Moon phase: Fourth Quarter
Color: Green

Moon Sign: Capricorn
Incense: Nutmeg

☽ Friday
Holocaust Remembrance Day
Waning Moon
New Moon 7:07 pm
Color: Purple

Moon Sign: Capricorn
Moon enters Aquarius 3:37 am
Incense: Violet

---

28 Saturday
Lunar New Year (Rooster)
Waxing Moon
Moon phase: First Quarter
Color: Black

Moon Sign: Aquarius
Incense: Patchouli

29 Sunday
Feast of St. Gildas
Waxing Moon
Moon phase: First Quarter
Color: Orange

Moon Sign: Aquarius
Moon enters Pisces 11:10 am
Incense: Frankincense

30 Monday
Martyrs' Day (Indian)
Waxing Moon
Moon phase: First Quarter
Color: White

Moon Sign: Pisces
Incense: Neroli

31 Tuesday
Independence Day (Nauru)
Waxing Moon
Moon phase: First Quarter
Color: Scarlet

Moon Sign: Pisces
Moon enters Aries 4:46 pm
Incense: Ylang-ylang

January Birthstones

By her in January born
No gem save Garnets should be worn;
They will ensure her constancy,
True friendship, and fidelity.

Modern: Garnet   Zodiac (Capricorn): Ruby

February Birthstones

The February-born shall find
Sincerity, and peace of mind,
Freedom from passion and from care,
If they the Amethyst will wear.

Modern: Amethyst   Zodiac (Aquarius): Garnet

February

1 Wednesday
St. Brigid's Day (Irish)
Waxing Moon
Moon phase: First Quarter
Color: Brown

Moon Sign: Aries
Incense: Marjoram

2 Thursday
Imbolc • Groundhog Day
Waxing Moon
Moon phase: First Quarter
Color: Crimson

Moon Sign: Aries
Moon enters Taurus 8:50 pm
Incense: Carnation

◐ Friday
St. Blaise's Day
Waxing Moon
Second Quarter 11:19 pm
Color: Rose

Moon Sign: Taurus
Incense: Orchid

4 Saturday
Independence Day (Sri Lankan)
Waxing Moon
Moon phase: Second Quarter
Color: Gray

Moon Sign: Taurus
Moon enters Gemini 11:44 pm
Incense: Magnolia

5 Sunday
Constitution Day (Mexican)
Waxing Moon
Moon phase: Second Quarter
Color: Yellow

Moon Sign: Gemini
Incense: Heliotrope

6 Monday
Bob Marley's birthday (Jamaican)
Waxing Moon
Moon phase: Second Quarter
Color: Silver

Moon Sign: Gemini
Incense: Rosemary

7 Tuesday
Feast of St. Richard the Pilgrim
Waxing Moon
Moon phase: Second Quarter
Color: Red

Moon Sign: Gemini
Moon enters Cancer 2:03 am
Incense: Cedar

February

8 **Wednesday**
Prešeren Day (Slovenian)
Waxing Moon
Moon phase: Second Quarter
Color: Topaz

Moon Sign: Cancer
Incense: Lavender

9 **Thursday**
St. Maron's Day (Lebanese)
Waxing Moon
Moon phase: Second Quarter
Color: Green

Moon Sign: Cancer
Moon enters Leo 4:41 am
Incense: Balsam

☺ **Friday**
Feast of St. Scholastica
Waxing Moon
Full Moon 7:33 pm
Color: Purple

Moon Sign: Leo
Incense: Rose

11 **Saturday**
National Foundation Day (Japanese)
Waning Moon
Moon phase: Third Quarter
Color: Blue

Moon Sign: Leo
Moon enters Virgo 8:52 am
Incense: Pine

12 **Sunday**
Abraham Lincoln's birthday
Waning Moon
Moon phase: Third Quarter
Color: Gold

Moon Sign: Virgo
Incense: Juniper

13 **Monday**
Parentalia (Roman)
Waning Moon
Moon phase: Third Quarter
Color: Lavender

Moon Sign: Virgo
Moon enters Libra 3:43 pm
Incense: Clary sage

14 **Tuesday**
Valentine's Day
Waning Moon
Moon phase: Third Quarter
Color: Gray

Moon Sign: Libra
Incense: Ginger

February

15 Wednesday
Susan B. Anthony Day
Waning Moon
Moon phase: Third Quarter
Color: Yellow

Moon Sign: Libra
Incense: Honeysuckle

16 Thursday
Feast of St. Juliana of Nicodemia
Waning Moon
Moon phase: Third Quarter
Color: Turquoise

Moon Sign: Libra
Moon enters Scorpio 1:41 am
Incense: Jasmine

17 Friday
Quirinalia (Roman)
Waning Moon
Moon phase: Third Quarter
Color: Pink

Moon Sign: Scorpio
Incense: Mint

◖ Saturday
St. Bernadette's Third Vision
Waning Moon
Fourth Quarter 2:33 pm
Color: Black

Moon Sign: Scorpio
Moon enters Sagittarius 1:52 pm
Sun enters Pisces 6:31 am
Incense: Sandalwood

19 Sunday
Flag Day (Turkmenian)
Waning Moon
Moon phase: Fourth Quarter
Color: Amber

Moon Sign: Sagittarius
Incense: Almond

20 Monday
Presidents' Day
Waning Moon
Moon phase: Fourth Quarter
Color: Ivory

Moon Sign: Sagittarius
Incense: Hyssop

21 Tuesday
Feralia (Roman)
Waning Moon
Moon phase: Fourth Quarter
Color: Maroon

Moon Sign: Sagittarius
Moon enters Capricorn 2:08 am
Incense: Basil

February ♓

22 Wednesday
Caristia (Roman)
Waning Moon
Moon phase: Fourth Quarter
Color: White

Moon Sign: Capricorn
Incense: Lilac

23 Thursday
Mashramani Festival (Guyana)
Waning Moon
Moon phase: Fourth Quarter
Color: Purple

Moon Sign: Capricorn
Moon enters Aquarius 12:17 pm
Incense: Apricot

24 Friday
Maha Shivaratri
Waning Moon
Moon phase: Fourth Quarter
Color: Coral

Moon Sign: Aquarius
Incense: Cypress

25 Saturday
St. Walburga's Day (German)
Waning Moon
Moon phase: Fourth Quarter
Color: Indigo

Moon Sign: Aquarius
Moon enters Pisces 7:24 pm
Incense: Rue

☽ Sunday
Zamboanga Day (Filipino)
Waning Moon
New Moon 9:58 pm
Color: Orange

Moon Sign: Pisces
Incense: Hyacinth

27 Monday
Independence Day (Dominican)
Waxing Moon
Moon phase: First Quarter
Color: White

Moon Sign: Pisces
Moon enters Aries 11:52 pm
Incense: Lily

28 Tuesday
Mardi Gras (Fat Tuesday)
Waxing Moon
Moon phase: First Quarter
Color: Black

Moon Sign: Aries
Incense: Cinnamon

March

1 Wednesday
Ash Wednesday
Waxing Moon
Moon phase: First Quarter
Color: Topaz

Moon Sign: Aries
Incense: Marjoram

2 Thursday
Read Across America Day
Waxing Moon
Moon phase: First Quarter
Color: Green

Moon Sign: Aries
Moon enters Sagittarius 2:43 am
Incense: Clove

3 Friday
Doll Festival (Japanese)
Waxing Moon
Moon phase: First Quarter
Color: Pink

Moon Sign: Taurus
Incense: Alder

4 Saturday
St. Casimir's Fair (Polish and Lithuanian)
Waxing Moon
Moon phase: First Quarter
Color: Gray

Moon Sign: Taurus
Moon enters Gemini 5:05 am
Incense: Sage

☽ Sunday
Navigium Isidis Festival (Roman)
Waxing Moon
Second Quarter 6:32 pm
Color: Gold

Moon Sign: Gemini
Incense: Frankincense

6 Monday
Alamo Day (Texan)
Waxing Moon
Moon phase: Second Quarter
Color: Lavender

Moon Sign: Gemini
Moon enters Cancer 7:54 am
Incense: Neroli

7 Tuesday
Vejovis Festival (Roman)
Waxing Moon
Moon phase: Second Quarter
Color: Scarlet

Moon Sign: Cancer
Incense: Ylang-ylang

March

8 Wednesday
International Women's Day
Waxing Moon
Moon phase: Second Quarter
Color: White

Moon Sign: Cancer
Moon enters Leo 11:45 pm
Incense: Bay laurel

9 Thursday
Teachers' Day (Lebanese)
Waxing Moon
Moon phase: Second Quarter
Color: Purple

Moon Sign: Leo
Incense: Myrrh

10 Friday
Tibet Uprising Day
Waxing Moon
Moon phase: Second Quarter
Color: Rose

Moon Sign: Leo
Moon enters Virgo 5:07 pm
Incense: Vanilla

11 Saturday
Johnny Appleseed Day
Waxing Moon
Moon phase: Second Quarter
Color: Black

Moon Sign: Virgo
Incense: Patchouli

☻ Sunday
Purim
Waxing Moon
Full Moon: 10:54 am
Color: Amber

Moon Sign: Virgo
Incense: Eucalyptus
Daylight Saving Time begins at 2 am

13 Monday
Feast of St. Leander of Seville
Waning Moon
Moon phase: Third Quarter
Color: Silver

Moon Sign: Virgo
Moon enters Libra 1:28 am
Incense: Rosemary

14 Tuesday
Pi Day
Waning Moon
Moon phase: Third Quarter
Color: Maroon

Moon Sign: Libra
Incense: Bayberry

March

15 Wednesday
Fertility Festival (Japanese)
Waning Moon
Moon phase: Third Quarter
Color: Brown

Moon Sign: Libra
Moon enters Scorpio 11:11 am
Incense: Honeysuckle

16 Thursday
St. Urho's Day (Finnish-American)
Waning Moon
Moon phase: Third Quarter
Color: Crimson

Moon Sign: Scorpio
Incense: Mulberry

17 Friday
St. Patrick's Day
Waning Moon
Moon phase: Third Quarter
Color: Purple

Moon Sign: Scorpio
Moon enters Sagittarius 11:00 pm
Incense: Thyme

18 Saturday
Sheelah's Day (Irish)
Waning Moon
Moon phase: Third Quarter
Color: Indigo

Moon Sign: Sagittarius
Incense: Pine

19 Sunday
Minna Canth's birthday (Finnish)
Waning Moon
Moon phase: Third Quarter
Color: Yellow

Moon Sign: Sagittarius
Incense: Marigold

◖ Monday
Ostara • Spring Equinox
Waning Moon
Fourth Quarter 11:58 am
Color: White

Moon Sign: Sagittarius
Moon enters Capricorn 11:31 am
Sun enters Aries 6:29 am
Incense: Narcissus

21 Tuesday
Harmony Day (Australian)
Waning Moon
Moon phase: Fourth Quarter
Color: Black

Moon Sign: Capricorn
Incense: Ginger

March ♈

22 Wednesday
World Water Day
Waning Moon
Moon phase: Fourth Quarter
Color: Topaz

Moon Sign: Capricorn
Moon enters Aquarius 10:28 pm
Incense: Lilac

23 Thursday
Pakistan Day
Waning Moon
Moon phase: Fourth Quarter
Color: Green

Moon Sign: Aquarius
Incense: Nutmeg

24 Friday
Denver March Powwow (ends March 26)
Waning Moon
Moon phase: Fourth Quarter
Color: Coral

Moon Sign: Aquarius
Incense: Yarrow

25 Saturday
Tolkien Reading Day
Waning Moon
Moon phase: Fourth Quarter
Color: Blue

Moon Sign: Aquarius
Moon enters Pisces 6:06 am
Incense: Ivy

26 Sunday
Prince Kuhio Day (Hawaiian)
Waning Moon
Moon phase: Fourth Quarter
Color: Orange

Moon Sign: Pisces
Incense: Juniper

☽ Monday
World Theatre Day
Waning Moon
New Moon 10:57 pm
Color: Ivory

Moon Sign: Pisces
Moon enters Aries 10:11 am
Incense: Clary sage

28 Tuesday
Weed Appreciation Day
Waxing Moon
Moon phase: First Quarter
Color: Gray

Moon Sign: Aries
Incense: Cedar

March

29 Wednesday
Feast of St. Eustace of Luxeuil
Waxing Moon
Moon phase: First Quarter
Color: Yellow

Moon Sign: Aries
Moon enters Taurus 11:48 am
Incense: Lavender

30 Thursday
Seward's Day (Alaskan)
Waxing Moon
Moon phase: First Quarter
Color: Turquoise

Moon Sign: Taurus
Incense: Balsam

31 Friday
César Chávez Day
Waxing Moon
Moon phase: First Quarter
Color: White

Moon Sign: Taurus
Moon enters Gemini 12:40 pm
Incense: Violet

March Birthstones

Who in this world of ours, her eyes
In March first opens, shall be wise.
In days of peril, firm and brave,
And wear a Bloodstone to her grave.

Modern: Aquamarine
Zodiac (Pisces): Amethyst

April ♈

1 Saturday
All Fools' Day • April Fools' Day   Moon Sign: Gemini
Waxing Moon   Incense: Sandalwood
Moon phase: First Quarter
Color: Black

2 Sunday
The Battle of Flowers (French)   Moon Sign: Gemini
Waxing Moon   Moon enters Cancer 2:27 pm
Moon phase: First Quarter   Incense: Almond
Color: Yellow

☾ **Monday**
Feast of St. Mary of Egypt   Moon Sign: Cancer
Waxing Moon   Incense: Hyssop
Second Quarter 2:39 pm
Color: Silver

4 Tuesday
Tomb-Sweeping Day (Chinese)   Moon Sign: Cancer
Waxing Moon   Moon enters Leo 6:13 pm
Moon phase: Second Quarter   Incense: Basil
Color: Red

5 Wednesday
Children's Day (Palestinian)   Moon Sign: Leo
Waxing Moon   Incense: Honeysuckle
Moon phase: Second Quarter
Color: Brown

6 Thursday
Chakri Memorial Day (Thai)   Moon Sign: Leo
Waxing Moon   Incense: Jasmine
Moon phase: Second Quarter
Color: Crimson

7 Friday
Motherhood and Beauty Day (Armenian)   Moon Sign: Leo
Waxing Moon   Moon enters Virgo 12:20 am
Moon Phase: Second Quarter   Incense: Rose
Color: Purple

April

8 Saturday
Buddha's birthday
Waxing Moon
Moon phase: Second Quarter
Color: Gray

Moon Sign: Virgo
Incense: Rue

9 Sunday
Valour Day (Filipino)
Waxing Moon
Moon phase: Second Quarter
Color: Gold

Moon Sign: Virgo
Moon enters Libra 8:34 am
Incense: Marigold

10 Monday
Siblings Day
Waxing Moon
Moon phase: Second Quarter
Color: White

Moon Sign: Libra
Incense: Lily

☺ Tuesday
Passover begins
Waxing Moon
Full Moon: 2:08 am
Color: Black

Moon Sign: Libra
Moon enters Scorpio 6:42 pm
Incense: Cinnamon

12 Wednesday
Children's Day (Bolivian and Haitian)
Waning Moon
Moon phase: Third Quarter
Color: Topaz

Moon Sign: Scorpio
Incense: Lilac

13 Thursday
Thai New Year (ends April 15)
Waning Moon
Moon phase: Third Quarter
Color: Turquoise

Moon Sign: Scorpio
Incense: Apricot

14 Friday
Good Friday
Waning Moon
Moon phase: Third Quarter
Color: Coral

Moon Sign: Scorpio
Moon enters Sagittarius 6:27 am
Incense: Orchid

161

April

15 Saturday
Fordicidia (Roman)
Waning Moon
Moon phase: Third Quarter
Color: Indigo

Moon Sign: Sagittarius
Incense: Sage

16 Sunday
Easter
Waning Moon
Moon phase: Third Quarter
Color: Amber

Moon Sign: Sagittarius
Moon enters Capricorn 7:05 pm
Incense: Heliotrope

17 Monday
Yayoi Matsuri (Japanese)
Waning Moon
Moon phase: Third Quarter
Color: Lavender

Moon Sign: Capricorn
Incense: Rosemary

18 Tuesday
Passover ends
Waning Moon
Moon phase: Third Quarter
Color: Scarlet

Moon Sign: Capricorn
Incense: Ginger

◗ Wednesday
Primrose Day (British)
Waning Moon
Fourth Quarter 5:57 am
Color: White

Moon Sign: Capricorn
Moon enters Aquarius 6:52 am
Sun enters Taurus 5:27 pm
Incense: Marjoram

20 Thursday
Drum Festival (Japanese)
Waning Moon
Moon phase: Fourth Quarter
Color: Purple

Moon Sign: Aquarius
Incense: Clove

21 Friday
Tiradentes Day (Brazilian)
Waning Moon
Moon phase: Fourth Quarter
Color: Pink

Moon Sign: Aquarius
Moon enters Pisces 3:43 pm
Incense: Mint

April

22 Saturday
Earth Day
Waning Moon
Moon phase: Fourth Quarter
Color: Brown

Moon Sign: Pisces
Incense: Magnolia

23 Sunday
St. George's Day
Waning Moon
Moon phase: Fourth Quarter
Color: Gold

Moon Sign: Pisces
Moon enters Aries 8:32 pm
Incense: Almond

24 Monday
St. Mark's Eve
Waning Moon
Moon phase: Fourth Quarter
Color: Ivory

Moon Sign: Aries
Incense: Neroli

25 Tuesday
Robigalia (Roman)
Waning Moon
Moon phase: Fourth Quarter
Color: Gray

Moon Sign: Aries
Moon enters Taurus 9:56 pm
Incense: Geranium

☽ Wednesday
Chernobyl Remembrance Day (Belarusian)
Waning Moon
New Moon 8:16 am
Color: Yellow

Moon Sign: Taurus
Incense: Lavender

27 Thursday
Freedom Day (South Africa)
Waxing Moon
Moon phase: First Quarter
Color: Green

Moon Sign: Taurus
Moon enters Gemini 9:39 pm
Incense: Carnation

28 Friday
Floralia (Roman)
Waxing Moon
Moon phase: First Quarter
Color: Rose

Moon Sign: Gemini
Incense: Alder

April

29 **Saturday**
Showa Day (Japanese)
Waxing Moon
Moon phase: First Quarter
Color: Blue

Moon Sign: Gemini
Moon enters Cancer 9:48 pm
Incense: Rue

30 **Sunday**
Walpurgis Night • May Eve
Waxing Moon
Moon phase: First Quarter
Color: Orange

Moon Sign: Cancer
Incense: Juniper

April Birthstones

She who from April dates her years,
Diamonds shall wear, lest bitter tears
For vain repentance flow; this stone
Emblem for innocence is known.

Modern: Diamond
Zodiac (Aries): Bloodstone

May

1   **Monday**
Beltane • May Day
Waxing Moon
Moon phase: First Quarter
Color: Gray

Moon Sign: Cancer
Incense: Clary sage

☾   **Tuesday**
Teacher Appreciation Day
Waxing Moon
Second Quarter 10:47 pm
Color: Maroon

Moon Sign: Cancer
Moon enters Leo 12:12 am
Incense: Cedar

3   **Wednesday**
Roodmas
Waxing Moon
Moon phase: Second Quarter
Color: Topaz

Moon Sign: Leo
Incense: Bay laurel

4   **Thursday**
Bona Dea (Roman)
Waxing Moon
Moon phase: Second Quarter
Color: Turquoise

Moon Sign: Leo
Moon enters Virgo 5:47 am
Incense: Balsam

5   **Friday**
Cinco de Mayo (Mexican)
Waxing Moon
Moon phase: Second Quarter
Color: Rose

Moon Sign: Virgo
Incense: Vanilla

6   **Saturday**
Martyrs' Day (Lebanese and Syrian)
Waxing Moon
Moon phase: Second Quarter
Color: Indigo

Moon Sign: Virgo
Moon enters Libra 2:20 pm
Incense: Sage

7   **Sunday**
Pilgrimage of St. Nicholas (Italian)
Waxing Moon
Moon phase: Second Quarter
Color: Amber

Moon Sign: Libra
Incense: Hyacinth

May

8 Monday
Furry Dance (English)
Waxing Moon
Moon phase: Second Quarter
Color: Silver

Moon Sign: Libra
Incense: Rosemary

9 Tuesday
Lemuria (Roman)
Waxing Moon
Moon phase: Second Quarter
Color: Red

Moon Sign: Libra
Moon enters Scorpio 1:01 am
Incense: Ylang-ylang

Wednesday
Independence Day (Romanian)
Waxing Moon
Full Moon 5:42 pm
Color: Yellow

Moon Sign: Scorpio
Incense: Honeysuckle

11 Thursday
Ukai season opens (Japanese)
Waning Moon
Moon phase: Third Quarter
Color: Purple

Moon Sign: Scorpio
Moon enters Sagittarius 12:59 pm
Incense: Nutmeg

12 Friday
Florence Nightingale's birthday
Waning Moon
Moon phase: Third Quarter
Color: Pink

Moon Sign: Sagittarius
Incense: Orchid

13 Saturday
Pilgrimage to Fátima (Portuguese)
Waning Moon
Moon phase: Third Quarter
Color: Blue

Moon Sign: Sagittarius
Incense: Sandalwood

14 Sunday
Carabao Festival (Spanish)
Waning Moon
Moon phase: Third Quarter
Color: Orange

Moon Sign: Sagittarius
Moon enters Capricorn 1:37 am
Incense: Frankincense

May

15 **Monday**
Festival of St. Dymphna
Waning Moon
Moon phase: Third Quarter
Color: Ivory

Moon Sign: Capricorn
Incense: Narcissus

16 **Tuesday**
Feast of St. Honoratus
Waning Moon
Moon phase: Third Quarter
Color: Black

Moon Sign: Capricorn
Moon enters Aquarius 1:50 pm
Incense: Basil

17 **Wednesday**
Norwegian Constitution Day
Waning Moon
Moon phase: Third Quarter
Color: White

Moon Sign: Aquarius
Incense: Lavender

○ **Thursday**
Battle of Las Piedras Day (Uruguayan)
Waxing Moon
Fourth Quarter 8:33 pm
Color: Crimson

Moon Sign: Aquarius
Moon enters Pisces 11:52 pm
Incense: Mulberry

19 **Friday**
Mother's Day (Kyrgyzstani)
Waning Moon
Moon phase: Fourth Quarter
Color: Coral

Moon Sign: Pisces
Incense: Thyme

20 **Saturday**
Feast of St. Aurea of Ostia
Waning Moon
Moon phase: Fourth Quarter
Color: Gray

Moon Sign: Pisces
Sun enters Gemini 4:31 pm
Incense: Patchouli

21 **Sunday**
Navy Day (Chilean)
Waning Moon
Moon phase: Fourth Quarter
Color: Yellow

Moon Sign: Pisces
Moon enters Aries 6:10 am
Incense: Marigold

May

22 Monday
Victoria Day (Canada)
Waning Moon
Moon phase: Fourth Quarter
Color: Lavender

Moon Sign: Aries
Incense: Neroli

---

23 Tuesday
Tubilustrium (Roman)
Waning Moon
Moon phase: Fourth Quarter
Color: Scarlet

Moon Sign: Aries
Moon enters Taurus 8:33 am
Incense: Cinnamon

---

24 Wednesday
Education and Culture Day (Bulgarian)
Waning Moon
Moon phase: Fourth Quarter
Color: Brown

Moon Sign: Taurus
Incense: Marjoram

Thursday
Missing Children's Day
Waning Moon
New Moon 3:44 pm
Color: Green

Moon Sign: Taurus
Moon enters Gemini 8:15 am
Incense: Myrrh

---

26 Friday
Pepys's Commemoration (English)
Waxing Moon
Moon phase: First Quarter
Color: Purple

Moon Sign: Gemini
Incense: Rose

---

27 Saturday
Ramadan begins
Waxing Moon
Moon phase: First Quarter
Color: Black

Moon Sign: Gemini
Moon enters Cancer 7:25 am
Incense: Pine

---

28 Sunday
Feast of St. Germain
Waxing Moon
Moon phase: First Quarter
Color: Gold

Moon Sign: Cancer
Incense: Eucalyptus

May

29 Monday

Memorial Day
Waxing Moon
Moon phase: First Quarter
Color: Silver

Moon Sign: Cancer
Moon enters Leo 8:12 am
Incense: Lily

30 Tuesday

Dragon Boat Festival (Chinese)
Waxing Moon
Moon phase: First Quarter
Color: White

Moon Sign: Leo
Incense: Geranium

31 Wednesday

Shavuot
Waxing Moon
Moon phase: First Quarter
Color: Topaz

Moon Sign: Leo
Moon enters Virgo 12:16 pm
Incense: Lilac

May Birthstones

Who first beholds the light of day,
In spring's sweet flowery month of May,
And wears an Emerald all her life,
Shall be a loved, and happy wife.

Modern: Emerald
Zodiac (Taurus): Sapphire

June

♊

◐ **Thursday**
Rice Harvest Festival (Malaysian)
Waxing Moon
Second Quarter 8:42 am
Color: Purple

Moon Sign: Virgo
Incense: Apricot

2 **Friday**
Republic Day (Italian)
Waxing Moon
Moon phase: Second Quarter
Color: Pink

Moon Sign: Virgo
Moon enters Libra 8:04 pm
Incense: Mint

3 **Saturday**
Feast of St. Clotilde
Waxing Moon
Moon phase: Second Quarter
Color: Indigo

Moon Sign: Libra
Incense: Rue

4 **Sunday**
Flag Day (Estonian)
Waxing Moon
Moon phase: Second Quarter
Color: Orange

Moon Sign: Libra
Incense: Heliotrope

5 **Monday**
Constitution Day (Danish)
Waxing Moon
Moon phase: Second Quarter
Color: Ivory

Moon Sign: Libra
Moon enters Scorpio 6:46 am
Incense: Narcissus

6 **Tuesday**
National Day of Sweden
Waxing Moon
Moon phase: Second Quarter
Color: Scarlet

Moon Sign: Scorpio
Incense: Ginger

7 **Wednesday**
Vestalia begins (Roman)
Waxing Moon
Moon phase: Second Quarter
Color: Brown

Moon Sign: Scorpio
Moon enters Sagittarius 6:59 pm
Incense: Lavender

June

♊

8 Thursday
World Oceans Day
Waxing Moon
Moon phase: Second Quarter
Color: White

Moon Sign: Sagittarius
Incense: Carnation

☺ **Friday**
Heroes' Day (Ugandan)
Waxing Moon
Full Moon 9:10 am
Color: Rose

Moon Sign: Sagittarius
Incense: Violet

---

10 Saturday
Portugal Day
Waning Moon
Moon phase: Third Quarter
Color: Black

Moon Sign: Sagittarius
Moon enters Capricorn 7:36 am
Incense: Ivy

---

11 Sunday
Kamehameha Day (Hawaiian)
Waning Moon
Moon phase: Third Quarter
Color: Gold

Moon Sign: Capricorn
Incense: Marigold

---

12 Monday
Independence Day (Filipino)
Waning Moon
Moon phase: Third Quarter
Color: White

Moon Sign: Capricorn
Moon enters Aquarius 7:45 pm
Incense: Hyssop

---

13 Tuesday
St. Anthony of Padua's Day
Waning Moon
Moon phase: Third Quarter
Color: Red

Moon Sign: Aquarius
Incense: Cedar

---

14 Wednesday
Flag Day
Waning Moon
Moon phase: Third Quarter
Color: Yellow

Moon Sign: Aquarius
Incense: Honeysuckle

June

15 Thursday
Vestalia ends (Roman)
Waning Moon
Moon phase: Third Quarter
Color: Turquoise

Moon Sign: Aquarius
Moon enters Pisces 6:17 am
Incense: Balsam

16 Friday
Bloomsday (Irish)
Waning Moon
Moon phase: Third Quarter
Color: Coral

Moon Sign: Pisces
Incense: Vanilla

◖ Saturday
National Day (Icelandic)
Waning Moon
Fourth Quarter 7:33 am
Color: Gray

Moon Sign: Pisces
Moon enters Aries 1:55 pm
Incense: Pine

18 Sunday
Waterloo Day (British)
Waning Moon
Moon phase: Fourth Quarter
Color: Orange

Moon Sign: Aries
Incense: Almond

19 Monday
Juneteenth
Waning Moon
Moon phase: Fourth Quarter
Color: Silver

Moon Sign: Aries
Moon enters Taurus 5:53 pm
Incense: Lily

20 Tuesday
Flag Day (Argentinian)
Waning Moon
Moon phase: Fourth Quarter
Color: Maroon

Moon Sign: Taurus
Incense: Bayberry

21 Wednesday
Litha • Summer Solstice
Waning Moon
Moon phase: Fourth Quarter
Color: Topaz

Moon Sign: Taurus
Moon enters Gemini 6:44 pm
Sun enters Cancer 12:24 am
Incense: Bay laurel

June

22 Thursday
Teachers' Day (El Salvadoran)
Waning Moon
Moon phase: Fourth Quarter
Color: Green

Moon Sign: Gemini
Incense: Clove

Friday
St. John's Eve
Waning Moon
New Moon 10:31 pm
Color: Purple

Moon Sign: Gemini
Moon enters Cancer 6:07 pm
Incense: Yarrow

24 Saturday
St. John's Day
Waxing Moon
Moon phase: First Quarter
Color: Blue

Moon Sign: Cancer
Incense: Sandalwood

25 Sunday
Ramadan ends
Waxing Moon
Moon phase: First Quarter
Color: Amber

Moon Sign: Cancer
Moon enters Leo 6:06 pm
Incense: Frankincense

26 Monday
Pied Piper Day (German)
Waxing Moon
Moon phase: First Quarter
Color: Lavender

Moon Sign: Leo
Incense: Rosemary

27 Tuesday
Seven Sleepers' Day (German)
Waxing Moon
Moon phase: First Quarter
Color: Gray

Moon Sign: Leo
Moon enters Virgo 8:41 pm
Incense: Basil

28 Wednesday
Paul Bunyan Day
Waxing Moon
Moon phase: First Quarter
Color: White

Moon Sign: Virgo
Incense: Lilac

29 Thursday
Haro Wine Battle (Spain)
Waxing Moon
Moon phase: First Quarter
Color: Crimson

Moon Sign: Virgo
Incense: Jasmine

 Friday
The Burning of the Three Firs (French)
Waxing Moon
Second Quarter 8:51 pm
Color: Coral

Moon Sign: Virgo
Moon enters Libra 3:02 am
Incense: Cypress

June Birthstones

Who comes with summer to this earth,
And owes to June her hour of birth,
With ring of Agate on her hand,
Can health, wealth, and long life command.

Modern: Moonstone or Pearl
Zodiac (Gemini): Agate

July

1 Saturday
Mt. Fuji climbing season opens (Japanese)
Waxing Moon
Moon phase: Second Quarter
Color: Brown

Moon Sign: Libra
Incense: Magnolia

2 Sunday
World UFO Day
Waxing Moon
Moon phase: Second Quarter
Color: Gold

Moon Sign: Libra
Moon enters Scorpio 12:59 pm
Incense: Eucalyptus

3 Monday
Dog Days of Summer begin
Waxing Moon
Moon phase: Second Quarter
Color: Gray

Moon Sign: Scorpio
Incense: Neroli

4 Tuesday
Independence Day
Waxing Moon
Moon phase: Second Quarter
Color: White

Moon Sign: Scorpio
Incense: Cinnamon

5 Wednesday
Tynwald Day (Manx)
Waxing Moon
Moon phase: Second Quarter
Color: Topaz

Moon Sign: Scorpio
Moon enters Sagittarius 1:08 am
Incense: Marjoram

6 Thursday
San Fermín begins (Spanish)
Waxing Moon
Moon phase: Second Quarter
Color: Turquoise

Moon Sign: Sagittarius
Incense: Balsam

7 Friday
Star Festival (Japanese)
Waxing Moon
Moon phase: Second Quarter
Color: Purple

Moon Sign: Sagittarius
Moon enters Capricorn 1:45 pm
Incense: Alder

July

8 Saturday
Feast of St. Sunniva
Waxing Moon
Moon phase: Second Quarter
Color: Blue

Moon Sign: Capricorn
Incense: Pine

☺ Sunday
Battle of Sempach Day (Swiss)
Waxing Moon
Full Moon 12:07 am
Color: Yellow

Moon Sign: Capricorn
Incense: Hyacinth

---

10 Monday
Nicola Tesla Day
Waning Moon
Moon phase: Third Quarter
Color: Ivory

Moon Sign: Capricorn
Moon enters Aquarius 1:35 am
Incense: Clary sage

---

11 Tuesday
Mongolian Naadam Festival (ends May 13)
Waning Moon
Third Quarter 8:52 pm
Color: Red

Moon Sign: Aquarius
Incense: Cedar

---

12 Wednesday
Malala Day
Waning Moon
Moon phase: Third Quarter
Color: Brown

Moon Sign: Aquarius
Moon enters Pisces 11:51 am
Incense: Lilac

---

13 Thursday
Feast of St. Mildrith
Waning Moon
Moon phase: Third Quarter
Color: Green

Moon Sign: Pisces
Incense: Mulberry

---

14 Friday
Bastille Day (French)
Waning Moon
Moon phase: Third Quarter
Color: White

Moon Sign: Pisces
Moon enters Aries 7:52 pm
Incense: Thyme

July

15 Saturday
St. Swithin's Day
Waning Moon
Moon phase: Third Quarter
Color: Black

Moon Sign: Aries
Incense: Sage

◑ Sunday
Fiesta de la Tirana (Chilean)
Waning Moon
Fourth Quarter 3:26 pm
Color: Orange

Moon Sign: Aries
Incense: Almond

17 Monday
Luis Muñoz Rivera Day (Puerto Rican)
Waning Moon
Moon phase: Fourth Quarter
Color: Lavender

Moon Sign: Aries
Moon enters Taurus 1:04 am
Incense: Lily

18 Tuesday
Nelson Mandela International Day
Waning Moon
Moon phase: Fourth Quarter
Color: Scarlet

Moon Sign: Taurus
Incense: Ylang-ylang

19 Wednesday
Flitch Day (English)
Waning Moon
Moon phase: Fourth Quarter
Color: White

Moon Sign: Taurus
Moon enters Gemini 3:31 am
Incense: Lavender

20 Thursday
Binding of Wreaths (Lithuanian)
Waning Moon
Moon phase: Fourth Quarter
Color: Crimson

Moon Sign: Gemini
Incense: Myrrh

21 Friday
National Day (Belgian)
Waning Moon
Moon phase: Fourth Quarter
Color: Rose

Moon Sign: Gemini
Moon enters Cancer 4:09 am
Incense: Alder

July

22 Saturday
St. Mary Magdalene's Day
Waning Moon
Moon phase: Fourth Quarter
Color: Indigo

Moon Sign: Cancer
Sun enters Leo 11:15 am
Incense: Sandalwood

Sunday
Mysteries of St. Cristina (Italian)
Waning Moon
New Moon 5:46 am
Color: Amber

Moon Sign: Cancer
Moon enters Leo 4:34 am
Incense: Juniper

24 Monday
Gion Festival second Yamaboko parade (Japanese)
Waxing Moon
Moon phase: First Quarter
Color: Silver

Moon Sign: Leo
Incense: Narcissus

25 Tuesday
Illapa Festival (Incan)
Waxing Moon
Moon phase: First Quarter
Color: Gray

Moon Sign: Leo
Moon enters Virgo 6:32 am
Incense: Geranium

26 Wednesday
St. Anne's Day
Waxing Moon
Moon phase: First Quarter
Color: Yellow

Moon Sign: Virgo
Incense: Honeysuckle

27 Thursday
Sleepyhead Day (Finnish)
Waxing Moon
Moon phase: First Quarter
Color: Purple

Moon Sign: Virgo
Moon enters Libra 11:37 am
Incense: Clove

28 Friday
Independence Day (Peruvian)
Waxing Moon
Moon phase: First Quarter
Color: Pink

Moon Sign: Libra
Incense: Orchid

July

29 Saturday
St. Olaf Festival (Faroese)
Waxing Moon
Moon phase: First Quarter
Color: Gray

Moon Sign: Libra
Moon enters Scorpio 8:23 pm
Incense: Patchouli

 Sunday
Micman Festival of St. Ann
Waxing Moon
Second Quarter 11:23 am
Color: Yellow

Moon Sign: Scorpio
Incense: Marigold

31 Monday
Feast of St. Ignatius
Waxing Moon
Moon phase: Second Quarter
Color: White

Moon Sign: Scorpio
Incense: Rosemary

July Birthstones

The glowing Ruby shall adorn
Those who in warm July are born;
Then will they be exempt and free
From love's doubt, and anxiety.

Modern: Ruby
Zodiac (Cancer): Emerald

August

1 Tuesday
Lammas
Waxing Moon
Moon phase: Second Quarter
Color: Black

Moon Sign: Scorpio
Moon enters Sagittarius 8:01 am
Incense: Bayberry

2 Wednesday
Porcingula (Pecos)
Waxing Moon
Moon phase: Second Quarter
Color: White

Moon Sign: Sagittarius
Incense: Lilac

3 Thursday
Flag Day (Venezuelan)
Waxing Moon
Moon phase: Second Quarter
Color: Crimson

Moon Sign: Sagittarius
Moon enters Capricorn 8:37 pm
Incense: Nutmeg

4 Friday
Constitution Day (Cook Islands)
Waxing Moon Waxing
Moon phase: Second Quarter
Color: Coral

Moon Sign: Capricorn
Incense: Mint

5 Saturday
Carnival of Bogotá
Waxing Moon
Moon phase: Second Quarter
Color: Indigo

Moon Sign: Capricorn
Incense: Rue

6 Sunday
Hiroshima Peace Memorial Ceremony
Waxing Moon
Moon phase: Second Quarter
Color: Amber

Moon Sign: Capricorn
Moon enters Aquarius 8:15 am
Incense: Almond

☺ Monday
Republic Day (Ivorian)
Waxing Moon
Full Moon 2:11 pm
Color: White

Moon Sign: Aquarius
Incense: Hyssop

August

8 Tuesday
Farmers' Day (Tanzanian)
Waning Moon
Moon phase: Third Quarter
Color: Gray

Moon Sign: Aquarius
Moon enters Pisces 5:56 pm
Incense: Ginger

9 Wednesday
Nagasaki Peace Memorial Ceremony
Waning Moon
Moon phase: Third Quarter
Color: Yellow

Moon Sign: Pisces
Incense: Bay laurel

10 Thursday
Puck Fair (ends Aug. 12; Irish)
Waning Moon
Moon phase: Third Quarter
Color: Purple

Moon Sign: Pisces
Incense: Jasmine

11 Friday
Mountain Day (Japanese)
Waning Moon
Moon phase: Third Quarter
Color: Pink

Moon Sign: Pisces
Moon enters Aries 1:22 am
Incense: Violet

12 Saturday
Glorious Twelfth (United Kingdom)
Waning Moon
Moon phase: Third Quarter
Color: Blue

Moon Sign: Aries
Incense: Sage

13 Sunday
Women's Day (Tunisian)
Waning Moon
Moon phase: Third Quarter
Color: Yellow

Moon Sign: Aries
Moon enters Taurus 6:40 am
Incense: Frankincense

☽ Monday
Independence Day (Pakistani)
Waning Moon
Fourth Quarter 9:15 pm
Color: Lavender

Moon Sign: Taurus
Incense: Lily

August

15 **Tuesday**
Bon Festival (Japanese)
Waning Moon
Moon phase: Fourth Quarter
Color: Maroon

Moon Sign: Taurus
Moon enters Gemini 10:06 am
Incense: Cinnamon

---

16 **Wednesday**
Xicolatada (French)
Waning Moon
Moon phase: Fourth Quarter
Color: Topaz

Moon Sign: Gemini
Incense: Honeysuckle

---

17 **Thursday**
Black Cat Appreciation Day
Waning Moon
Moon phase: Fourth Quarter
Color: Turquoise

Moon Sign: Gemini
Moon enters Cancer 12:13 pm
Incense: Apricot

---

18 **Friday**
St. Helen's Day
Waning Moon
Moon phase: Fourth Quarter
Color: Purple

Moon Sign: Cancer
Incense: Cypress

---

19 **Saturday**
Vinalia Rustica (Roman)
Waning Moon
Moon phase: Fourth Quarter
Color: Black

Moon Sign: Cancer
Moon enters Leo 1:55 pm
Incense: Ivy

---

20 **Sunday**
St. Stephen's Day (Hungarian)
Waning Moon
Moon phase: Fourth Quarter
Color: Gold

Moon Sign: Leo
Incense: Heliotrope

☽ **Monday**
Consualia (Roman)
Waning Moon
New Moon 2:30 pm
Color: Ivory

Moon Sign: Leo
Moon enters Virgo 4:25 pm
Incense: Clary sage

August ♍

22 Tuesday
Feast of the Queenship of Mary (English)
Waxing Moon
Moon phase: First Quarter
Color: Scarlet

Moon Sign: Virgo
Sun enters Virgo 6:20 pm
Incense: Basil

23 Wednesday
National Day (Romanian)
Waxing Moon
Moon phase: First Quarter
Color: Brown

Moon Sign: Virgo
Moon enters Libra 9:05 pm
Incense: Marjoram

24 Thursday
St. Bartholomew's Day
Waxing Moon
Moon phase: First Quarter
Color: Green

Moon Sign: Libra
Incense: Carnation

25 Friday
Liberation of Paris
Waxing Moon
Moon phase: First Quarter
Color: Rose

Moon Sign: Libra
Incense: Rose

26 Saturday
Heroes' Day (Namibian)
Waxing Moon
Moon phase: First Quarter
Color: Gray

Moon Sign: Libra
Moon enters Scorpio 4:53 am
Incense: Magnolia

27 Sunday
Independence Day (Moldovan)
Waxing Moon
Moon phase: First Quarter
Color: Amber

Moon Sign: Scorpio
Incense: Eucalyptus

28 Monday
Qixi Festival (Chinese)
Waxing Moon
Moon phase: First Quarter
Color: Silver

Moon Sign: Scorpio
Moon enters Sagittarius 3:48 pm
Incense: Narcissus

August ♍

 Tuesday
St. John's Beheading   Moon Sign: Sagittarius
Waxing Moon   Incense: Cedar
Second Quarter 4:13 am
Color: Red

---

30 **Wednesday**
St. Rose of Lima Day (Peruvian)   Moon Sign: Sagittarius
Waxing Moon   Incense: Lavendar
Moon phase: Second Quarter
Color: Topaz

---

31 **Thursday**
La Tomatina (Valencian)   Moon Sign: Sagittarius
Waxing Moon   Moon enters Capricorn 4:18 am
Moon phase: Second Quarter   Incense: Mulberry
Color: White

August Birthstones

Wear Sardonyx, or for thee
No conjugal felicity;
The August-born without this stone,
'Tis said, must live unloved, and lone.

Modern: Peridot
Zodiac (Leo): Onyx

September ♍

1 Friday
Wattle Day (Australian)
Waxing Moon
Moon phase: Second Quarter
Color: Purple

Moon Sign: Capricorn
Incense: Yarrow

---

2 Saturday
St. Mammes's Day
Waxing Moon
Moon phase: Second Quarter
Color: Blue

Moon Sign: Capricorn
Moon enters Aquarius 4:06 pm
Incense: Sandalwood

---

3 Sunday
National Feast of San Marino
Waxing Moon
Moon phase: Second Quarter
Color: Yellow

Moon Sign: Aquarius
Incense: Hyacinth

---

4 Monday
Labor Day
Waxing Moon
Moon phase: Second Quarter
Color: Gray

Moon Sign: Aquarius
Incense: Neroli

---

5 Tuesday
Ghost Festival (Chinese)
Waxing Moon
Moon phase: Second Quarter
Color: Maroon

Moon Sign: Aquarius
Moon enters Pisces 1:28 am
Incense: Ginger

☺ 6 Wednesday
Unification Day (Bulgaria)
Waxing Moon
Full Moon 3:03 am
Color: White

Moon Sign: Pisces
Incense: Honeysuckle

---

7 Thursday
Independence Day (Brazilian)
Waning Moon
Moon phase: Third Quarter
Color: Crimson

Moon Sign: Pisces
Moon enters Aries 8:01 am
Incense: Balsam

September ♍

8 **Friday**
International Literacy Day
Waning Moon
Moon phase: Third Quarter
Color: Coral

Moon Sign: Aries
Incense: Orchid

---

9 **Saturday**
Remembrance for Herman the Cheruscan (Asatru)
Waning Moon
Moon phase: Third Quarter
Color: Indigo

Moon Sign: Aries
Moon enters Taurus 12:23 pm
Incense: Sage

---

10 **Sunday**
National Day (Belizean)
Waning Moon
Moon phase: Third Quarter
Color: Gold

Moon Sign: Taurus
Incense: Juniper

---

11 **Monday**
Coptic New Year
Waning Moon
Moon phase: Third Quarter
Color: Silver

Moon Sign: Taurus
Moon enters Gemini 3:29 pm
Incense: Rosemary

---

12 **Tuesday**
Mindfulness Day
Waning Moon
Moon phase: Third Quarter
Color: Red

Moon Sign: Gemini
Incense: Ylang-ylang

◑ **Wednesday**
The Gods' Banquet (Roman)
Waning Moon
Fourth Quarter 2:25 am
Color: Brown

Moon Sign: Gemini
Moon enters Cancer 6:12 pm
Incense: Lilac

---

14 **Thursday**
Holy Cross Day
Waning Moon
Moon phase: Fourth Quarter
Color: Green

Moon Sign: Cancer
Incense: Clove

September ♍

15 Friday
International Day of Democracy
Waning Moon
Moon phase: Fourth Quarter
Color: Pink

Moon Sign: Cancer
Moon enters Leo 9:09 pm
Incense: Thyme

16 Saturday
Independence Day (Mexican)
Waning Moon
Moon phase: Fourth Quarter
Color: Gray

Moon Sign: Leo
Incense: Patchouli

17 Sunday
Von Steuben's Day
Waning Moon
Moon phase: Fourth Quarter
Color: Orange

Moon Sign: Leo
Incense: Almond

18 Monday
Constitution Day
Waning Moon
Moon phase: Fourth Quarter
Color: Ivory

Moon Sign: Leo
Moon enters Virgo 12:52 am
Incense: Clary sage

19 Tuesday
Feast of San Gennaro
Waning Moon
Moon phase: Fourth Quarter
Color: White

Moon Sign: Virgo
Incense: Geranium

☽ Wednesday
Feast of St. Eustace
Waning Moon
New Moon 1:30 am
Color: Topaz

Moon Sign: Virgo
Moon enters Libra 6:06 am
Incense: Lavender

21 Thursday
Islamic New Year • Rosh Hashanah
Waxing Moon
Moon phase: First Quarter
Color: Purple

Moon Sign: Libra
Incense: Jasmine

September

22 Friday
Mabon • Fall Equinox
Waxing Moon
Moon phase: First Quarter
Color: Rose

Moon Sign: Libra
Moon enters Scorpio 1:40 pm
Sun enters Libra 4:02 pm
Incense: Vanilla

23 Saturday
Feast of St. Padre Pio
Waxing Moon
Moon phase: First Quarter
Color: Blue

Moon Sign: Scorpio
Incense: Rue

24 Sunday
Schwenkenfelder Thanksgiving (German-American)
Waxing Moon
Moon phase: First Quarter
Color: Amber

Moon Sign: Scorpio
Incense: Marigold

25 Monday
Doll Memorial Service (Japanese)
Waxing Moon
Moon phase: First Quarter
Color: Lavender

Moon Sign: Scorpio
Moon enters Sagittarius 12:01 am
Incense: Lily

26 Tuesday
Feast of Santa Justina (Mexican)
Waxing Moon
Moon phase: First Quarter
Color: Scarlet

Moon Sign: Sagittarius
Incense: Cinnamon

◖ Wednesday
Meskel (Ethiopian and Eritrean)
Waxing Moon
Second Quarter: 10:54 pm
Color: Yellow

Moon Sign: Sagittarius
Moon enters Capricorn 12:24 pm
Incense: Bay laurel

28 Thursday
Chrysanthemum Festival (Japanese)
Waxing Moon
Moon phase: Second Quarter
Color: Turquoise

Moon Sign: Capricorn
Incense: Carnation

29 **Friday**
Michaelmas
Waxing Moon
Moon phase: Second Quarter
Color: Coral

Moon Sign: Capricorn
Incense: Rose

---

30 **Saturday**
Yom Kippur
Waxing Moon
Moon phase: Second Quarter
Color: Black

Moon Sign: Capricorn
Moon enters Aquarius 12:40 am
Incense: Magnolia

September Birthstones

A maiden born when autumn leaves
Are rustling in September's breeze,
A Sapphire on her brow should bind;
'Twill cure diseases of the mind.

Modern: Sapphire
Zodiac (Virgo): Carnelian

October ♎

1   Sunday
Armed Forces Day (South Korean)
Waxing Moon
Moon phase: Second Quarter
Color: Orange

Moon Sign: Aquarius
Incense: Juniper

2   Monday
Gandhi's Birthday
Waxing Moon
Moon phase: Second Quarter
Color: White

Moon Sign: Aquarius
Moon enters Pisces 10:26 am
Incense: Narcissus

3   Tuesday
German Unity Day
Waxing Moon
Moon phase: Second Quarter
Color: Red

Moon Sign: Pisces
Incense: Bayberry

4   Wednesday
Mid-Autumn Festival (Chinese)
Waxing Moon
Moon phase: Second Quarter
Color: Topaz

Moon Sign: Pisces
Moon enters Aries 4:40 pm
Incense: Lilac

☺ Thursday
Sukkot begins
Waxing Moon
Full Moon 2:40 pm
Color: Green

Moon Sign: Aries
Incense: Myrrh

6   Friday
German-American Day
Waning Moon
Moon phase: Third Quarter
Color: Rose

Moon Sign: Aries
Moon enters Taurus 7:56 pm
Incense: Violet

7   Saturday
Nagasaki Kunchi Festival (ends Oct. 9)
Waning Moon
Moon phase: Third Quarter
Color: Blue

Moon Sign: Taurus
Incense: Sage

October

♎

8 Sunday
Arbor Day (Namibian)
Waning Moon
Moon phase: Third Quarter
Color: Gold

Moon Sign: Taurus
Moon enters Gemini 9:44 pm
Incense: Eucalyptus

9 Monday
Columbus Day • Indigenous Peoples' Day
Waning Moon
Moon phase: Third Quarter
Color: Lavender

Moon Sign: Gemini
Incense: Clary sage

10 Tuesday
Finnish Literature Day
Waning Moon
Moon phase: Third Quarter
Color: Scarlet

Moon Sign: Gemini
Moon enters Cancer 11:38 pm
Incense: Cinnamon

11 Wednesday
Sukkot ends
Waning Moon
Moon phase: Third Quarter
Color: Yellow

Moon Sign: Cancer
Incense: Marjoram

☽ Thursday
National Festival of Spain
Waning Moon
Fourth Quarter 8:25
Color: Turquoise

Moon Sign: Cancer
Incense: Balsam

13 Friday
Fontinalia (Roman)
Waning Moon
Moon phase: Fourth Quarter
Color: Pink

Moon Sign: Cancer
Moon enters Leo 2:41 am
Incense: Cypress

14 Saturday
National Education Day (Polish)
Waning Moon
Moon phase: Fourth Quarter
Color: Black

Moon Sign: Leo
Incense: Pine

October

---

15 **Sunday**
The October Horse (Roman)
Waning Moon
Moon phase: Fourth Quarter
Color: Yellow

Moon Sign: Leo
Moon enters Virgo 7:19 am
Incense: Frankincense

---

16 **Monday**
The Lion Sermon (British)
Waning Moon
Moon phase: Fourth Quarter
Color: Silver

Moon Sign: Virgo
Incense: Neroli

---

17 **Tuesday**
Dessalines Day (Haitian)
Waning Moon
Moon phase: Fourth Quarter
Color: White

Moon Sign: Virgo
Moon enters Libra 1:35 pm
Incense: Cedar

---

18 **Wednesday**
Feast of St. Luke
Waning Moon
Moon phase: Fourth Quarter
Color: Brown

Moon Sign: Libra
Incense: Bay laurel

☽ **Thursday**
Mother Teresa Day (Albanian)
Waning Moon
New Moon 3:12 pm
Color: Purple

Moon Sign: Libra
Moon enters Scorpio 9:41 pm
Incense: Nutmeg

---

20 **Friday**
Feast of St. Acca
Waxing Moon
Moon phase: First Quarter
Color: Coral

Moon Sign: Scorpio
Incense: Orchid

---

21 **Saturday**
Diwali
Waxing Moon
Moon phase: First Quarter
Color: Indigo

Moon Sign: Scorpio
Incense: Patchouli

October ♏

22 Sunday
Jidai Festival (Kyoto)
Waxing Moon
First Quarter 3:14 pm
Color: Amber

Moon Sign: Scorpio
Moon enters Sagittarius 7:57 am
Incense: Marigold

23 Monday
Sukkot ends
Waxing Moon
Moon phase: First Quarter
Color: Ivory

Moon Sign: Sagittarius
Sun enters Scorpio 1:27 am
Incense: Lily

24 Tuesday
United Nations Day
Waxing Moon
Moon phase: First Quarter
Color: Maroon

Moon Sign: Sagittarius
Moon enters Capricorn 8:12 pm
Incense: Ginger

25 Wednesday
St. Crispin's Day
Waxing Moon
Moon phase: First Quarter
Color: Yellow

Moon Sign: Capricorn
Incense: Lavender

26 Thursday
Death of Alfred the Great
Waxing Moon
Moon phase: First Quarter
Color: Crimson

Moon Sign: Capricorn
Incense: Apricot

☾ Friday
Feast of St. Abbán
Waxing Moon
Second Quarter 6:22 pm
Color: Purple

Moon Sign: Capricorn
Moon enters Aquarius 8:59 am
Incense: Mint

28 Saturday
Ohi Day (Greek)
Waxing Moon
Moon phase: Second Quarter
Color: Gray

Moon Sign: Aquarius
Incense: Ivy

29   **Sunday**
National Cat Day
Waxing Moon
Moon phase: Second Quarter
Color: Gold

Moon Sign: Aquarius
Moon enters Pisces 7:46 pm
Incense: Heliotrope

---

30   **Monday**
John Adams's birthday
Waxing Moon
Moon phase: Second Quarter
Color: Lavender

Moon Sign: Pisces
Incense: Rosemary

---

31   **Tuesday**
Halloween • Samhain
Waxing Moon
Moon phase: Second Quarter
Color: Black

Moon Sign: Pisces
Incense: Basil

October Birthstones

October's child is born for woe,
And life's vicissitudes must know;
But lay an Opal on her breast,
And hope will lull those foes to rest.

Modern: Opal or Tourmaline
Zodiac (Libra): Peridot

November ♏

1 **Wednesday**
All Saints' Day • Día de los Muertos
Waxing Moon
Moon phase: Second Quarter
Color: Topaz

Moon Sign: Pisces
Moon enters Aries 2:43 am
Incense: Marjoram

2 **Thursday**
All Souls' Day
Waxing Moon
Moon phase: Second Quarter
Color: White

Moon Sign: Aries
Incense: Clove

3 **Friday**
St. Hubert's Day (Belgian)
Waxing Moon
Moon phase: Second Quarter
Color: Purple

Moon Sign: Aries
Moon enters Taurus 5:46 am
Incense: Rose

☺ **Saturday**
Loy Krathong Lantern Festival (Thai)
Waxing Moon
Full Moon 1:23 am
Color: Black

Moon Sign: Taurus
Incense: Magnolia

5 **Sunday**
Guy Fawkes Night (British)
Waning Moon
Moon phase: Third Quarter
Color: Yellow

Moon Sign: Taurus
Moon enters Gemini 5:26 am
Incense: Almond
Daylight Saving Time ends at 2 am

6 **Monday**
St. Leonard's Ride
Waning Moon
Moon phase: Third Quarter
Color: Silver

Moon Sign: Gemini
Incense: Hyssop

7 **Tuesday**
Election Day (general)
Waning Moon
Moon phase: Third Quarter
Color: Scarlet

Moon Sign: Gemini
Moon enters Cancer 5:45 am
Incense: Ylang-ylang

8   Wednesday
World Urbanism Day   Moon Sign: Cancer
Waning Moon   Incense: Lilac
Moon phase: Third Quarter
Color: Brown

9   Thursday
Fateful Day (German)   Moon Sign: Cancer
Waning Moon   Moon enters Leo 7:29 am
Moon phase: Third Quarter   Incense: Carnation
Color: Turquoise

◗   Friday
Martin Luther's Birthday   Moon Sign: Leo
Waning Moon   Incense: Vanilla
Fourth Quarter 3:36 pm
Color: Rose

11   Saturday
Veterans Day   Moon Sign: Leo
Waning Moon   Moon enters Virgo 11:41 pm
Moon phase: Fourth Quarter   Incense: Sandalwood
Color: Gray

12   Sunday
Feast Day of San Diego (Tesuque Puebloan)   Moon Sign: Virgo
Waning Moon   Incense: Eucalyptus
Moon phase: Fourth Quarter
Color: Gold

13   Monday
Festival of Jupiter (Roman)   Moon Sign: Virgo
Waning Moon   Moon enters Libra 6:26 pm
Moon phase: Fourth Quarter   Incense: Clary sage
Color: White

14   Tuesday
Feast of St. Lawrence O'Toole   Moon Sign: Libra
Waning Moon   Incense: Geranium
Moon phase: Fourth Quarter
Color: Maroon

November ♏

15 Wednesday
Seven-Five-Three Festival (Japanese)
Waning Moon
Moon phase: Fourth Quarter
Color: Yellow

Moon Sign: Libra
Incense: Bay laurel

16 Thursday
St. Margaret of Scotland's Day
Waning Moon
Moon phase: Fourth Quarter
Color: Green

Moon Sign: Libra
Moon enters Scorpio 3:19 am
Incense: Balsam

17 Friday
Queen Elizabeth's Accession Day
Waning Moon
Moon phase: Fourth Quarter
Color: Purple

Moon Sign: Scorpio
Incense: Alder

☽ Saturday
Independence Day (Moroccan)
Waning Moon
New Moon 6:42 am
Color: Indigo

Moon Sign: Scorpio
Moon enters Sagittarius 1:59 pm
Incense: Sage

19 Sunday
Garifuna Settlement Day (Belizean)
Waxing Moon
Moon phase: First Quarter
Color: Amber

Moon Sign: Sagittarius
Incense: Hyacinth

20 Monday
Revolution Day (Mexican)
Waxing Moon
Moon phase: First Quarter
Color: Ivory

Moon Sign: Sagittarius
Incense: Lily

21 Tuesday
Feast of the Presentation of Mary
Waxing Moon
Moon phase: First Quarter
Color: Red

Moon Sign: Sagittarius
Moon enters Capricorn 2:14 am
Sun enters Sagittarius 10:05 pm
Incense: Cedar

22 Wednesday
St. Cecilia's Day
Waxing Moon
Moon phase: First Quarter
Color: White

Moon Sign: Capricorn
Incense: Lavender

23 Thursday
Thanksgiving Day
Waxing Moon
Moon phase: First Quarter
Color: Crimson

Moon Sign: Capricorn
Moon enters Aquarius 3:14 pm
Incense: Jasmine

24 Friday
Evolution Day
Waxing
Moon phase: First Quarter
Color: Coral

Moon Sign: Aquarius
Incense: Thyme

25 Saturday
Feast of St. Catherine of Alexandria
Waxing
Moon phase: First Quarter
Color: Blue

Moon Sign: Aquarius
Incense: Rue

☾ Sunday
Constitution Day (Indian)
Waxing Moon
Second Quarter 12:03 pm
Color: Gold

Moon Sign: Aquarius
Moon enters Pisces 12:03 pm
Incense: Frankincense

27 Monday
Feast of St. Virgilius
Waxing Moon
Moon phase: Second Quarter
Color: Lavender

Moon Sign: Pisces
Incense: Neroli

28 Tuesday
Republic Day (Chadian)
Waxing Moon
Moon phase: Second Quarter
Color: Gray

Moon Sign: Pisces
Moon enters Aries 11:30 am
Incense: Bayberry

November

29 **Wednesday**
William Tubman's birthday (Liberian)
Waxing Moon
Moon phase: Second Quarter
Color: Brown

Moon Sign: Aries
Incense: Lilac

30 **Thursday**
St. Andrew's Day (Scottish)
Waxing Moon
Moon phase: Second Quarter
Color: Turquoise

Moon Sign: Aries
Moon enters Taurus 3:38 pm
Incense: Mulberry

November Birthstones

Who first come to this world below,
With drear November's fog, and snow,
Should prize the Topaz's amber hue,
Emblem of friends, and lovers true.

Modern: Topaz or Citrine
Zodiac (Scorpio): Beryl

December

1 Friday
Feast for Death of Aleister Crowley (Thelemic)
Waxing Moon
Moon phase: Second Quarter
Color: Pink

Moon Sign: Taurus
Incense: Orchid

2 Saturday
Republic Day (Laotian)
Waxing Moon
Moon phase: Second Quarter
Color: Blue

Moon Sign: Taurus
Moon enters Gemini 4:21 pm
Incense: Ivy

3 Sunday
St. Francis Xavier's Day
Waxing Moon
Full Moon 10:47 am
Color: Amber

Moon Sign: Gemini
Incense: Marigold

4 Monday
Feasts of Shango and St. Barbara
Waning Moon
Moon phase: Third Quarter
Color: Silver

Moon Sign: Gemini
Moon enters Cancer 3:37 pm
Incense: Narcissus

5 Tuesday
Krampus Night (European)
Waning Moon
Moon phase: Third Quarter
Color: Maroon

Moon Sign: Cancer
Incense: Ginger

6 Wednesday
St. Nicholas's Day
Waning Moon
Moon phase: Third Quarter
Color: White

Moon Sign: Cancer
Moon enters Leo 3:37 pm
Incense: Lavender

7 Thursday
Burning the Devil (Guatemalan)
Waning Moon
Moon phase: Third Quarter
Color: Green

Moon Sign: Leo
Incense: Clove

December

8 **Friday**
Feast of the Immaculate Conception
Waning Moon
Moon phase: Third Quarter
Color: Rose

Moon Sign: Leo
Moon enters Virgo 6:09 pm
Incense: Mint

9 **Saturday**
Anna's Day (Sweden)
Waning Moon
Moon phase: Third Quarter
Color: Black

Moon Sign: Virgo
Incense: Pine

10 **Sunday**
Alfred Nobel Day
Waning Moon
Fourth Quarter 2:51 am
Color: Orange

Moon Sign: Virgo
Incense: Juniper

11 **Monday**
Pilgrimage at Tortugas
Waning Moon
Moon phase: Fourth Quarter
Color: Gray

Moon Sign: Virgo
Moon enters Libra 12:01 am
Incense: Rosemary

12 **Tuesday**
Fiesta of Our Lady of Guadalupe (Mexican)
Waning Moon
Moon phase: Fourth Quarter
Color: Scarlet

Moon Sign: Libra
Incense: Ylang-ylang

13 **Wednesday**
Hanukkah begins
Waning Moon
Moon phase: Fourth Quarter
Color: Brown

Moon Sign: Libra
Moon enters Scorpio 8:59 am
Incense: Marjoram

14 **Thursday**
Forty-Seven Ronin Memorial (Japanese)
Waning Moon
Moon phase: Fourth Quarter
Color: Turquoise

Moon Sign: Scorpio
Incense: Balsam

15 Friday
Consualia (Roman)
Waning Moon
Moon phase: Fourth Quarter
Color: Coral

Moon Sign: Scorpio
Moon enters Sagittarius 8:07 pm
Incense: Violet

---

16 Saturday
Las Posadas begin (end Dec. 24)
Waning Moon
Moon phase: Fourth Quarter
Color: Gray

Moon Sign: Sagittarius
Incense: Patchouli

---

17 Sunday
Saturnalia (Roman)
Waning Waning Moon
Moon phase: Fourth Quarter
Color: Yellow

Moon Sign: Sagittarius
Incense: Heliotrope

☽ Monday
Feast of the Virgin of Solitude
Waning Moon
New Moon 1:30 am
Color: White

Moon Sign: Sagittarius
Moon enters Capricorn 8:33 am
Incense: Clary sage

---

19 Tuesday
Opalia (Roman)
Waxing Moon
Moon phase: First Quarter
Color: Red

Moon Sign: Capricorn
Incense: Cinnamon

---

20 Wednesday
Hannukah ends
Waxing Moon
Moon phase: First Quarter
Color: Topaz

Moon Sign: Capricorn
Moon enters Aquarius 9:29 pm
Incense: Bay laurel

---

21 Thursday
Yule • Winter Solstice
Waxing Moon
Moon phase: First Quarter
Color: Crimson

Moon Sign: Aquarius
Sun enters Capricorn 11:28 am
Incense: Myrrh

December

22 Friday
Feasts of SS. Chaeremon and Ischyrion　　　Moon Sign: Aquarius
Waxing Moon　　　　　　　　　　　　　　　Incense: Rose
Moon phase: First Quarter
Color: Pink

23 Saturday
Larentalia (Roman)　　　　　　　　　　　Moon Sign: Aquarius
Waxing Moon　　　　　　　　　Moon enters Pisces 9:42 am
Moon phase: First Quarter　　　　　　　　　　Incense: Sage
Color: Blue

24 Sunday
Christmas Eve　　　　　　　　　　　　　　Moon Sign: Pisces
Waxing Moon　　　　　　　　　　　　　　Incense: Almond
Moon phase: First Quarter
Color: Gold

25 Monday
Christmas Day　　　　　　　　　　　　　　Moon Sign: Pisces
Waxing Moon　　　　　　　　　Moon enters Aries 7:27 pm
Moon phase: First Quarter　　　　　　　　Incense: Hyssop
Color: Ivory

○ Tuesday
Kwanzaa begins (ends Jan. 1)　　　　　　　Moon Sign: Aries
Waxing Moon　　　　　　　　　　　　　　Incense: Cedar
Second Quarter 4:20 am
Color: White

27 Wednesday
St. Stephen's Day　　　　　　　　　　　　Moon Sign: Aries
Waxing Moon　　　　　　　　　　　　　　Incense: Lilac
Moon phase: Second Quarter
Color: Yellow

28 Thursday
Feast of the Holy Innocents　　　　　　　　Moon Sign: Aries
Waxing Moon　　　　　　　　　Moon enters Taurus 1:23 am
Moon phase: Second Quarter　　　　　　　Incense: Nutmeg
Color: Green

December

29 Friday
Feast of St. Thomas à Becket
Waxing Moon
Moon phase: Second Quarter
Color: Purple

Moon Sign: Taurus
Incense: Yarrow

---

30 Saturday
Republic Day (Madagascan)
Waxing Moon
Moon phase: Second Quarter
Color: Indigo

Moon Sign: Taurus
Moon enters Gemini 3:31 am
Incense: Rue

---

31 Sunday
New Year's Eve
Waxing Moon
Moon phase: Second Quarter
Color: Orange

Moon Sign: Gemini
Incense: Eucalyptus

December Birthstones

If cold December gives you birth,
The month of snow, and ice, and mirth,
Place in your hand a Turquoise blue;
Success will bless whate'er you do.

Modern: Turquoise or Blue Topaz
Zodiac (Sagittarius): Topaz

Fire Magic

Kicking It Up a Notch: After Pagan 101

by Susan Pesznecker

At some point in our spiritual lives—whether we practice Wicca, Druidism, Heathenry, herbalism, Witchcraft, or any other of the often lumped-together Pagan practices—we find we've dealt with all of the introductory content we can get our hands on. We've read books, explored web pages, talked to people, dabbled in practice, and maybe visited a group or festival or two. We've taken the first few steps, but now we're unsure of what to do next. We take a deep breath, look around, and say, "Well. That was interesting. Now what?"

It's time to take things to the next level.

But that's often not as simple as it sounds. Store shelves are filled with Pagan 101 books geared toward the newbie, because it's that excited neophyte who buys those materials. That's where the big money is, so those books keep getting written. As for the web, enter "Pagan" or "Witch" or "Heathen" into a search engine and you'll reap a million or more hits. But the quality is often low. Most will be overly simplistic, biased, incomplete, or poorly cited, and some will contain material that's inaccurate and possibly even dangerous. Even worse, many will charge money for memberships that promise the sharing of "mysteries" or "secret initiations," again drawing in novices as easy prey.

What's a frustrated practitioner to do? How does one climb out of the 101 rut and find a new direction?

1. Begin with Self-Inventory

Consider your own Pagan origins. How did you begin your explorations? Were you born into a family that practices, or did you find the path on your own? Have you been practicing for years, or are you an eager beaver who wants more and wants it now? What path or tradition most interests you and why? Think back to what sparked your interest when you first began. Are you still feeding this flame, or does it need rekindling? Going back to your own beginnings and answering these questions can help you think about what it is you wanted at first, what you want now, and how to take new steps in that direction.

Use tools to help with the inventory. You can use your favorite method of divination to assess your progress or path. Or take a long walk outside, auguring the natural signs and considering the ways they speak to you. Meditation is a terrific way to reflect too. Neuroscience has shown that meditation directly affects the brain and, in turn, affects our ability to do magick and work with all things spiritual. Ponder a question you need answered, slip into a meditative trance, and see what develops.

Journaling is another valuable tool for insights. When you write by hand, you stimulate a specific part of your brain that heightens your attention and makes you more aware of your surroundings and internal thoughts. Freewriting—writing for five to ten minutes without stopping—can bring deep memories bubbling to the surface. Journaling about your path, your questions, the work and rituals you do, and your discoveries helps cement memory and stimulates forward movement. Using your journal as a sort of diary of progress will help in this way, too.

Researching your family tree and DNA may also help you direct your work. I had heard my family included a Native American background; I was interested in taking this further, but found through a DNA test that I have no Native American blood. On the other hand, I discovered that I was one-third Irish, which meshed neatly with my growing curiosity about Celtic culture. These discoveries fascinated me and helped shape my direction.

2. Explore Robust Source Materials

It's almost impossible to be a student of anything spiritual without a lot of reading. Push past the 101 shelves and look for advanced topics: books and essays on ethics, advanced practices, Pagan education, creating and managing magickal groups, building community, and so forth. Read books or visit sites from a number of different disciplines or paths; study their similarities and differences and apply their ideas to your own workings. Read other types of closely related books, too, such as mythology, art and medieval history, astronomy, and folklore. By

looking outside your own magickal sphere, your world-view broadens and becomes more complex.

How do you find reliable materials? The academic standard for resource materials is that they should be written by people with experience, academic degrees and credentials, or a publication history in the subject area. This is where belonging to an experienced community can help: ask your peers whom they recommend and whom they don't recommend. If you're on your own, use the web to investigate each author, finding out where that person has studied, what that person's experience level is, and so forth. Book reviews may also be helpful in some cases.

As for web-based materials, here are a few hints to help you locate reliable sources:

Avoid material that doesn't give the author's name.
Look for works that cite and list their sources.

As a rule, the more recent the source, the better—excluding archival-type materials.

The .edu domain is linked to educational institutions; materials on .edu sites can be trusted. Domains of .com and .org are available for anyone to purchase and may be less reliable.

Anything posted on a college or professional library site is prevetted and trustworthy.

Beware of sites that provide a blank "Contact Us" box but don't share their contact information. Nine out of ten times, your information goes straight to spam-bots or e-mail lists.

Try to look past Wikipedia. In the academic community, Wikipedia and other wikis aren't regarded as authoritative sources. Why? Because they're not always written by actual experts in that area and thus don't meet rigorous authoritative criteria. That said, all Wikipedia articles end with fabulous source lists—don't miss those.

Your intermediate or advanced explorations will be buoyed by research. Pick one or two areas that interest you and dive in. Find good materials, read them, then go to their bibliographies and read those texts. Take good notes and finish each research session with journaling, letting your mind sort through the new ideas. Carry a small notebook to capture questions as they occur.

Do you have museums nearby? You can explore paintings, ancient manuscripts, tools, costumes, and other artifacts that might inspire your work or help you understand it more completely.

3. Take Classes

Taking a formal class from a knowledgeable teacher can be inspiring and fun. Most local community colleges offer classes in mythology, comparative religions, ethics, ancient history, and classical languages, as well as all of the arts, writing included. Traditional universities cost more but offer even more classes. Literature classes are wonderful options, particularly those that delve into areas you're interested in, such as women's studies, mythology, fantasy, and more.

You might take the plunge into an online learning community or a massive open online course (MOOC). If you decide to study online, be aware that it's very different from the face-to-face setting. Online learners must be good at pushing themselves forward and managing their time well. There's less direct instructor-student interaction in online classes too, and this must be carefully considered.

4. Join or Form a Community

There's real value in belonging to a community—especially a face-to-face community in which you engage with real people in real time. I'm not negating cybercommunities: I belong to several myself, and they can be wonderful in their own ways. But in my opinion, nothing beats working in real space with other humans on the same journey. Working side by side with others is a great way to experience new ideas and approaches, and the encouragement provided will benefit everyone. You might also formalize the experience by entering into a tutelage or apprenticeship, leading to certification or initiation.

A friend of mine said, "But I live in a small town. There aren't any people like me anywhere around." And I say, "Au contraire." The people are there; if you're there, they're there, too. You just haven't found them yet.

Now, to be sure, some people on Pagan paths live in conservative communities and are uncomfortable expressing their beliefs or practices publicly. Such decisions are individual oncs, but I promise you that the

people are there. How to find them? The Internet can be a big help in finding like-minded folks, as can word of mouth. If you live in a more relaxed setting, you shouldn't have any trouble finding people to work and study with. Check out community publications and bulletin boards. Visit a public ritual or a local festival, or explore meetup-type groups. Good times await.

5. Teach!

When I was working on my teaching credentials, I spent lots of time on the interactions between teaching and learning. What stuck with me was that no one learns by just watching: we learn by doing. And the best way to "do" is to demonstrate and to teach another person. We learned the saying, "Each one see one, do one, teach one." What does that mean? You start by watching someone else demonstrate the skill. Then, you learn to do it yourself. And then, you cement your knowledge by teaching it to someone else. There's no better way to develop expertise, and by teaching others, you pay forward the gift of those who taught you.

6. And What about UPG?

Unverified personal gnosis, also known as UPG, refers to a sudden aha moment that changes or informs a person's spiritual process. Some people feel UPG demonstrates improved or heightened awareness and is therefore essential to forward movement. Others feel UPG is bogus and distracts people from the "real" path. Only you can decide what role UPG will play in your work. Be sure to journal when it occurs; this will help you go back and reflect on it as time passes, which can be quite important. Who knows? You might be inspired to create something new.

7. Last but Not Least, Work Every Day

Many people confine their magickal practices and studies to the sabbats or esbats or work a charm or prayer when they need something, yet they don't carry out any sort of daily practices. Daily work is vital: it inspires curiosity, encourages learning, and builds skill. Whether you engage in reading, energy work, altar craft, divination, journaling, ritual, or something else, do a little every day. It makes a difference.

~

Best wishes as you continue to inspire your journey— may it be exciting!

City Protection Magic

by Ash Wennsday Everell

When you live in the city, you often find that you need heavy-duty protection that's rarely prescribed in basic texts. Just today, I was yelled at several times and spat upon during the two-block walk to the grocery store, something that doesn't really happen when I'm outside of the city center. For every lucky duck who can escape into their own yard when in need of a respite, there's another who has to brave two hours of public transit to get to the park.

A particular point of interest for Witches in the city is the sheer amount of stimuli that barrages us from every quarter. Aside from adjusting your lifestyle to ensure your own personal safety in the city, by avoiding dark alleys alone or locking your door when you're home, the mental environment for a city Witch can get quite tough. If you're an empathic type, being subject to literally thousands of people vying for prime psychic space is tiring as all get-out.

The result is that adjustments ought to be made to the way we protect ourselves in the city. Closing ourselves off entirely is often not an option in the city, as many of us live in these hubs to network and partake in the greater city community, whether it be at a work function or an industry mixer. The city environment offers a host of unique opportunities to flex our personal protective muscle!

Around the Apartment

The easiest way to get psychically protected is to secure your home. Beyond the usual locks and alarms, living in the city offers a whole slew of options for apartments.

The inside of your front door is a great place to put a protective ward. A small, stick-on hook, usually sold in grocery and convenience stores, can be temporarily stuck on to a wall, where dried herbs, wreaths, or even a broom could be held,

warding the doorway from negative energies. It would be lovely to hang a bundle of rowan berries for protection, perhaps on a broom decorated by everyone in the house. It can be secured by a brick-brown ribbon for security and can even be sealed and stamped with wax to make a neat bundle. You can buy herbs from the supermarket and tie them upside down to dry in windows, if you live in an arid area, and incorporate them into bundled wards for other doors in your house.

Every apartment (and home) has a unique soul. Find your apartment's special nooks and crannies and work with them to protect both your home's spirit and yours.

A Little Natural Magic

Don't let apartment space keep you from growing a container garden! Rail planters can be bought and hung on the bottom or rail of your window or balcony. If you're above the ground floor, this is an excellent chance to grow vining plants. For an extra kick of protection magic, choose plants with a grounding or shielding element. Yarrow is a great choice, and basil and sage make for friendly container plants too. You can even plant smaller globe radishes in between your taller crops. Not only will they be practical, you'll be able to catch their magical scent when the breeze blows by your open window as well!

If your apartment is secure but you still feel a little exposed psychically, a cleansing may be in order. Expose every corner of your apartment to the elements: A candle for fire, incense or a scented oil for air, salt for earth, and water for the ubiquitous water. Sprinkle mixed saltwater and waft the incense through your house counterclockwise, to rid it of negative energies. Finish by drawing a line across your threshold with the saltwater to seal the circuit. This should bring your home together and help it draw from the elements to protect itself and its inhabitants!

Self-Protection

Leave all that negative energy at the door when you come home. Envision any little nasties that have clung on to you dissipating at the gate to your home as you cross the threshold. If you need a quick shower after going out to wash off all the pollution gunk and any lingering residual negatives, cold water will break any psychic links and leave you cool and refreshed.

Of course, one needs the most protection when out and about. An easy way to help with this is to find a gemstone that is known for its grounding or protective qualities, such as hematite or amethyst, and consecrate it on your altar, envisioning a protective crystal layer of the gem solidifying around you. You can see through it, but it is completely bulletproof. It's the hardest substance around!

Once you're done, you can take the stone and touch it whenever you need to summon the protective crystal. You can also wear bracelets and jewelry with chip and inset gems in order to more actively "put on" your crystal armor before leaving the house.

A Heavy-Duty Banishing Ritual

If, on occasions, you *do* feel inundated with negative energies, choose this spell on a waning Moon. This is a strong,

stark, yet effective banishing that should wash away all energies maligning the user. It's particularly effective on the dark Moon, whose position behind the dark veil of sky is particularly suitable for protection. Using the element of water, we can banish and block negative energies to keep them from accumulating—especially those that could get picked up along the way in high-traffic areas.

It's a good idea to start with a nice, long salt bath to cleanse yourself and relax—light some candles of your choice while you do, if you like—before embarking on this spell.

You will need:

A large, shallow bowl: glass is best, but a cauldron also works
Three black candles: 4-inch or chime candles are perfect
Salt

Water

A brown paper bag: these can be scavenged after grocery shopping or getting food delivered

Matches

If your tradition calls for a circle to be cast, you can do so now. Add the water to the bowl and sprinkle a pinch of salt into it to cleanse the liquid.

Take a black candle, and light it, realizing it represents all that seek to break your protection. Slowly, push it farther and farther away from you, watching all swipes at your home and person wane away. If it helps, say these words:

You are going!
You are fading!
You are gone!

When the candle is as far away as you can reach, take it and push it into the water end-first. Extinguish it and watch it go out completely. Break the candle in half and put it in the bag (you may like to sprinkle some salt over it to cleanse between each candle).

Repeat this with the other candles, for a total of three times, breaking them all and discarding them in the paper bag. Once done, sprinkle salt over the candles in the bag to decharge them, roll up the paper bag, and throw it out of the house. This is key—make the trip to the dumpster or the trash chute, and feel the negative energies just wash away.

The key to protection in the city is working with the resources you have. Frequently, when books make mention of not needing protection magic "this serious" and you live in a place where brains cross wires like telephones, don't be afraid to break out the big guns. After all, your most precious asset is yourself!

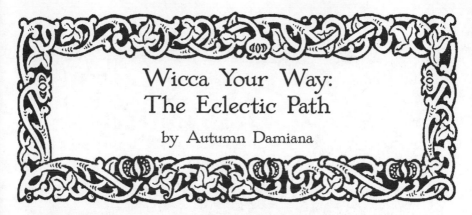

Wicca Your Way:
The Eclectic Path

by Autumn Damiana

What is Eclectic Wicca? The joke is that if you ask ten Eclectic Wiccans what they believe, you will get ten answers. This is (hopefully) a playful jab at Eclecticism, but it is partly true. Eclectic Wicca has become an umbrella term for ideals and practices that don't fall under established Wiccan traditions, such as British Traditional Wicca, Celtic Wicca, or the Dianic Path. It is surrounded by controversy, and everyone seems to have an opinion about it. Critics will even go so far as to say that Eclectics have no place in Wicca at all. But why is this?

To begin, Eclectic Wiccans don't give much credence to lineage, hierarchy, or a degree system. They usually don't feel the need to use oathbound material, secrecy, or require coven members to go through the prescribed "year and a day" of training. Some Eclectics may not even follow traditionally accepted Wiccan ritual methods or may interpret teachings differently. One of the most disputed ideas in Eclectic Wicca is that of self-initiation, because some believe that "only a Witch can make another Witch." Another debated issue is the assumption that Eclectic Wiccans just throw together any aspects of spirituality that they like to create a tailor-made religion.

In an effort to determine exactly what Eclectic Wicca is, I thought it might be best to start by getting an idea of what actual Wiccans and Witches had to say about it. I decided to interview several individuals about their beliefs and practices, and I have included some of their contributions throughout this article. (Please note that all names have been changed and quotes have been paraphrased.)

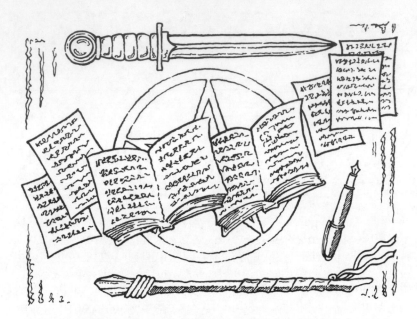

Interviews of Eclectics by Type

Solitary Eclectic: As the largest group, Solitaries evolved out of necessity before the Internet helped connect far-flung Wiccans with other Solitaries, groups, and covens. However, some are now actively choosing to be Solitary, because it has become its own path and offers self-governance and freedom of choice. Zoe is one such individual. "I'm self-educated in the Craft and began as a Solitary, but now I plan on staying that way. It works for me because I don't have to depend on anyone else."

Eclectic Wiccan Witch: "Wiccan" and "Witch" are often used synonymously, especially by Eclectics, who may blend their personal Witchcraft practices with their Wiccan practice. While Alex is a hereditary Witch, he noted, "The Witchcraft that I grew up with in my household could be construed as Eclectic Wicca. At one point I identified as that because I didn't know what else to call it."

Eclectic coven member: New covens often advertise as "Eclectic." Many of these are offshoots of more traditional covens or may contain members from several different traditions. Interestingly, a lot of more recent Eclectic covens are being started by younger Wiccans as a reaction to the strict mentality of their elders. "I was part of an Eclectic coven because I already had a background in Paganism, Druidry, and Witchcraft," said Jeremy. "Eclecticism was exciting because it offered me the ability to do ritual with a group while still exploring other forms of spirituality."

Neo-Wiccan: Some believe that there are really only two types of Wicca: British Traditional and everything else that came later—and sometimes the "everything else" is called Neo-Wicca to distinguish between the two. "I left a traditional coven that I had been initiated into as a Third Degree member," said Kate. "I now identify as a Witch, but I still hold some Wiccan beliefs. Does this make me a 'Neo-Wiccan'? I don't like that label, but it may be true."

Eclectic organizations: Church of Universal Eclectic Wicca (CUEW), Covenant of Unitarian Universalist Pagans (CUUPS), and the Aquarian Tabernacle Church (ATC) are three of the most well-known organizations that some Eclectics belong to. According to Michelle, "I came to Wicca through Christianity. I know that many others have done the same, especially Catholics, but for me it happened in the Unitarian church."

Mixing Pantheons

Plenty of Wiccans see nothing wrong with mixing pantheons, which may be one of the reasons that they are drawn to Eclecticism in the first place. Nevertheless, the ones I interviewed have a few boundaries. "Do I think that the gods care if I mix pantheons? Not really," said Michelle. "But I try to work ritual with only one pantheon at a time."

Jeremy thought that "it probably doesn't matter if you mix them, but it also keeps you from learning more than offhand knowledge of any particular one."

Zoe had a more permissive attitude: "Mixing pantheons is frowned upon in more structured forms of Wicca. But if you are not part of a circle that forbids it or you are Solitary, then why not?"

Kate commented, "I think it matters when you are trying to work with pantheons that don't mesh well. I don't feel like Odin is going to play nice with Ra."

Alex chimed in, "This is a question of whether or not you are a 'hard' or 'soft' polytheist. In that argument, it has more to do with whether or not you think it is disrespectful to the gods."

Cultural Appropriation

The term "cultural appropriation" describes when someone from one culture adopts something from another culture and often has a negative connotation, especially when a dominant culture absorbs the beliefs and/or practices from one that it has conquered. A perfect example is the dominant Caucasian culture of the United States borrowing from the indigenous Native American culture. However, Kate observed, "This is not a new thing; the pagan tribes of Europe gave way to Christianity, which obviously appropriated their holidays and some of their customs. But no one in our present culture takes this very seriously."

Jeremy also had this to say: "I would like to think that any spiritual tradition that I'm attracted to should not be dictated by my color, nationality, or race. When I was Wiccan, it was all about being Celtic. My racial ancestors were likely Celtic, but Stregheria really appealed to me even though it had nothing to do with my background." He went on to say, "It's possible that I might have a connection to this tradition because of a past-life experience."

Michelle had this to add: "It is one thing to adopt ideas from another culture, so long as you don't attempt to claim that culture as your own. You can learn some really beautiful teachings from the Huichol, for example. But don't go claiming that you're a Huichol shaman just because you spent five days in the desert taking peyote."

Eclectic Ethics

The CUEW outlines what they call the "Five Points of Wiccan Belief" on their website. Three of these are fairly self-explanatory ethics: Self-Responsibility, Constant Improvement, and Attunement (to the Divine in everything and the cycles of life.) The other two beliefs, the Wiccan Rede and the law of return (sometimes called the law of three), are recognized by all Wiccans. However, there are, of course, variations.

On the rede, Alex said, "The rede theoretically outlines what Wiccans should and should not do. I take issue over summing up the entire poem in the phrase 'harm none.' It's too reductionist, and it's not realistic. Plants and animals have to die every day just so we can eat, which is obviously causing harm to them."

Zoe shrugged and said, "I try to keep the rede in mind, but I always took it as good advice, not commandments."

Kate agreed. "I believe that every spell I cast does interfere with others' free will on some level, so I interpret the law of return and the rede a little differently. But this also makes me very, very careful what I attach my energy to. I do believe that 'what goes around comes around,' as they say, and it may not even be in this lifetime." She also adds, "And by the way—that cause and effect principle is not the law of karma. Too many Wiccans go around saying this, and it's not what karma means."

Jeremy's response about the law of return was more blunt: "If you are worried about bad energy coming back to you, then you should take a hard look at all of your intentions and motives. Because if these aren't good, then I don't believe that adding a little 'disclaimer' to the end of your spell is going to fix anything." What about the idea that "a Witch who cannot hex cannot heal"? According to Jeremy, "This just means that you should have a good working knowledge of magic, which by itself is not positive or negative. Knowing about hexes is not the same as casting them."

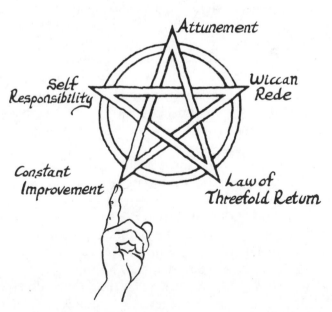

Alex concurred and added, "Is defensive magic considered a hex? Because if someone is threatening me or mine, I won't hesitate to protect them, especially on a magical level."

Opinions on Other Practices

Christian Wicca: This is another very controversial idea among Eclectics. Is it possible to be both Christian and Wiccan? Kate questioned, "Why would you want to? I left traditional Wicca because I found it to be too 'churchy' already."

Michelle smiled and said, "There are Christian Wiccans. I met some in both the Unitarian and Quaker churches. Although, Christianity as they believe it is radically different from everyone else's. I guess you could say that they are Eclectic Christians?"

Jeremy said, "I can see aspects of Christianity that might fit with Wicca, but you're more of a Witch if you try to blend these two."

Alex claimed that "both of these religions essentially contradict each other. There is no good reason to be both."

Zoe wryly observed, "Most say you can't be a Christian Wiccan, because Christians believes in their 'one true God above all others,' which Wiccans don't. So the Christians say we are all worshipping Satan. Is Satanic Wicca a thing, then? No, because we don't believe in him, either. So all this tells me is that if one path is valid, then they both are. Because frankly, Christian Wicca seems just as bizarre to me as the idea of Satanic Wicca."

Cyber-Wiccan: Zoe said, "Isn't this just a Solitary with an Internet connection? Whether you are part of an online school earning your degrees or connecting with other Wiccans or even participating in online circles or whatever, you are still a Solitary."

Chaos magic: "Wiccans can practice Chaos Magic. However, there are also Chaos Magicians, and they have a valid path, but it doesn't really have anything to do with religion. It has to do with magic," said Kate.

"Anything goes" view: Alex had this to say: "People have this idea that Eclectic Wiccans read a book or two and then just do whatever the hell they want. If only it were that easy."

Zoe agreed. "Ours is automatically an initiatory experience because we have to do all the work ourselves, especially as Solitaries. There is no single way in Eclectic Wicca that you can look to for guidance."

Jeremy pointed out that "most Eclectics 'go where they are called' so to speak, so they do cherry-pick from other religions. But isn't it better that their practices are so meaningful as a result?"

Kate said, "Eclectic Wicca is not for everyone. Even with a coven or group, it's not the free and easy shortcut that it seems to be. You still have to work hard, study hard, and then forge your own path in the process. But if it weren't challenging, it might not be as fulfilling, either."

And last, Michelle concluded, "You can tweak a recipe quite a bit before it changes what you are making. Eclectic Wicca is the same—it allows for adjustments, but it's still Wicca."

The Power of Spell Building

by Charlynn Walls

A foundational aspect of many spiritual pathways is the construction and use of spells, either working in conjunction with ritual or as part of a daily devotional act. Through spells we can affect our daily lives and set into motion the change we wish to see. However, building momentum in our spells is a sometimes overlooked aspect of the process, and it is useful when we need our spells to build potency and continue to expand.

For spell building to work, you have to clearly envision the entirety of the spell and begin constructing it with that in mind. By doing so, you will choose the most appropriate times to add to your spell. You will also choose what elements to add during those times.

Spell building is for long-term magickal goals that will take time to come to fruition. As with other types of magickal workings, you will want to support your spellwork with practical, real-world effort, which will reinforce the energies you are putting forth into your spell.

Purpose of Spells

Spells help manifest a desired change. Typically the change starts as thought and becomes a physical manifestation. First, you will need to decide why you need to do the spell. Setting your intention when you determine the purpose for your magickal working is crucial because it will influence when and how you will start expanding the initial spell. You are taking the potential in yourself and around you and giving it a magickal push to start moving toward your desired outcome.

Build the Foundation: Spell Creation

Creating spells can seem like a daunting task, and there are dozens of books devoted to how to properly craft a spell. However, the main thing to realize is that through putting the spell together, you are taking control of the situation.

Spell building is based on a solid foundation spell. In this phase you are creating the base spell that you will continue to build on. You will want to make sure that you consider the following components needed for the spell:

Identify the purpose or intent.
Determine what materials are needed.
Consider the timing of the spell.
Ascertain how you will build energy and release it.

Increasing the Magick: Spell Building

Spell building is based on the stacking of spells. You take your initial spell and continue to expand on it by continually adding elements to it over a predetermined amount of time. Stacking your spells like this has some advantages.

Rather than doing several one-shot spells that quickly lose their momentum or deviate from the original intent, you are allowing the energy to continue to flow by adding additional spells to it.

In order for it to be effective you will need to key into the spell's overall purpose. Will you be working for protection, prosperity, or another goal? After the goal is set, you need to determine how long you will carry out the work. Will you be doing daily work for a week after the initial spell was cast? Or do you need to continue to renew and add to the magick for several months?

With the purpose of the spell and the time frame set firmly in mind, you will next need to determine how you will amplify the energy of your initial spell. Adding the use of candles, sigils, crystals, poppets, or other magickal focus appropriate to your purpose in any combination can give the original spell a boost. The components can be added based on your timetable and can include specific times of day or Moon phases if desired.

Putting Together the Pieces

One purpose that lends itself well to spell building is protection magick. This is a spell that is easily renewed and amplified in order to keep the energy flowing so that the protections remain in place. What follows is an example that could be used for protecting your home and property throughout the course of a year. You will want to make sure that you own the property or plan to be at the home for an extended time. The spell-building stages were chosen as examples of how different magickal components could all be tied back to protection.

Purpose: Protection of property and family
Materials Needed:
Initial Spell: Four stones (examples: obsidian, black tourmaline, onyx, and hematite); small spade for digging
Spell Building, Stage 1: Black candles; carving tool; protection sigil

Spell Building, Stage 2: Offering bowl or cauldron; sage, angelica, juniper, sandalwood

Spell Building, Stage 3: Full Moon water; chalice

Spell Building, Stage 4: Broom

Spell Building, Stage 5: Offering bowl or cauldron; graveyard dirt

Timing: Saturday or waning Moon, midnight

Building Energy: Using a chant

Spell-Building Length: One year

Initial Spell

To begin the foundation spell, you will want to walk the boundaries of your property. This can be done at any time. You will want to get a feel for the location of the natural breaks in the land's energy and use those points to place your four anchor points that will help secure the protection magick to the area, as they will store the energy and form a perimeter around the property.

After identifying the areas you want to use, wait until either a waning Moon or a Saturday at midnight—times the protective energies will be most conducive. You can use any protection stone or combination of stones for this purpose. I like utilizing a combination of obsidian, black tourmaline, onyx, and hematite, as they all resonate protective energies.

When you are ready to begin the spell, start with the spot for the northernmost anchor point. Taking your spade, place the stone about one foot into the soil if possible. This will keep the stone from being accidentally dislodged. While doing so, you will say,

With strength of stone, my will is set to protect my home.

You will continue clockwise to the next anchor point while repeating the process of placing the stone and continuing the chant. Repeat the pattern until all of the stones have been placed into the soil. When all the stones are set, close the initial spell by saying,

All evil intent is barred; the energies gathered protect and guard.

Every couple of months you will renew and amplify the energy by rewalking the boundaries. Each time there will be a new component that will lend its unique energies to those you already established.

Stage 1

Two months after your initial spell, you will want to increase the protective energies on the property. Choose either a Saturday at midnight or the evening of the waning Moon. You can create a protection sigil for carving into a black candle. This can be as elaborate as you would like, or it can be a simple pentagram.

Again starting at the northernmost anchor point, take your black candle and use the carving tool (I use a bamboo skewer for convenience) to engrave the sigil into the candle. When you have finished, light your candle and walk from anchor to anchor in a clockwise motion. At each point, pour a little of the candle wax onto the ground as you say,

With strength sealed in stone, my will is set to protect my home.

When you get to the last point, you can again end with this:

All evil intent is barred; the energies gathered protect and guard.

Stage 2

Two months after the stage 1 spell, you will again add to the protective magick. The timing will again be a Saturday or waning Moon at midnight. Begin with the northernmost anchor point. This time you will combine a protection herb for each anchor point in an offering bowl. You will utilize the chant from the initial spell as you sprinkle the herb mixture in a large circle, making sure to leave a little extra at the anchor points. Say,

With strength grown in stone, my will is set to protect my home.

When you get to the last point, you can again end with this:

All evil intent is barred; the energies gathered protect and guard.

Stage 3

Two months after the stage 2 spell, when the timing is closest to a Saturday or evening of the waning Moon, you will again add to the protective magick. This time you will utilize Full Moon water that was collected and blessed previously. The water will enhance the protective energies already in place.

Place the water in a chalice for ease of working with it. You will start with the northernmost anchor point and begin sprinkling the water around the property line as you walk the boundaries. Again you will utilize the chant from the initial spell and end it as before:

With strength of Moon stored in stone, my will is set to protect my home.

When you get to the last point, you can again end with this:

All evil intent is barred; the energies gathered protect and guard.

Stage 4

Two months after the stage 3 spell, you will reinforce the protective magick by banishing negativity. Take the broom to the northernmost anchor point. Begin sweeping the negative energy out of the boundaries of your property. Continue around the perimeter and chant,

> *With negativity banished from strength of stone, my will is set to protect my home.*

When you get to the last point, you can again end with this:

> *All evil intent is barred; the energies gathered protect and guard.*

Stage 5

Two months after the stage 4 spell, you will add another layer to the protective magick. Place graveyard dirt that was previously collected into an offering bowl or cauldron. Proceed to the northernmost anchor point and begin sprinkling the boundary line with the graveyard dirt as you move around the property. This chant will be used to help anchor the protective energies of the ancestors to the anchor points:

> *With strength of ancestors anchored in stone, my will is set to protect my home.*

When you get to the last point, end with this:

> *All evil intent is barred; the energies gathered protect and guard.*

If you wish to continue to renew the energy after the year, you can do so. The protective magick will still be potent as long as you continue to add to it on a regular basis. At this point you can repeat the cycle or continue to add new elements into the rotation.

Should you choose to stop the spell building, the spells will slowly fade with time. If you were renting or plan to move at some point from the property, you would want to remove the anchor points and take them with you to your next place of residence. They could then be placed inside the new home or anchored on the new property.

Conclusion

Spell building is not a magickal working you would consider for a regular ritual situation. The energy boost is for those times when you need to continue the magickal work on a longer-term basis in order to help achieve your magickal goals.

Typically, magick finds the path of least resistance and the quickest form of release. By prolonging the magick, you are ensuring that the energy is being consistently renewed and amplified, which helps ensure that the output is directed more adequately to your need.

However, it is a lot of work to plan out the aspects of these spells to ensure the best affect. There will be a lot of preplanning for this type of energy work to make sure that the foundation spell is sufficient and to plan how you will continue to amplify the spells that will build upon it.

Spell building is difficult to undo because it takes as much effort—if not more—to undo as to create. The spells, if not renewed, will slowly fade on their own over time because the power has been layered, ensuring longevity.

Spellwork, especially spell building, is not for the faint of heart. It is work! But the results can be staggering if you give it the due consideration that it requires.

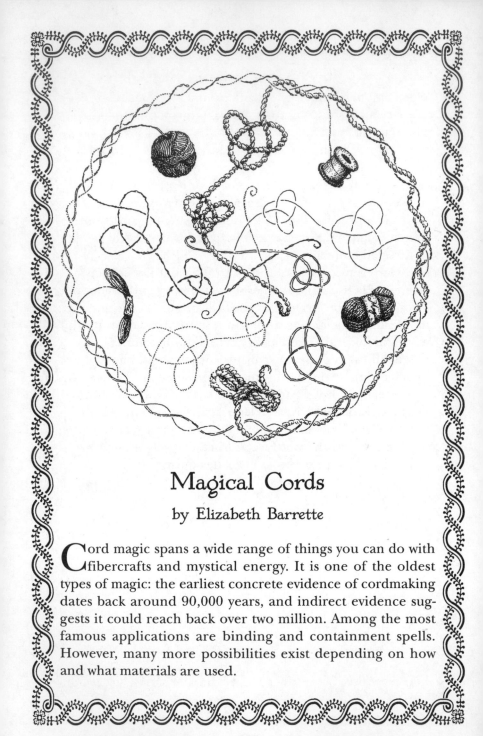

Magical Cords

by Elizabeth Barrette

Cord magic spans a wide range of things you can do with fibercrafts and mystical energy. It is one of the oldest types of magic: the earliest concrete evidence of cordmaking dates back around 90,000 years, and indirect evidence suggests it could reach back over two million. Among the most famous applications are binding and containment spells. However, many more possibilities exist depending on how and what materials are used.

Thread, String, and Rope

"Cord" can refer to any strand of twisted fibers. Twisting them together makes a stronger line that stays put and holds other things in place. To make a thicker diameter, several pieces may be twined together in such configurations as two-ply or three-ply rope. Other times a sheath may be woven around a central bundle of cords. Embroidery floss is designed to come apart so that you may decide how many strands to use at once.

The size of the cord influences what you can do with it. Thread is fine and smooth. It can't hold much weight but it is very discreet; you can stitch or tie a charm that will be unnoticeable from a few steps away. String offers a great balance between something that is lightweight yet fairly strong. It's easy to carry string with you for emergency magical needs. Thread and yarn may be knitted, crocheted, woven, or made into fabric. Rope is very sturdy and lasts a long time. It also provides a visual signal, such as knots on a boundary marker, when you want people to see what you're doing or during a group ritual.

Generally, use the thinnest cord that will do the job. It's less bulky and expensive that way. Choose the size based on what it needs to do. If you want it to flex or lie smooth, thinner is better. Thread is usually the only size to disappear well. If it needs to hold weight, thicker is better. For knots, string and rope let you see more clearly what you're doing.

Materials

Cord comes in many types. Common fibers include cotton, linen, wool, and silk. Rope adds some coarser options, such as jute and hemp, but those require careful handling because they are prickly. For most magical purposes, you want natural fibers like these. They tend to work well with magic, although silk is notable as a magic insulator. Synthetic fibers include acrylic, nylon, and polyester. These work best for technomagic and tend to insulate against natural magic. As with most types of artifact crafting, use the best materials you can get, preferably new rather than reused. If you use inferior materials, the magic will burn through them quickly, causing the fibers to fall apart. Here are some materials, their positive and negative qualities, and any notes on magical function:

Acrylic: Dyes brightly and stays colorfast, lightweight yet bulky, luxurious feel, good draping, resistant to odors and mildew, good insulation, excellent moisture management. Can stretch and shrink, forms static electricity, pills easily, breaks down under extreme heat.

Cotton: Breathable, soft yet durable, versatile, hypoallergenic. Dyes tolerably well but not colorfast, shrinks, wrinkles, mildew prone. (Woven cotton rope such as a clothesline is good for tying and untying knots, but after wetting, it's harder to untie.)

Hemp: Strong, hypoallergenic, eco-friendly, breathable, resistant to ultraviolet light. Can be scratchy, dyes with dull colors and not colorfast, wrinkles. (Best choice for imaginative or psychedelic work.)

Jute: Cheap, eco-friendly, strong, breathable, antistatic. Brittle, sheds fibers, scratchy, drapes poorly, weak when wet, dyes poorly, is prone to microbial decay.

Linen: Strong, stronger when wet, withstands high temperatures, antistatic, no pilling or lint. Wrinkles, not very durable, drapes poorly, low elasticity, expensive.

Nylon: Dyes easily, cleans easily, strong, resilient, abrasion resistant. Stains easily, fades in sunlight, too slippery to knot.

Polyester: Dyes easily, colorfast, strong, shiny, lightweight, does not shrink or stretch, mildew resistant. Does not breathe, eco-hostile, stains easily, stiff, holds knots poorly but better than nylon.

Silk: Dyes beautifully, nonallergenic, soft, shiny, luxurious, breathable, durable, makes secure knots, lightweight. Stains easily, needs special care, tangles, very expensive. (Insulates against magic.)

Wool: Dyes well, strong and warm (even more so when wet), breathable, tear resistant, elastic, luxurious. Colors tend to be dull, deteriorates in sunlight, pills easily, itchy, vulnerable to mold and mildew. (Best choice for animal magic.)

Colors

Most types of cord can be dyed in desired hues. Wool grows naturally in a range of black, brown, gray, white, and reddish tones. By choosing an appropriate color, you can add energy and make sure the cord resonates with its intended purpose. Here are some colors and their correspondences:

White: purification, positive energy, unity, consecration, general purpose, youth

Gray: balance, moderation, contemplation, diffusion, technology

Black: binding, negative energy, concealment, wisdom, protection, reversing

Brown: nourishing, grounding, animals, stability, body, earth

Gold: eternity, unchanging, masculine energy, the Sun, the God

Silver: rebirth, cycles, feminine energy, the Moon, the Goddess

Pink: friendship, affection, platonic love, emotional healing
Red: passionate love, intense energy, fire, life force, adulthood
Orange: creativity, self-expression, ambition, vigor, travel
Yellow: joy, communication, uplifting, new beginnings, air
Green: nature, plants, healing, prosperity, luck, abundance
Blue: soothing, sleep, dreams, justice, willpower, focus, truth, mind, water
Violet: magic, psychic power, divine connection, endings, spirit, elders

Spinning and Braiding

In order to work cord magic, first you need the cord. Spinning, in which you twist fibers into a long spiral, is the most popular way of creating it. Some fibers can also be braided, or you can spin cords and then braid them. Use the cords for hanging things, tying knots, or other purposes.

Spinning channels power through a spiral motion. It can be done slowly with a hook, faster with a drop-spindle, or quite briskly with a spinning wheel. Most cord today is spun by machine, and it works fine for magic. However, for maximum impact, you can make your own. Use fiber with good "catch," such as wool, so that it spins easily.

Braiding crosses strands so they stay together. You can make use of number magic as you combine three or more strands. Make a solid-colored braid, or choose colors to represent the different energies. A three-strand braid might feature maiden, mother, and crone. A four-strand braid might use earth, air, fire, and water. Among the simplest cord magic spells is making a braid while holding your intent in mind.

Knotting

Knots can be used to capture energy. Some have a specific theme, such as the "true love" knot. Many spells are done with a plain overhand knot. One of the oldest spells recorded is for sailors. They would take a rope outside during a strong wind and tie knots in it to bind that power. When a ship was becalmed at sea, they would untie one or more of the knots to raise wind for traveling.

Knots are also used to secure the loose end at the conclusion of many fibercrafts such as braiding. Note that once you make the final knot, it seals the magic in place. If you cut that knot off, the magic will run out. This is actually useful: if you make a mistake in the magic, you can cut it loose, and still salvage the mundane craft. Just make a new knot to keep the work from unraveling.

Celtic knotwork represents infinity and connections. It may use plain lines or shape them into animals and people. This type of knotwork uses cords to make handles, pendants, bracelets, and other items. It's also beautiful when the cords are knotted and stitched onto pillows or quilts. Different images may evoke the Triple Goddess, the Horned God, the White Stag, or other mythic figures.

Latch hook is a simple craft that involves knotting short yarns around a canvas base to create a patterned rug. This pairs well with a mantra or chant, which you repeat each time you tie a knot. That repetition adds power, like filling a pool one bucket at a time. It works great for making coven rugs with magical designs, such as a pentacle.

A good knot spell is to visualize something upsetting you, then tie an overhand knot in a black cord. Put all your negative feelings into that knot. Yell at it or stomp on it if you wish. Then go soothe yourself with a bath, a hot meal, or whatever helps you relax. Later come back and untie the knot to release the energy, and it will help you work through the problem.

Knitting and Crochet

These types of fibercraft rely on making yarn into a great big sheet of knots by using a tool. The tools, whether knitting needles or crochet hooks, can help you tune the magic if they are made out of wood or metal, and you can use the correspondences for that material as well as the yarn itself. For technomagic, you might prefer aluminum or plastic. Think of this as your magic wand, and speak the incantation as you work.

Next, consider the shape. You can work in a spiral, a triangle, squares, rows, and so forth. There are even pentagram patterns! This works well for flat objects such as altar cloths, rugs, afghans, etc. You can work in positive energy for things like warming or comforting spells. It's also possible to knit or crochet pieces that are later fastened together to make stuffed animals, fitted garments, and other projects.

You can even use the wand motion as your primary casting and the yarn as a disguise. This works for such things as banishing or shielding in a public place, where you want people to respect your space. Point the tip of your wand at them and imagine flicking them away. When you finish your project, you'll also have a scarf or whatever that is good for the same shielding or banishing.

Weaving

Woven fabric typically has warp (lengthwise threads) and weft (woven around the warp threads), although finger-weaving uses the same strands for both purposes in a diagonal pattern. When you weave, you can easily switch colors to make pictures or other patterns. "Shot silk" uses warp of one color and weft of a contrasting color, so that the fabric seems to change tones as it moves, perfect for working magic with fire and water (red and blue) or earth and air (brown and yellow).

If you're weaving a rug, stole, altar cloth, or other strip design, then you also have the option of using knots. Gather the warp threads together in small bundles, focus your intent, and then tie the knot. Say a mantra over each one as you do so. In this manner you may anchor many little parts of a spell as you work your way across the two raw ends of the cloth.

Conclusion

Cord magic is really based in hearth magic, something you do as you make it, rather than a quick spell with premade components. It's an everyday application of mystical energy that you can use to make your life easier or just a little more enchanted. You can pick and choose the type of materials, size of cord, and finished project based on your needs.

Bear in mind that fibercraft is a kind of moving meditation, and cord magic of all kinds requires sustained focus. In mundane crafts, you can let your thoughts wander; in magic, you must keep the purpose in mind while you are working. Therefore, start with small projects to build up your stamina; you might start with a potholder charmed against burning or dropping. Later, break large projects into specific stages with good stopping points to anchor the energies temporarily. A quilt might be made one square at a time, each with a different well-wishing on it. Some people find that it helps to play suitable music or nature sounds to help maintain their concentration on the theme.

Look around your sacred space to see what kind of magical items you could make with thread, yarn, or rope. Choose something and give it a try!

The Magic of Characters in Dreams: Artistic Inspiration and Dream Spells

by Shawna Galvin

Most people experience characters, stories, and more in their dreams. They talk about them, like in stories, and tell them to others. As a writer, I've used characters in my dreams over the years in fiction, poetry, and in other aspects of creating art, such as painting and making altered books. I've returned to journals I've kept over the years, and used dreams I'd written down in them in the past, not knowing then that they would become part of art.

Dreaming of ourselves or as someone else within a dream or of strangers entering the dream fascinates me, and I make creative use of many dreams I've had both recently and years ago. Dreams have been a popular topic of study, and a number of people use dreams for making art—music, stories, paintings, poetry, and even inventions. I often take scenes and characters from my dreams and turn them into poetry or stories, just as things in the waking world (such as overheard dialogue, new experiences, or an atmospheric setting) are often used for art.

I've written down hundreds of dreams over the years, and the ones I use within fictional stories include settings, plot lines, characters, and entire other worlds presented in my dreams. I am also intrigued that people I have never seen before or don't even know enter my dreams and become a huge part of or an entire story I write. Or sometimes, I am that other character, but me—I am living that character's life in my dream. I am soaring through that person's point of view. Other times, I am a fly on the wall, watching the story unfold before me in my dream.

I have dreams about people I know or who have passed away, and I have so many types of dreams—scary, disturbing, lovely, spiritual, and magical. We spend so much time asleep in our lives that it only makes sense that we would connect with other realms. Dreams are mysterious; I think we have the ability to time travel or soul travel in dreams, and I believe I have done so.

I have always been interested in the story or particular scenes within dreams, along with the feelings, colors, settings, people,

interactions, and time periods. When my mother passed away, I was in the final semester of graduate school, studying creative writing. I found an article she had clipped about dreams, "Writers Finding Muse in Dreams." The writer of the article, Jordan Lite, talks about how literary publicist Naomi Epel wrote a book, *Writers Dreaming*, in which one of her own dreams inspired her to interview twenty-six writers, such as Stephen King, about how they use dreams in their writing. In the article, Epel said that most creative people "trust" the dream "information when it comes up," and I have read about, learned about, and met many writers who have trusted and used their dreams. She elaborates, "Many people don't remember their dreams every day, but when a big dream occurs, [writers] listen [and] go with their process of exploration." For example, the article states, William Styron dreamed of a young woman tattooed with concentration camp numbers and the next day wrote the beginning of *Sophie's Choice*.

Many writers, such as my late friend and coworker Rick Hautala, write in the morning. He said he would not eat, shower, or do anything when he woke up, except go right to his typewriter in the hypnagogic state to write. Writer Dennis Lehane said the same thing of his own writing process, that perhaps that is why some writers were or are known to use alcohol or other substances: to put them in that dream-like state to write in. Maya Angelou used to play solitaire to "hypnotize herself"; she would play cards to relax her mind as she would go into a creative zone to put herself in another world, writes Lite. Mary Shelley's dream inspired her story *Frankenstein; or, The Modern Prometheus.* The more I got to know fellow and late writers, the more I realized how dreams play a huge part of many writers' lives.

Nightmares and Negative Energy in Dreams

Nightmares can sometimes haunt our dreams and even our waking life. One in particular happened to me in a hotel room several years ago while visiting San Francisco and Alcatraz. I didn't connect the two right away, but I think some negative energy came back with me. I cannot prove it, but I certainly believe this, as I experienced a most malevolent presence. It felt as though someone was pushing down on me, I woke up inside my dream, yet I think I was also awake. In my mind, I demanded the evil presence to leave, telling it that it was unwelcome. I said prayers and visualized white light surrounding me. At the same time, I felt as though I was paralyzed; I couldn't move or wake up from that dream for a long time. Like Poe said, life is "but a dream within a dream." That was the second time in my life I had a dream of an evil presence that seemed so real. The first case happened in the late 1980s. I wrote it down, had to sleep with my light on for days after, and used the dream in my first novel, *The Ghost in You,* decades later.

Dream Spells and Nightmare Protection

I come from an Irish and English background, with a touch of Mic Mac Indian, and using crystals, dream catchers, and prayer have been part of my upbringing. I furthered my studies for about ten years while taking meditation classes, experiencing polarity and spiritual readings, and also becoming a Reiki II practitioner. I've always used universal light force energy as protection to keep bad dreams away or to help get a good night's sleep. In the two worst nightmares of my life, where both times an evil presence came to me, I stood up to them. The experiences were terrifying, but I do not allow evil spirits in my life. I am not immune to evil, but I have learned to use tools such as imagining a white light around me, my house, loved ones, and even my car for protection.

Dream catchers are something my family has always had around, and I even remember making them in summer camp. My son has had one hanging in his room since he was old enough to recall his first nightmares, mainly about an alien living in the basement of our over-200-year-old house at the time. The dream catcher has come with us to our new house as well, hanging up in his window. Dream catchers, which originated with the Ojibwe people and Native American cultures and beliefs in general, are both magical and spiritual. A dream catcher is said to attract dreams to its web. The good spirits find their way through the center hole and float along the sacred feathers to the people sleeping below. The evil spirits get caught in the web and are melted by the morning Sun. Patron of thc Arts, a website on art and creativity, has a guide to making your own dream catchers (www.patronofthearts .com/2015/02/meaning-magic-drcamcatchers).

If a bad dream occurs, one can still clear out negative energy after a nightmare lingers on in the mind, even if that energy extends to one's surroundings. Back when I was in San Francisco and felt that horrible presence, which felt like an evil spirit in

my dream, I smudged my home with white sage to clear out any residual parts of that energy when I arrived back in Maine. I felt at peace afterward and believe that this ritual worked. White sage smudging is something I'd learned to use back when I was practicing Reiki and other spiritual transformations in my life. After having a nightmare that really hangs on, I burn my white sage smudge stick and walk around my house fanning the smoke to each corner of the rooms as best I can with my hand or a feather, and think good intentions. I also visualize white light surrounding myself, my family, and my home as protection. Sometimes I say prayers, but mainly I trust my instincts and use good intentions only. Smudging with white sage is good to use for any feelings of negativity that arise.

Traveling in Dreams

I'm fascinated by the fantasy worlds I visit when I dream and by the ones that seem real, like when friends and loved ones who have passed visit; it feels mystical to connect to them this way. Sometimes in dreams I feel like I'm traveling in another dimension—communicating with this world and another world. They often take me back in time to other lands, perhaps in a parallel world. Other times, they are a mixture of this world and another world, as in Gabriel García Márquez's stories of magical realism.

Dream worlds can be mysterious, bizarre, shadowy, and surreal, and they often feel like a real place separate from experiences in the waking world. And from these, for me, many stories, ideas, poems, and other forms of writing art can spring forward.

Some dreamers have out-of-body experiences or perform astral projection. I have dreams where I am outside of myself, looking upon a dream world story as it unfolds. I am like a wallflower, observing. This type of observation in dreams has become a part of my and other authors' writing. Ebenezer Scrooge of *A Christmas Carol* was awakened from his dreams (or was he?) and traveled around to his past, present, and possible future. Dorothy was knocked unconscious by her bedroom window during the tornado, and what dreams did that bring her! Or perhaps she wasn't dreaming and really did soul-travel to the Land of Oz.

Lucid dreams can offer powerful inspiration as well. Ryan Hurd, a dream studies specialist, explains that galantamine, which is supposed to promote dreaming sleep as well as lucid dreaming, "has been used for centuries in China as a memory enhancer, and was even noted by the ancient Greeks for its powerful mind-inducing effects." He writes that it is also used for some Alzheimer's patients to increase memory. (Consult your physician before taking any sort of alternative supplement.)

Many people try to control or train their mind to have lucid or other kinds of dreams. I have found that the best way to get the most out of dreaming is to write down my dreams. There is no magic spell for this—just try to catch them before they slip away. I've lost a few because I couldn't remember them; I was too tired to write them down after waking in the middle of the night, and they drifted away, as memories of dreams often do.

As I finished writing this, a close friend, who was also a writer, had been fighting cancer and was under the impression she was doing better. Then, just like that, the cancer spread like wildfire. She was told she had a few weeks, maybe a month, to live, but passed away days later.

Two days before she passed, a book release party was held for my small publishing company, through which my friend published a story based on true experiences. I imagined her walking in to the party, feeling better, but that didn't happen. Instead, I learned of her latest development and prognosis. I had planned to go visit her the following Monday morning, as I knew she'd be surrounded by hospice and such, but I wanted to hold her hand for a moment and give her a picture that my son drew of hers while they were in preschool together. Saturday evening, perhaps into the twilight hours of Sunday morning, I had a dream that my friend and I were walking through Rome in the summer, by ancient architecture, but it was also blended with Portland, near where we both live. I woke that morning, feeling that perhaps she had already passed, and we would continue to roam around in dreams together from there. We also shared a love of the B-52's song "Roam," which is pretty much about soul-travel. Perhaps the dream of us in Rome was a symbol of us being able to roam around the world in our dreams.

Later that Sunday morning, I was told she was probably going to pass that very day. It was later in the evening when I had that feeling she had let go, and indeed it was so. Since then, I've had

247

dreams of my friend, and I often talk to her in my mind. I feel her presence, treasure life, and know she'd want me to experience life to its fullest as I have been lately. I've been inspired to write new things using my dreams since she passed, and some of my dreams about her have led me to new creative endeavors in my writing.

Pay attention to your dreams. The more you do so, the more of a ritual it becomes to write them down; perhaps tell them to others, write a poem, or make a picture or collage about them—do something that helps you to remember and use your dream. I think the more one pays attention to dreams, without forcing or trying to control them, the more likely one will be to have lucid or other types of dreams. They might not come every night; they might come on certain Moons, or certain days of the year, or at random. For those nights they don't come, just focus on getting enough sleep and be grateful for the rest. A nice relaxing spell you might try follows next.

A Dream Box Spell: Folk Magic

This dream spell can be done during a Full Moon or anytime you like. I choose colors at my own working altar. I like to work with lavender scent and herb and a soft lavender color, because it is associated with relaxation, peaceful sleep, insight, and dream work.

For Your Altar

Spread out a cloth to place your items on. Anyplace you want to set up an altar is fine, as long as you feel comfortable. I prefer a sacred space that keeps me close to my ancestors.

Set out your dream box, perhaps a small bundle of lavender, a candle to light during your ceremony, lavender essential oil, and a small statue or charms that have meaning for you. This is a place for you to create your own sacred space, so add whatever you like to your altar.

For Your Dream Box

You can really have fun with this, as you can choose any sort of box you like. You can select a decorative box and even embellish and customize one of your own. Let creativity flow when putting the dream box together on your altar. You can collect things to put into the box and adapt this dream spell for many purposes. Perhaps you are working on the art of lucid dreaming, or maybe you'd like to dream about a loved one who has passed. Whatever the purpose, an easy way to make your intention clear is to write it down, roll it up, tie a ribbon around the scroll, and place in the dream box. Other things one might place in the box are a piece of amethyst; a handful of dried, loose lavender; aromatherapy, such as few drops of essential oil; a photograph; a piece of jewelry; a specific tarot card; or whatever has meaning for you.

Clearing Your Space

I always begin and end rituals and spells by clearing the space and bringing positive energy in. The use of white light visualization to surround a space and smudging with white sage are two things I prefer, along with a prayer sometimes.

Place the box under your bed before falling asleep, say the following chant, and dream away. This is a wonderful way to start paying attention to your dreams and start a dream journal. You can add to or modify this however you like. You might even have a dream catcher nearby as well.

May the universe guide my dreams tonight.
Be with me, peaceful, restful sleep.
Let my mind be eased;

Let my body be calm.
Let in the sight of night,
And let the dream be clear.
Let my troubles drift away,
And let me dream.

When to Do This Spell

Do this during a Full Moon. You might want to smudge or do some kind of closing ceremony the next morning or during the day. Try visualizing a pure, healing white light surrounding the area around your bed or smudging with white sage, drawing and keeping positive energy in while ridding it of any negative energy. End by thanking your dreams, spirits, or whatever guidance you believe in for the experience.

For Further Study

Hurd, Ryan. "Galantamine: Reviewing the Lucid Dreaming Pill." Dreamstudies.org. Accessed on November 6, 2015. http://dreamstudies.org/galantamine-review-lucid-dreaming-pill.

Lehane, Dennis. "You and Me This Morning Talks to Dennis Lehane." YouTube video, 6:13. October 19, 2012. https://www.youtube.com/watch?v=e45cnK43FJ8.

Lite, Jordan. "Writers Finding Muse in Dreams." Associated Press. August 12, 1999. http://www.apnewsarchive.com/1999/Writers-Finding-Muse-in-Dreams/id-d438dfb9b521cfff8f41bcef19bd8942.

Witch Jars Rebooted for the Modern Witch

by Cassius Sparrow

Witch jars and witch bottles have been in use for centuries. In fact, the earliest record of witch bottle use dates back to 1681 in England. During this time, they've garnered for themselves a sort of reputation for being used in "witch warfare" as a counterattack to curses and malevolent magic. In this regard, they can be used for both offensive and defensive magic: as a reaction to hexes and curses by negating them (or returning them to their caster) and by protecting against further attempts of harm. Witch jars are some of the best items in a witch's arsenal of protective magic.

However, relegating witch jars to a simple category of "protective magic" limits the multitude of ways that they can be used across every category of magic imaginable. Witch jars are a self-contained, ongoing spell. They are one of the most adaptive forms of magic available to witches: as long as the bottle or jar is not broken, the spell is continually cast. This means that witch jars no longer have to be buried in some secret place and dug up every time a witch moves. They can be placed in a cupboard or closet or hidden away in the attic, as long as they are safe and out of harm's way. Since they are a form of "passive magic," there are no serious, taxing, or exhausting rituals for the caster to endure, and there's no mess to clean up after, as all the spell reagents are contained neatly within the jar. The contents of the jar can be as simple or complex as the caster wishes and can be tailored to be more general, all-encompassing magic or to be very specific and definite. Because they are versatile and can be adapted to suit a witch's location and variety of available ingredients, witch jars are an excellent starting point for any witch wishing to write his or her own spells and are a great way to experiment with more personal spells to add to a witch's grimoire.

Even in this modern age of Witchcraft, there is still a need for discretion within the magical community and among practitioners of Witchcraft. Witch jars provide a sort of discretion that more elaborate spells cannot. As said before, everything is neatly contained within the jar or bottle, and nothing is more innocuous looking than a simple jar. Completed jars are small enough to be hidden away easily, and there is no need to bury them—which comes as a huge relief to any witch without a yard or easily accessible garden or one who does not want to risk being caught digging a hole on possibly private property in order to hide the spell. Jars and bottles are easy to come by, and recycling pasta and salsa jars or glass beverage bottles makes this magic both cost-effective and eco-friendly by keeping more trash out of landfills.

While witch jars can still be used as passive protective magic, there's no end to the possibilities and versatility of their use. The contents can be used to cast spells of prosperity, healing, luck, hexes, cleansing, banishing, and even attracting love. Protective uses can be expanded to include nonmagical maladies, such as spells against nightmares, bad luck, anxiety, depression, financial problems, and troublesome people or spirits.

Writing a witch jar spell is as simple as knowing what you need and what you want the end result of the spell to be, and understanding the necessary items you will need to cast it. Herbs, oils, written petitions, physical representations, symbols, incense, candles—all of these are common spell ingredients and all are acceptable additions to the contents of the spell jar. If you have experience creating your own spells, then you'll know what it is you will need to include in the anatomy of your witch jar. You can adapt spells to easily be contained within a jar, or you can glean ideas from other witch jar spells in order to create your own. Once you get into the habit of using witch jars in your spellwork, the rest will come easy.

A Witch Jar for Prosperity

You will need the following:

Basil (fresh or dried)
Mint (fresh or dried)
Cinnamon
Sea salt
Four coins of any denomination (pennies will work)
Paper and pen
A green or white candle
Basil oil (optional)

Start your jar by adding a single layer of sea salt. If you are using fresh herbs, shred them now and add a layer

of basil first, then a layer of mint. See the green herbs as money coming to you, filling your wallet and your bank account. Add another layer of sea salt. If you are using a cinnamon stick, rather than ground cinnamon, break it into pieces and scatter it over the second layer of salt; otherwise, sprinkle your ground cinnamon over this layer, using it as a means of drawing prosperity to you. Write your petition for prosperity on the paper:

> *As this jar is filled with treasures, so too will my life be filled with prosperity. So shall it be.*

Fold the paper four times, and anoint it with basil oil if you are using it. Add it to the jar, and add the four coins. Add two more layers of basil and mint. Seal the jar and burn the candle on top (do not leave burning candles unattended), allowing the dripping wax to further seal the jar with your intent. Aloud, repeat your petition:

This jar is sealed, my spell is cast, prosperity shall come to me and fill my life as I have filled this jar. So shall it be.

Give the jar a shake, dispersing the layers and see prosperity in all forms being dispersed to you. You can either keep the jar on your altar or workspace or put it away for safekeeping. When you feel the need for an extra boost of prosperity, take it out and give it another shake, while repeating your petition.

"The Way Is Convoluted": A Spell to Banish Bad Luck
You will need the following:

Paper and pen or a printed image of a maze
Salt
Rue, lavender, rosemary, powdered dragon's blood, and
  chamomile
Three cloves of garlic
Olive oil or an uncrossing oil of your choice
Lucky charm (optional)
A black candle and a white candle
Sandalwood incense
Fresh water
Soap (either a new bar or a few drops of liquid soap)

This is a two-part spell that starts with a symbolic cleansing of your bad luck so far and banishing of bad luck, and it ends with a petition to draw good luck to you in the future. Light the sandalwood incense. Start your jar by drawing an X or a protective sigil of your choice on the inside of the jar with your oil (you can use your finger or a paintbrush). Say this aloud:

Bad luck has plagued me but no longer. The way is convoluted, and it shall not find me.

Wash your hands with the water and soap; dispose of the dirty water immediately. Draw a maze on the paper unless you are using a printed image of a maze. Fold the paper in thirds and repeat this:

The way is convoluted, and bad luck shall not find me.

Pass the paper and your hands through the smoke. Add the maze to the jar and sprinkle it with a liberal layer of salt. Peel and crush the three cloves of garlic for the next layer in the jar. Next, layer the powdered dragon's blood and rue (for protection), chamomile (for peace), rosemary and then lavender (for drawing good luck). Say this aloud and with intent:

Bad luck has plagued me but no longer. The way is convoluted, and it shall not find me. The wheel of fate is turning, and only good luck and good will shall find me now. So shall it be.

If you are including a lucky charm (anything that you associate with luck or that has been particularly lucky for you) add it to the jar now and seal your jar. On top of the jar, burn the black candle first, banishing the negativity that has been following you. When it is done, burn the white candle over the black wax, drawing good fortune and good luck to you and your home. When it has burned out, put the jar in a dark, secret place, and be careful not to disperse the layers so that the maze stays hidden at the bottom of the jar.

⌇

Witch jars are an old form of magic, reliable and well-founded in their antiquity, but can and should be used in modern forms of witchcraft, as they are adaptable both in practice and in path. Any type of witch, from kitchen witches to faery craft practitioners to urban witches, can find a use for witch jars and bottles. The only limit to their usage lies in the imagination and the needs of the witch using them.

The Blue Sphinx

by Estha K. V. McNevin

Related in world animistic folklore to the beguiling mystery of our own happiness, the Sphinx protects but also casts down her adjudications upon our lives here on earth. Our Lady of the ROTA is often invisible to the uninitiated eye and is fixed in Jupiter's cherubic hegemonies, the elemental spirits, of which she is absolutely composed. Proposing the riddle of karma and the dharmic cycles directly ahead of us on the trundle, she observes everything. The Sphinx is the ruling intelligence of the sacred mysteries and the keeper of the secret names of God. Featured masterfully in the Rider-Waite Tarot on Trump X, the Wheel of Fortune, this mythological pictograph of adaptive mastery is every magician's very own terrifying and resplendent confidant.

Secret Society Spiritualism

As a symbolic puzzle key of universal order, the Sphinx is faithfully allied with supernatural abilities of keen perception and is patroness of the sacred mystery cults of Egypt. Contemporary ceremonial organizations are filled with the esoteric, linguistic, and mathematical code of the ancient civilizations. The framework of our modern tarot formula relies heavily on the Victorian translations and Gnostic work of secret esoteric societies like the Golden Dawn.

In the 1880s, members of this fraternal occult tradition translated volumes of the world's most beloved mystical texts. In a spectacle of typical mid-Victorian zeal, they took to the academic study and ritual practice of the corpus of global humanities, binding this work to the starry belt of the zodiac. An intriguing portion of these ceremonial texts included the Kabbalistic rituals and Hebrew studies of Eliphas Levi. His extensive astrological and alchemical work reflected the bohemian math and science advances of Ottoman academia. Levi's symbolic tables were translated from the Gnostic works of John Dee and Heinrich Cornelius Agrippa. His universal code became essential in the creation of one of the first pictorial decks, the Italian Sola-Busca Tarot.

Commissioned sometime in the late fifteenth century, this Renaissance deck provided the framework for a global obsession with neoclassical art, and certainly explains our modern penchant for the reclaimed mythic symbolism of antiquity. A member of the Golden Dawn, artist Pamela Colman Smith studied and worked on a near-replica Edwardian version, the Rider-Waite Tarot, published in 1910. Smith's depiction of the nemes-clad Blue Sphinx appeared Technicolor in its own time, and as a pictograph of the ethics of occult philosophy, it remains second to none.

The Nemes and Uraeus

The Sphinx and her traditional headdress, the *nemes* (pronounced neh-may), were both popularized during the First Dynasty, sometime around 3100 BCE, following the unification of the southern dry lands of Upper Egypt with the contrasting northern wetlands of Lower Egypt. The lightweight, loom-woven linens were a common feature of the Nile Delta and were produced in a variety of warp-and-weft patterns. Warp is the lengthwise or longitudinal thread in a roll, while weft is the transverse thread, symbolic of the unseen fabric of reality. Egyptian spirituality prized weavers as cocreators of our world. Artfully pleated to reveal semitransparent repetitions of light and silhouette, this Gnostically woven fabric proved an impressive Copper Age luxury. The nemes (a striped linen headdress) was paired with an uraeus (the sculpted rearing cobra), both bound to the head with finely woven gold cord sacred to Nut and Isis. The snake was a revered form of the goddess Wadjet, patroness of the Nile and wife of Hapi, god of flooding.

When worn together, the uraeus and nemes became a crowning symbol of unity and sovereignty in the Old Kingdom. They were used most notably to shroud a pharaoh legally with the primordial power of creation. The twofold mystical sibling allegories of the Nile civilization are aboriginal to the region. Religious rituals used the nemes in the reenacting of creation and venerated the paradoxical dualism of something from nothing, life from death. Priests and shamans officiated public ceremonies and administered epic celebrations, which kept the living in constant contact with the dead.

The systematic privileges of ordered society, and the regimented administration of shamanic ritual offerings, known only to a few, were outwardly obscured in the hieroglyphic art and richly sculpted architecture of monolithic polytheism. One could say that the mysteries of the cosmos were hidden in plain sight!

A common depiction is the story of creation, illustrating humanity's rise—out of the waters of life and into our leafy longboats built to fish upon the divine and celestial Nile, a perfect mirror of the heavens. Plants such as flax, papyrus, lotus, and palm that grew naturally along the river all came to symbolize complex esoteric themes of self-discipline, enlightenment, and immortality. Ceremonially woven linen was profoundly connected to the magical spirit of the river. According to the mythology of the Egyptian Book of the Dead, the goddess Neith, using celestial mathematics, secretly wove the first Nile linen cloth; her name bears the hieroglyph for the loom.

Wearing a pharaoh's headdress equips the Sphinx with the unlimited authority of a deity. It designates her as God's right hand (the Hand of Fate), thus placing her in a position of active sulfuric alchemical command. She is the volatile and primordial master of chance and willpower. As the keeper of the keys of mastery, she is a capable yet unpredictable patroness, benign until ignited into an explosive and transformative act.

The Sphinx's nemes is pleated in a style similar to the celebrated Fourth Dynasty Pharaoh Khufu, patron of engineering and the architectural arts. Khufu was the builder of the Great Pyramid of Giza, which was constructed between 2540 and 2560 BCE. Many scholars now believe that it was actually his son Khafre who built the Sphinx to further honor and serve his immortal father in the afterlife. Archeologists unearthed wooden longboats hidden for centuries beneath the paws of the monument that were offered for Khufu's cosmic journey.

The nemes elevated political leaders as gods of truth, innovation, and stability. They were often depicted in hieroglyphic art as living gods on earth, adored as lions amongst men and entombed as cosmological immortals upon death. Egypt later came to idealize funeral ceremony and transfiguration as the foundation of its civilization. The nemes worn by the Sphinx trademarks a guardian of both temple and tomb, imbued with the divine right of adaptive predominance and adorned with fine Nile linen: the regalia of mystic ascension.

Shrouded in Jupiterian Obscurity

The blue, athletic body of the lioness Sphinx reveals her link with the power and prowess of the Roman "King God" Jupiter, whose planetary colors are King Scale sky blue and Queen Scale violet. According to Chic Cicero and Sandra Tabatha Cicero, Sachiel is the ancient Semitic spirit of providence and the archangel of Jupiter, ruler of Thursday. His name means "covering of God," an idea that is highly applicable to the nemes-clad Sphinx. In the Greek mythos, the Sphinx appeared as Hera's Aethiopian monster of justice who was brought from the Gulf of Aqaba to Thebes as an eternal punishment for the unscrupulous abduction of young boys. She devoured the delusional, consumed the ignorant, restored the learned, and rewarded the wise.

The Sphinx lived on Theban ignorance until challenged by the plucky Oedipus, as told to us by Sophocles in *Oedipus Rex*. In a violent rush of wit she asks, "Which creature has one voice and yet becomes four-footed and two-footed and three-footed?" After careful thought, he replies, "Man, who crawls on all fours as a baby, then walks on two feet as an adult, and

then uses a walking stick in old age." Although answering correctly didn't save Oedipus from his incestuous fate foretold by the Oracle at Delphi, it did free the people of Thebes from the Sphinx, who, as a result of Oedipus's response, is said to have laid herself upon a high rock and died.

Throughout the Hellenistic occupation of Egypt, Greece continued New Kingdom traditions, which gave rise to many different types of Sphinxes. The Hieracosphinx, for example, was sacred to the cult of Osiris and Horus, and was a figure of wisdom, Egyptian law, and justice. Worshiped by academics and priests alike, the Hieracosphinx was entrusted with dominion over technology on earth and governmental administration. To mark this he was given the head of a falcon.

The Criosphinx, also popular, was a guardian of the cult of Amon. This icon bore the head of a ram and the body of a lion. The lord of truth was a hidden one, and Criosphinx relates to the Berber spirit Jinn who is also closely connected to the Arabic idea of Genie. Jinn, like Amon, is the unseen force ruling over fertility and the wind.

The Anatomy of Life and Everything in It

The Sphinx is an inspirational key and a brilliant tool of learning. When meditated upon, she becomes a guardian of evocative hidden power and teaches all students the humble wisdom of adaptive learning. She is forever whispering in the ears of pupils who dare to explore the ancient mysteries, "*Panta rhei ki ouden mani.*" (Everything is changing; nothing is stagnant.) And, while full of the beneficent potential of Jupiter, she is paradoxically bound to the primal energy of female Saturn who devours all those who fall short of the mark or who fail to adapt.

When expounding on the nature of Trump X in the Book of Thoth, Aleister Crowley explains, "This card is attributed to the planet Jupiter, 'the Greater Fortune' in astrology. It corresponds to the [Hebrew] letter Kaph, which means the palm of the hand, in whose lines, according to another tradition, the fortune of the owner may be read. It would be narrow to think of Jupiter as good fortune; he represents the element of luck. The incalculable factor."

Kaph is the hand that spins the wheel. It represents the letter *K* and is traceable in the shape of the Sphinx's body, mystically eliciting the mechanics of the universe. Typhon, an evil serpentine god, slithers down the Wheel of Fortune's left-hand side, moving lustfully toward indulgence. Anubis, loyal friend to all and psychopomp god of the underworld, is lifted up by the power of his mercurial nature, energizing the Wheel with truth, the flooding force of effortless inertia. He appears sublimely suspended in a superhuman defiance of earthly law, which only the jackal-headed Anubis is capable of.

Crowley believed the three keepers of the Wheel were evocative of the three forces of circumstance related to the karmic philosophies of the gunas in Hinduism. Within Vedic philosophy, the stages of man correlate to the three virtues of integrity. Tamas he related to the darkness of Typhon, rajas to the energy of Anubis and excitement, and the sattvas to the calm, liberated intelligence of the Sphinx. These principles resemble our own resolution of karma and must be actively brought into a place of balance by the magician using the three magical virtues of all of ceremonial magic: "To will, to know, and to dare to keep the mysteries silent."

The mysterious Blue Sphinx guards the world and its elements. She sits atop the Wheel like a lapis enigma, levying the ebb and flow of fate by the karmic law of her empirical scimitar. Her indiscriminate detachment is revealed in the placement of her left hand, on the cutting side of a sword's hilt. She stoically grips the blade, delivered from the lust of the result. And, like all good anthropomorphic monsters of antiquity, she devours the unworthy in her primal parable of fortune's infinite mythic riddle of justice. She bestows blessings at the temple entrance but only to the truly deserved; her obscure favor is the route of all earthly success.

In the myths of Assyria and Babylon, the Sphinx's tail was a great desert serpent who struck down the unworthy, devouring their sins along with them. Her commanding gaze seems to both start and stop time, but it is the code of the ROTA that makes her most beguiling to aspiring mystics.

ROTA

Often capitalized, this magickal rearrangement of the word TARO (which, in its cyclical path, becomes "tarot"), ROTA is also Latin for "wheel." The occult code of ROTA corresponds to Levi's alchemical wheel and is metaphorically used to encapsulate the study, practice, and mastery of the codex of Western esoterica. ROTA links the Wheel of Fortune to nature's own cycles of birth, life, death, and decay. The tarot is full of Hermetic gods, symbols, and ancestral philosophies, some of which may not have been otherwise preserved.

In my own ceremonial work as a devotional priestess, I use the tarot as a concise, modern Pagan holy book. For me the tarot is alive, filled with spirits from our ancient Pagan world, spirits who are also alive. The spirit of Blue Sphinx has been a true companion of my academic and occult studies: she holds the keys to math, science, astrology, and all systems of adaptive, healthy living. When I study, I allow her to engineer my course of research on a subject by asking her to naturally drive my curiosity. Meditating on her helps me to problem-solve and adapt to innovation or failure with equal merit.

The following key is designed to help readers understand each of the cherubic aspects of the Sphinx in relation to the elements and the role they play throughout the tarot. This is in an attempt to show a more complete model of her intricate symbolism. The Sphinx is a universal framework for elemental religious associations, designed to more effectively express the ancient gods of the natural human world—a time of paradisia lost, but a hidden lesson that we have not yet forgotten. The Sphinx peers out from the sands of time, ever embodying and observing the animistic formula of transmutation vital to our pagan understanding of sacred living and immortal dying.

T

    Hebrew language: Yod (light)
    Animus cherubim: Eagle
    Zodiac: Scorpio
    Planet: Mars
    Element: Fixed water
    Incense: Storax/styrax (related to benzoin)
    Human body zone: Neck
    Stone: Emerald
    Sphinx: Nemes
    Hindu guna: Sattvas (intelligent balance)
    Cabbalistic world: Atziluth (divine and archetypal)
    Location on X The Wheel of Fortune: Lower right
    Alchemical substance: Mercury

A

    Hebrew language: Heh (window)
    Animus cherubim: Lion
    Zodiac: Leo
    Planet: Sun

Element: Fixed fire
Incense: Frankincense
Human body zone: Heart
Stones: Ruby
Sphinx: Blue body
Hindu guna: Rajas (energy)
Cabbalistic world: Briah (archangelic and creative)
Location on X The Wheel of Fortune: Upper right
Alchemical substance: Sulfur

R

Hebrew language: Vau (priest)
Animus cherubim: Man
Zodiac: Aquarius
Planet: Saturn
Element: Fixed air
Incense: Galbanum
Human body zone: Genitals
Stones: Topaz
Sphinx: Serpentine tail
Hindu guna: Tamas (darkness)
Cabbalistic world: Assiah (material and active)
Location on X The Wheel of Fortune: Upper left
Alchemical substance: Azoth

O

Hebrew Language: Heh (window)
Animus cherubim: Bull
Zodiac: Taurus
Planet: Venus
Element: Fixed earth
Incense: Opoponax (related to myrrh)
Human body zone: Genitals
Stones: Topaz
Sphinx: Serpentine tail
Hindu guna: Tamas (darkness)
Cabbalistic world: Assiah (material and active)
Location on X The Wheel of Fortune: Lower left
Alchemical substance: Salt

The Power of a Complaining Fast

by Melissa Tipton

Complaining is a powerful act of magic. The catch? Complaining brings about precisely what you wish to avoid: the circumstance that you're complaining about in the first place! Have you ever noticed how chronic complainers have a never-ending supply of things to bemoan? That's no accident. By complaining, they are using intention and energy to manifest those unfortunate situations. This is why embarking on a complaining fast can be so transformative, allowing you to repattern your brain . . . and your life.

How does complaining qualify as an act of magic? Think about the ingredients for effective magic: You need a clearly defined intention, focus, and energy to power the working. Let's look at an example. Sabine is seriously thinking about breaking up with her boyfriend. She feels like he's not supportive, and he might even be cheating on her. Complaining about her boyfriend has become Sabine's favorite pastime, and she'll do it with anyone who'll listen. If she's alone, she's happy to continue complaining in her head, obsessively going over what isn't working in her relationship.

When Sabine is focused on what she views as the problem—her boyfriend—she is setting the intention of attracting what she doesn't like about her relationship. Granted, this isn't an intention she would admit to consciously creating, but the act of repeatedly focusing on her unhappy situation is no different from someone visualizing a positive outcome that they wish to manifest. The difference, as my mother once heard a pastor say, is that "complaining is praying for what you *don't* want."

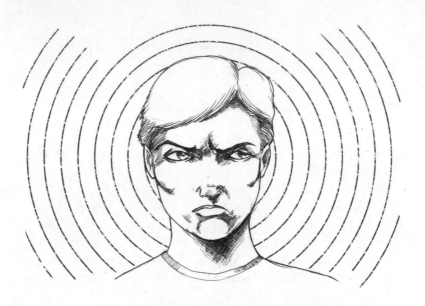

Intention, Focus, and Energy

So, it's clear that complaining is, in part, the process of crafting an intention. The next magical ingredient, focus, is also present. Think of how laser focused one can get in the throes of complaining. In the heat of complaining, even the most mild-mannered person will interrupt and monopolize the conversation, such is their fervor and focus on the object of their complaints.

What about the third ingredient, energy? It's easy to see how worked up we can get while complaining. Our anger, fear, or other intense emotions flare as we relive the scenario in our minds. All of this is energy. Our faces might flush, our eyes widen, and we talk faster and more aggressively. When we get caught up in the act of complaining, we are capable of generating a significant amount of energy, and if we're complaining to another person who is also getting worked up by our tirade, perhaps taking our side and asserting how wrong the perpetrator is, their energy adds further fuel to the fire.

How to Express Frustration

In order to successfully complete a complaining fast and channel your power into the things you *do* want, you need to understand why complaining is so enticing and why it can feel so difficult to stop. The first piece is emotional. When we experience something we deem unpleasant, emotions arise. This is natural and healthy, but where problems creep in is when we're uncomfortable experiencing those emotions *directly*. We might struggle with the fear that our anger will cause us to do something destructive or that our sadness will overwhelm us, but attempting to suppress our emotions causes far more damage than healthy expression ever could.

I want to emphasize the *healthy* in healthy expression. Punching someone in the face when you're angry isn't healthy; punching a pillow, however, might be just what you need. The key is to find authentic ways to experience your feelings without causing harm to yourself or others. There's also a fine line between acting out your feelings and truly experiencing them, and unless you are doing the latter, you will continue to struggle with a strong urge to complain.

Emotions must be experienced and released in order for us to maintain balance and harmony. Our attempts at avoiding our emotional experience are, in my belief, the root of all self-destructive behavior, such as perfectionism, over- or under-eating, and complaining. Specifically, when we complain, we distance ourselves from our emotional experience by creating a story about the experience, and this storytelling also gives us a false sense of control over the situation, both of which prevent us from being with the feelings, up close and personal. The irony is that if we were to simply feel our feelings, they would dissolve of their own accord. It is when we resist our emotions that they become stuck.

Here's an analogy: Picture a clear plastic tube. We'll simulate an emotion by using colored water. When something in life triggers us, an emotion arises and the colored water starts to flow through the tube. When we are uncomfortable with our emotions, we shut down, capping the tube at both ends in an attempt to keep the emotions out. The problem is that the water—the emotion—is *already* inside the tube, so capping it is achieving the exact opposite effect; the emotion is now trapped inside the tube. If, instead, we allow our emotional experience to unfold, the water will, of its own accord, flow in one end and out the other.

Every time we complain, we give the tube a good shake, agitating the emotions all over again. So, the first step in our complaining fast is to feel any emotions that arise rather than resist them. Psychologist Dr. Shefali Tsabary says, "It's important to note that there's a difference between reacting emotionally and feeling our feelings. Many of us assume that when we are angry or sad, we are feeling our feelings. On the contrary, we are often merely reacting. Truly feeling an emotion means being able to sit with the incoherence we experience at such a time, *neither venting it nor denying it, but simply containing it and being present with it*" (my italics).

Being present with your emotions, letting them rise and fall in your body and your mind without narrating the experience, is a courageous act of living authentically and reclaiming your power. When you're not spending massive amounts of energy capping the tube and resisting emotional flow, you can spend that energy on soul-affirming pursuits instead. By doing this, you are taking away one powerful incentive for complaining because, again, one of the main reasons we complain is to avoid our emotional experience. If you're not avoiding your emotions, your need to complain will decrease dramatically.

There's another reason why we complain, and understanding it provides the second step in our fast. Complaining fools us into thinking that we're doing something to solve the problem. I believe this fallacy comes from the fact that, deep in our spiritual DNA, we possess an ancestral knowing that words have power. Think of how many cultures throughout history have some version of spells, mantras, or other language-based power practices. Similarly, there is a part within all of us that recognizes the power of words; thus, complaining can feel seductively effective.

The problem, of course, is that words alone are not enough to create change. As we discussed, we know that our words, which represent our intention, must be coupled with focus and energy. And guess what? We also know that complaining fills all three of those requirements, so complaining certainly does "work," but not toward solving our problem; instead, it generates more of the same. In spite of feeling that we're doing something about the issue by complaining, all we're doing is "praying for what we don't want."

So, step one of our complaining fast is allowing our emotions to arise and sitting with those feelings, and step two is recognizing that, as much as we might think we're solving the issue by complaining about it, we're doing precisely the opposite. These two steps alone will bring about massive change. When you add the third step of our complaining fast, the actual abstinence from complaining, you fully reclaim your energy and power.

Abstaining from complaining is just what it sounds like. If the urge arises, choose in that moment to abstain. You might wear a rubber band around your wrist and snap it anytime you feel a complaint coming on. This resets your consciousness and gives you enough of a pause to choose a different course of action. I find that physically moving helps me make the shift. If I'm standing in the kitchen, on the verge of a complain-a-thon, I stop and walk into the living room, perhaps doing a silly dance while I'm at it. Find whatever helps you to press the pause button.

Committing to a complaining fast for a set amount of time, say, for one month, is a great way to repattern your habits, and journaling about the process will allow you to see how your energy is shifting from fueling undesirable situations to manifesting the life you want. This feedback is a potent motivator, fueling a positive loop: the more you see your life improving as you abstain from complaining, the less you will have to complain about, and around and around it goes, in one happy cycle.

For Further Study

Tsabary, Shefali. *The Conscious Parent: Transforming Ourselves, Empowering Our Children.* Vancouver: Namaste Publishing, 2010.

Water Magic

Sweet on You: Sweetening Magic

by Deborah Castellano

When you sweeten someone or something toward you, you are shaping your intention to be like a cube of pure, perfumed sugar. Your petition may be broad and more universal (e.g., *I want to find a partner who will love me and sex up my nights, I want to have enough money to keep me in the lifestyle I am accustomed to, I want to find myself in the career that would make me the happiest, I want opportunities to use my creative skills,* or *I want my coworkers to treat me nicely at work)* or as specific as you wish (e.g., *I want my husband to get back together with me, I want my children to treat me sweetly, I want my coworker to stop spreading rumors about me and instead to be considerate to me,* or *I want Stefan to love me).*

However, you do need to be sure to be clear about what you are doing. If you set a universal intention that is not person specific, you are not working your will over another person. If you set your intention to a specific person, then you *are* working your will over another person. Not everyone follows the same code of ethics; Hoodoo (the tradition that sweetening magic is native to) is unapologetically ambiguous when it comes to morals. Check your own personal moral compass and spend some time considering what you feel to be ethical and what you don't feel to be ethical. Part of the delight of being a Witch is choosing your own moral code to follow. It's always better to take more time than needed to consider a magical course of action than not enough time. Put another way, if you are out at a bar, you can always choose to drink more booze later, but you cannot drink less later. Choosing to drink more booze now instead of taking some time to consider your course of actions for the evening may (or may not) have unintended consequences. In magic, it's always best for your consequences to be as intended as possible.

The most commonly used form of sweetening magic is the honey jar (or honey pot). As it is encased in a jar, it's both a container spell and a sweetening spell. In Hoodoo as I was taught, when you work with a magical item like a honey jar, it isn't simply a jar full of lifeless components but a small spirit that you are slowly bringing to life with your constant attention and care. Much like a well-loved houseplant, a beloved pet, or a child, if you stop taking care of your honey jar, not only will your intention dim but the spirit itself will dim as well. It's a responsibility that should not be taken lightly, as you are the spirit's caregiver as well as your spirit's breath of life.

Make a Honey Jar

Start by deciding on your intention. Ideally, this intention should be able to be distilled down to a single sentence. Simplicity is key here because it will be a lot easier for your fledging spirit to successfully focus on one single clear intention and achieve results than to try to effect change based on a lengthily worded paragraph that drifts from intention to intention. Take as much time as you need to marinate on what your intention will be and how to best phrase it.

Decide which components you would like to use. What kind of sweetener will you use? Honey, sugar, agave syrup? What sized jar will you use? A tiny, hexagonal, glass honey jar? An antique mason jar? A jar that once housed hibiscus syrup and blooms?

What components will you utilize? To promote financial prosperity, try citrine, garnet, aventurine, malachite, and jade. To bring love, rose quartz, turquoise, moonstone,

and blue calcite. To bring luck, tiger's eye, amber, amazonite, and moss agate. To bring creativity, carnelian, celestite, amethyst, and amazonite. If you want your petition to happen more quickly, it's generally a good idea to use a "heating" herb such as ginger or cinnamon. If you want to sweeten gossips or frienemies to you, you can use slippery elm bark, alum powder, chia seed, and cloves. If you want to bring a lover back to you, you can use damiana, lavender, safflower petals, and balm of gilead. To get a new lover, you can use lemon leaves, lemon mint, and lovage root. For money magic, you can use allspice, basil, Irish moss, and patchouli. To keep a sweet home, you can use rosemary, alfalfa, blessed thistle, cumin seeds, and holly leaves. To improve your luck, you can use John the Conqueror, tonka beans, nutmeg, and star anise. To turn a court case in your favor, you can use calendula flowers, dill seed, Little John (to chew), and tobacco. You can also use loose incense such as crown of success, boss fix, come to me, fast luck, and house blessing incense. Local botanicas

and some Witch and Pagan shops will carry these. Original Botanica (www.originalbotanica.com) is a reputable source if in-person shopping is not an option. You can also add charms; personal effects; blood, saliva, hair, etc.; essential oils; and whatever else feels right to you.

Write your petition. Now that you have distilled your petition to a single sentence, write it down on a small piece of brown paper bag. Your pen should not leave the paper, even if you are dotting i's, crossing t's, or going to the next line. If your pen leaves the page, start over. Dust the paper with some of the herbs or incense you will be putting in the jar and roll it toward you. Fold it into a small square. Focus on your intention and gather up your will. Infuse your petition paper with your will by breathing into it.

Assemble your honey jar. Put the petition paper at the bottom of the jar (which should have a lid). Put the components in the jar. Fill the jar the rest of the way with your sweetener of choice and seal it.

Bring your jar to life. Choose a small chime candle in the color that would best fit your petition (green for luck, red for love, white for a sweet home, etc.). Etch it with the appropriate words or sigils that are relevant to your petition using a sewing pin or needle. Anoint it with an essential oil that is appropriate to your petition (rose for love, clove to stop gossip, lavender for a sweet home, basil for money, etc.). Anoint the candle using a downward motion, toward yourself. Put your honey jar in your kitchen sink. Light the candle and drip a little wax onto the top of the lid. Fix the chime candle to the lid in the melted wax. Let it burn out. Once the candle burns out, put the honey jar on your altar.

Take proper care of your honey jar. At least once a week, etch, anoint, and burn a chime candle on top of your honey jar so that it's properly fed. Watch how the candle burns to scry for an omen. Does it burn clear and easily without soot and without going out? Does it light easily? Then your objective is well on its way. If it has difficulty burning, sputters and spurts, and burns with a lot of soot, then your petition is going to be more difficult to obtain and will require more work and more attention.

If your petition is met, put your honey jar to rest. If your goal is obtained or has drastically changed, then you need to thank your honey jar for the service your spirit has given you by verbally thanking your jar and enumerating the successes you have obtained due to your spirit's hard work. Then, traditionally, you would bury your honey jar at a crossroads. If you have ecological concerns, you could put the sweetener and petition paper in your compost heap and recycle the jar. Wash off the stones, leave them on your windowsill for a Full Moon in a bowl of salt, and then gift them to friends.

In conclusion, while honey jars are a slow and steady kind of magic and can take a little while to show results, they are very much worth the effort, as they are loyal and devoted spiritual allies. My honey jar has helped me an incredible amount, especially when I was a strictly free-lance employee, to ensure that my bills were always paid and that there was always enough food in my tummy and electricity in my house, which was no mean feat, especially in a down economy. If you are willing to give your honey jar the time and attention that its spirit deserves, the spirit will be equally willing to give your petition the time and attention that it deserves as well.

Animal Apantomancy

by Blake Octavian Blair

Most magickal persons learn several methods of divination, and many of us are proficient with at least one. From tarot and oracle cards to pendulums, runes, flickering flames, mirrors, and more, there are numerous ways to divine the information you seek. However, people often forget that they still have means to divine even when they find themselves without their tools. Apantomancy is divination with found items at hand. I'm going to address an even more specific and even more accessible form of apantomancy, the branch that deals with chance sightings of animals in nature.

Many magickal and shamanic folks are of the mind that there is no such thing as chance or coincidence, so the term chance becomes a bit humorous. However, be that as it may, we will use it in the context that you have not mundanely exerted control or arranged what you will be seeing. The

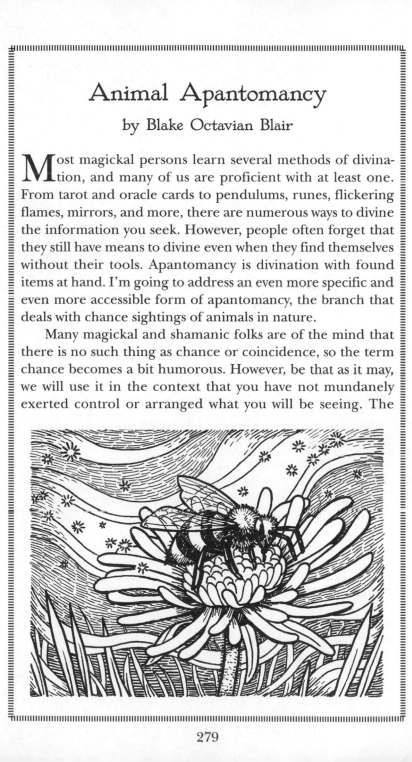

shamanic and magickal point of view is that the creatures you see have been sent to you with messages from the Divine—messages that are specific to you and your life. In the shamanic view, everything and all that is, is alive! This viewpoint also holds that all that is, is interconnected. Animals, in fact, are relations to us because we are simply human animals ourselves. Neither the bumblebee, the ant, nor the grizzly bear is a lesser being than a human. In fact, many would argue they are greater and perhaps more noble, in that they help the earth to thrive, participating in ecosystems, life cycles, and, in the case of the bee for example, pollination. Our animal relations live in harmony with nature. Humans, unfortunately, have a track record of destruction resulting from a severe superiority complex and a shortsightedness of our interconnectedness (but that tangent could serve as another article entirely). However, I briefly make this point for you to consider just how equal we are to our non-human relations and how much we have to learn from them on how to walk through life and also upon the planet. Engagement with these thoughts is important as we enter into this work.

Nature in the City

We as humans have a huge diversity of living situations. Some of us live in rural homes, surrounded by large expanses that are undeveloped by humans and filled with trees, wild plants, and wildlife that clearly outnumber the visible presence of humans. Others of us live in urban environments filled with tall buildings, swaths of paved streets and sidewalks, and perhaps a peppering of landscaped areas; and some areas are lucky enough to have beautiful, large, expansive parks and greenways. Fortunately for city dwellers like myself, our communities are not, in fact, devoid of nature. I currently live in a town in the Greater Boston area in Massachusetts. People who are not familiar with the Greater Boston area are unaware that we actually have quite a bit of natural and green space located throughout the area cities and towns. In fact, just a two-minute walk behind my midrise apartment building is a beautiful lake that is home to more than one hundred species of migratory birds. Though the type and amount of wildlife found in the city may differ a bit from more rural areas, it is indeed present. One must not discount creatures like the robin, pigeon, rabbit, squirrel, deer, hawks, owls, ducks, and more. These too are sacred creatures capable of being messengers of the Divine. One person's rural elk sighting is not more majestic that your urban viewing of a cardinal.

Practicing your skills at animal apantomancy is also a great way to connect deeper with the earth, the cycle of the seasons, and your spirits of place, and to deepen your connection and place within the web of life. Most of us favor one or more of the seasons over others. Some folks adore the heat of summer. Other folks prefer the coolness of fall and even love the snowy landscape of winter. However, balance is sacred and it is worth an attempt to connect to each season, seeing what it has to offer. An easy way to do that, even if it seems indirect, is to engage each season in animal apantomancy in nature. Make time each season to engage in a session of animal apantomancy—consider it a general check-in with the universe for any specific messages it has for you this season. Let's walk through an easy way to get set up for a session of this natural divination.

Observing Animals

Many prefer actually going outdoors if possible to perform the first observational part of the divination. If you can, head outside and find a comfortable spot where you have a nice vantage point of your surroundings. You can sit directly on the ground to connect as fully as possible with the earth; however, if you need or prefer to bring a blanket, cushion, or portable chair to sit on, that's perfectly acceptable as well. Don't let a bit of less-than-sunny weather deter you from heading outdoors. (In the scope of history, it seems a rather modern fad to allow a little chill or a misting of rain in the air to completely drive us indoors.) I implore you to

be *in nature* if at all possible: nature's various states are part of life's sacred experiences. If you cannot make it outside for any reason, however, you can also successfully perform the apantomancy from a seat indoors with a good window view of the outdoor landscape. Also bring along a journal or notebook and a reliable pen. Optional items include a favorite crystal, perhaps for clarity, and smudging supplies if you wish.

Once you are settled in your viewing spot, if you want to smudge, this is the time. Now, make a prayer to the universe, God and Goddess, Spirit, or however you wish to address the Divine, and ask it to present the messages to you that you most need to hear and apply to your life at this time. Then sit quietly and remain present for ten or fifteen minutes. Do not attempt to close your eyes or zone out in any sense; remain mentally present and observe your surroundings in a relaxed state. Take note of the wildlife you observe or even if any particular plant life sticks out very prominently to you and makes itself known. (While I'll often refer to this method as animal apantomancy, please do include beings from all branches of nature. Plant spirits have powerful messages for us, as do stones, clouds, bodies of water, etc.) Sit with your observations. Let your intuition and the spirits that came to you tell you what their meanings are and what they have to say to you. At the end of your observation period, make a prayer thanking the spirits and the Divine for the messages. Finish up journaling any notes about your observations. Then let the messages and meanings continue to digest over time. Make more notes and journal as necessary.

Interpreting Your Observation

It sounds incredibly simple, very free-form, and vague; however, it can be incredibly personal and powerful. This divinatory practice is about what the messages mean to *you* and not anyone else. You're the only one qualified to fully interpret the divination. The interaction was between you and the divine messengers—nobody else. A logical and strongly suggested second step to flesh out deeper meaning from the findings of the apantomancy session is to have a ceremonial or ritual session where you specifically meditate on the meanings of the animals you saw or take a shamanic journey for further clarification. Let's say you saw a flock of Canada geese flying in V formation. You can meditate on how that might apply to your life at this time, or if you are trained in shamanic journeying, you can actually travel into nonordinary reality and ask the spirit of Canada goose directly what it would like to tell you at this time. An important tip to this is to *not* consult any animal totem dictionaries or references for an extended period of time after your divination. Do your own explorations first. It is not relevant in this method of divination what another person thinks Canada geese mean. It is only relevant what they mean to you and what their message for you is at this time. Their message for you may not be the same as their message for another person. If later on in time you wish to look at a reference or two just to see if there are any commonalities or differences with your interpretations, that is fine. Just realize that differences do not mean errors in your interpretations. This type of divination is not a multiple choice exam where you must choose the correct answer—it is more of an open essay with no right or wrong answer, only your answer.

The layer of this divination that helps you to better connect to the cycle of the seasons and the earth is inherently present throughout the entire process. Animals have different activity patterns and natural behaviors during different times of the year. If you saw a deer nested down and resting in a field in the fall it would have a different meaning in your life than if you saw a herd of deer, complete with fawns, prancing at high speed out of the woods during another season. An important element not to overlook when peeling through the layers of meaning during and after the apantomancy observation is to look at the parallels of the natural behaviors and characteristics of the animal, not just the more esoteric messages it brings to you. Both types of messages are significant. If you witness an animal coming out of its den, what might that be telling you? If you see a bird of prey swoop down and snatch up a meal, does this parallel something currently in your life? Think about how you feel the actions in your life relate—the creature's message may be holding up a mirror to actions that you yourself are carrying out as well.

Apantomancy and the Sabbats

Many magical practitioners find it challenging to come up with fresh ideas and rites for solo Wheel of the Year sabbat observances. I find that doing an animal apantomancy session for a solo observance and "check-in" as the wheel turns is quite a nice experience. It can be your complete sabbat observance, or perhaps you can do it in addition to other planned activities. I find that the apantomancy session in nature, combined with the shamanic journey to the spirits afterward, is a powerful experience.

New connections to helping spirits can often be formed. You might wish to frame an image or find a statuette of any spirits, animals, or plants that were of specific significance during your experience to put on your altar for a time. This will serve as a tangible reminder of your connection to the spirit and give it a place of honor. Another detail you may wish to add, as a Wheel of the Year project, is to do this divination in the same spot each time. By doing it in the same location, you'll not only observe the "chance" meetings you'll have with the local flora and fauna but also watch as the landscape makes its shift, whether dramatic or subtle, from sabbat to sabbat. You might consider taking a snapshot of the landscape at each sitting to log the shift. You can print the photo and tape or paste it into your journal entry for each divination.

Interconnection and Exploration

There is a growing emphasis and movement in Pagandom to try to live more locally and to practice a Paganism that is more relevant to our lives where we live. For example, while many people live where it is blustery, cold, and snowy at Imbolc, many people don't see a single flake. In fact, their grass may be green, and they might be trekking out in not much more

overclothes than a sweater. However, the wheel is still turning, there are still changes in the nature that is local to them, and this nature-branded version of apantomancy will allow you to observe and experience those changes rather than settle on a preconceived notion. Also, by all means, if you are traveling for a holiday to a geographical region different from that of your home, take the opportunity to do a divination session in both your home location before you go and at your holiday destination. It is fascinating how it can deepen your connection with the natural world to stop and take note of the differences of each season in different geographical locations. It is simple and awe inspiring all at once to know that such diverse natural worlds can exist simultaneously. If you are in California and fly to Maine to see relatives for winter holidays, the dichotomy will be quite drastic. If you go from Florida to Arizona, it may or may not be a more subtle experience. Every combination will have its own beautiful uniqueness and add to your opportunities to glean wisdom from the spirits of the natural world.

Perhaps this article has seemed like a rather general guide into this nature-and-animal-based branch of apantomancy without a lot of specific direction. If that is the case, I am glad, as that serves to further honor the wonderful outlet for personalization that this method of divination provides to a practitioner. All you need is yourself as a human animal, one being in the interconnected web of life, and all that is in order to perform this divination. As the seasons change and the Wheel of the Year turns, I hope you, too, will seek out wisdom from all our relations.

Empathy and Magickal Work
by Raven Digitalis

Used commonly in metaphysical circles, the term empathy denotes the phenomenon of experiencing the emotional state of another (usually another person). While sympathy involves "feeling for," empathy can be called "feeling as." Empathy is concerned with sensing and *absorbing* the emotional energies of people, animals, or environments around you. Those who are particularly sensitive and who consistently absorb the emotions of others can be called empaths.

The Empathic Experience

Empathy isn't limited to metaphysical analysis. The empathic experience is physiological, being deeply embedded in our biology. Empathy is a daily experience that emotionally bonds humans (and other animals), ensuring our success as a species. If we didn't have empathy, we would be walking around in disconnected fogs of self-focused survivalism. As an evolutionary aid, empathy ensures the development of familial bonds and social cooperation.

Indeed, our brain's mirror neurons allow for an experience called emotional contagion. Do you ever unconsciously turn your head if the person you're talking to turns their head? Do you ever yawn if someone else yawns? These are example of emotional contagion, which is related to empathy. By "catching" external emotions, we can easily step into a state of reality separate from our own. From there, we can learn the interconnectedness of all things. This realization of nonseparateness is an ancient, mystical truth.

Empathy involves stepping into an alternate emotional landscape and having a compassionate response. It's not enough to

merely *feel* external emotions; true empathy requires that we respond with compassion. This ability can be an invaluable asset in our everyday lives and in our magickal work.

Empaths

With abilities sometimes considered to be related to psychic powers and ESP, empaths not only sense the emotions of a person, animal, or environment, but they instantaneously absorb or "catch" the surrounding emotional energy and take it on as their own. This can lead to depression and confusion if not controlled, yet it can also lead to deep levels of healing, compassion, and interpersonal engagement if harnessed and understood.

Though there are no strict rules to being an empath, certain experiences are undeniably shared among them. The same can be said for psychics or clairvoyant intuitives, who all share some abilities even though they are not tuned in to the same sensations and may receive, express, and channel their messages in different ways. All psychics function with some amount of empathy, and all empaths function with some amount of psychicism. Many empaths feel a direct correlation between magickal spirituality and their empathic abilities. However, as humans, we all possess some degree of empathetic ability that can also be used in magickal work with great success.

Empathy in Magick

While it's of utmost importance for us magickal folk to exercise emotional awareness and thought control, the experience of empathy can have resounding effects in our daily lives and in our magick.

It's not enough to simply realize that we are experiencing emotions while we are meditating or spellcasting—we have to own those feelings on a deep level. It's imperative for us magickal workers to follow our trains of thought and observe how our emotions develop. When an emotion has arisen, it's our duty to fully connect with that part of ourselves. The emotions we are feeling (or *aren't* feeling) will dictate the direction of our magickal intention. Because prayer, spellcraft, and magick are meant to be precise, we must have precision in our emotional awareness.

As we more accurately become aware of our emotional responses and their influence in our lives, we can actively choose which kinds of emotions give shape to our magickal work—and our daily perspectives. When we intentionally invoke empathy for others and for ourselves, the magickal work we perform becomes more spiritual and less "needy."

Hop online and you'll find countless spells for cursing someone into ill health, for manipulating people's freewill, for making someone's cattle barren, for causing explosive diarrhea—the list goes on. But when we add a component of self-awareness and emotional humility, practitioners of magick who are spiritually progressive can bypass all these karmic messes by empathically empowering our rituals. By humbly utilizing empathy, we can actively control our thoughts and can invoke a higher level of magickal experience whose energy is more karmically advanced—and thereby more deeply spiritual.

What follows is a list of common spellcasting intentions. Empathy can uniquely apply to each intention, strengthening and clarifying our connection to the energy at hand. In the course of our regular magickal practice, we can extend our own emotions into the situation we aim to influence. We can utilize empathy toward another person's emotions, toward our own emotions, or simply toward a certain energy, all of which can serve to strengthen our magickal work and keep it karmically pure.

Intentions

Clarity, Personal: The empathic key to invoking personal clarity first requires an objective view of what's cluttered. Bring your attention to the unclear situation at hand, empathizing with the manner you are perceiving the situation. Accept your feelings of struggle or confusion as natural and normal. After you've sat with this energy for a while, skillfully invite clarity into your sphere through any magickal methods you deem appropriate. (Planetary association: Sun)

Cleansing and Healing: Whether working for yourself or others, begin by emotionally merging with the scenarios you are working with. For example, when energetically cleansing a house, open yourself emotionally as you enter each room so that you can accurately perceive which areas need to be cleansed. Where do you find "pockets" of residual emotional energy? If you are performing healing work for another person, merge your consciousness with that individual's chakras, auric layers, and so on, in order to see which work should ensue (in addition to the

advice of a physician as needed). Additionally, exercise empathy by affirming your client's feelings and by providing emotional understanding alongside a good dose of optimistic hope. (Planetary association: Jupiter)

Communication: First, forgive yourself and any missteps you feel that you've taken in the course of communication. Extend this empathy to the other person or persons, stepping into their shoes and trying to consider the root of difficulty in communication. As part of your magickal work, vow to "see through the eyes of the other" in every conversation. (Planetary association: Mercury)

Cursing: Cursing is tricky because it's usually the last thing an empath wants to do, but it does have its time and place. For curses to be successful, the practitioner must make a concerned effort to emotionally connect with the other person's emotional body. Empathizing with the perspective and plight of the other allows one to step into their consciousness and cause influence accordingly. This can also allow the practitioner to reconsider the curse before acting on impulse. Also, keep in mind that a temporary binding spell is more benign and often a better option. (Planetary association: Mars)

Death Magick: Using a representation of death and dying, emotionally connect with the overarching energy of death through deep meditation, reflection, stillness, and the slowing of your breath. Both sorrowful and beautiful at once, death is the subtle plane of existence just behind life. Emotionally opening ourselves to this gentle energy connects us to the hidden realms and helps enrich our own perspectives on life. (Planetary association: Saturn)

Divination: Divination should be objective. For this reason, it is wise to not overly empathize with a querent (client), but to instead extend your emotional awareness to the spirits you are employing to assist with the divinatory work. (Planetary association: Moon)

Emotional Magick: When facing difficult emotions, empathy allows the practitioner to feel and accept the sensations that are being worked with. A bit of compassionate understanding goes a long way when faced with darker emotions like anger, shame, and sadness. When something is truly and deeply felt, it can allow the door of alchemical transformation to occur. Without the step of empathetic connection, emotionally charged magickal work falls incomplete. (Planetary association: Moon)

Employment: Emotionally step into the occupational situation you are seeking to manifest. Feel the emotions created within this job, not the details of the job (this can limit your intention). Sit in this energy as long as possible, pulling it toward you with joy. Invite this feeling to recur anytime you contemplate work. (Planetary association: Earth)

Faery Work: When working with the hidden realm of Fae, go to a natural environment where you can feel their presence. Gently channel your own emotions and cognitive awareness into their world, abandoning your own insecurities and sense of time. In order for communion to occur, you must try to see how they see and feel how they feel—but always come back to yourself, lest ye be taken away by the wee folk! (Planetary association: Moon)

Friendship: If working to rekindle a friendship, take time to understand the other person's motivations and perspectives. If inviting new friendship, feel the emotional qualities you seek in the other person while you perform sympathetic magick aimed at attracting this individual. (Planetary association: Venus)

Happiness and Inspiration: After feeling, accepting, and channeling your darker emotions, think back to times where you felt completely happy, secure, inspired, creative, and at ease with life. Next, forget about the details and simply sit with that emotion of personal fulfillment. Reinvoke this raw emotional energy when you are feeling down, discouraged, or pessimistic. (Planetary association: Sun)

Hex Breaking: If you're feeling safe and confident, place your emotional awareness into the curse or hex that may have been cast on yourself or your client. Try to objectively feel its intention. But *do not stop there,* or it becomes a dangerous situation. Use your magick to ground the curse into an inanimate object that you will bury, burn, or sink, or you can use a mirror to "return to sender." If you can first safely feel the intention that may have been cast, you can then take control of that energy and conduct it accordingly. (Planetary association: Jupiter)

Love: Undoubtedly the strongest force in the universe, love can be invoked by first loving yourself. The process of self-directed

compassion can be difficult in practice but should be applied daily. During those times that you feel content and confident with who you are, use magnetic magick to attract that same force from others in the world. Practiced regularly, it may surprise you to see the ways in which the vibration of love manifests itself. (Planetary association: Venus)

Memory and Study: When you are working to commit something to memory, utilize your emotions to forge a link with the information itself. Whether you're studying a period in history, a meticulous math problem, or a foreign language, get creative to draw some kind of emotional association with the details you're studying. We are likely to have better memorization abilities if we can associate minor emotional responses with cognitive information. (Planetary association: Mercury)

Prosperity and Luck: As a complicated subject linked to our survival, prosperity magick requires that we spend time emotionally disconnecting from ideas of worth. Reconsider idealizations you may have about both poverty and wealth. Aim to replace feelings of desperation with feelings of spiritual trust. Emotionally feel your worthiness and your ability to be financially responsible while you invoke energetic prosperity. Tap into overarching energies of abundance and draw that emotional fulfillment toward you as a daily routine. (Planetary association: Jupiter)

Protection: Emotionally merge into the need you have to create protection. It doesn't matter what is being protected: yourself, a client, a pet, a house, or a situation. The most important aspect of this magick is to feel the need and trust yourself while you craft the intention. (Planetary associations: Mars and Saturn)

Sleep and Dreaming: When working magick aimed at sleep or the realm of dreams, it's essential to make your thoughts "fuzzy." By calming the rational mind and letting the creative take hold, we begin to step into the terrain of the unconscious. Empathically, you may extend your emotions to the experience of sleeping itself. Feel the emotional fulfillment that comes from rejuvenating the body throughout the night. (Planetary association: Moon)

Spirit Work: Whether you're working with ghosts, deities, guides, or guardians, take some time to emotionally merge with their realm and sidestep your own fleeting emotions. Once you have empathized with their spiritual essence, step back into yourself and respectfully perform your work and communication. (Planetary association varies)

Travel: Empathically connect with your future self while you perform any magick associated with travel. See yourself happy, content, and safe in your destination. Draw an energetic link by feeling those emotions yourself in the present moment. Regularly reinforce the visualization before and during the course of travel. (Planetary association: Mercury)

Feel free to utilize these suggestions in your own magickal work and add to the list based on your own reflections and experiences. This list is designed to serve as an empathetic point of reference to incorporate with your personal spellcraft, ritual, prayer, meditation, and creative visualization.

For Further Study

Aron, Elaine N. *The Highly Sensitive Person: How to Thrive When the World Overwhelms You.* Secaucus, NJ: Birch Lane Press, 1996.

Belanger, Michelle. *The Psychic Energy Codex: Awakening Your Subtle Senses.* San Francisco, CA: Weiser, 2007.

Digitalis, Raven. *Esoteric Empathy: A Magickal & Metaphysical Guide to Emotional Sensitivity.* Woodbury, MN: Llewellyn, 2016.

McLaren, Karla. *The Art of Empathy: A Complete Guide to Life's Most Essential Skill.* Boulder, CO: Sounds True, 2013.

The Astrological Elements of Tarot: Sun Sign Readings for All

by Sally Cragin

When my grandmother gave me a set of tarot cards in the early 1970s, the first thing I did was mislay the instructions. This actually turned out to be a perfectly acceptable strategy for a preteen reader. I loved the Fool card and any of the cards with cats (the Queen of Wands, Strength). But most of them mystified me, and the set soon went into a drawer.

Decades later, I had done some reading on the history of the cards, and it seemed clear that the suits lined up with the astrological elements quite neatly: wands to fire signs (Aries, Leo, and Sagittarius), pentacles to earth signs (Taurus, Virgo, and Capricorn), swords to air signs (Gemini, Libra, and Aquarius), and cups to water signs (Cancer, Scorpio, and Pisces). When you line up the cards in suits (thirteen cards per suit, including a page, knight, queen, and king), you see a narrative unfold. For me as an astrologer, the cards now had extra significance.

When I do tarot workshops here in New England, I often have anywhere from twenty-four to fifty-six attendees, divided into small groups. My instructions always include giving yourself time to study the card. Who is on it—a man, woman, child? What is the person doing? What—or whom—does it "remind" you of? Finally, see how the next card corresponds to the previous ones.

So, if you're just learning tarot but are overwhelmed by the number of cards, just divide your deck and work with the suit that corresponds to your Sun sign.

Fire Signs and Tarot

Aries, Leo, and Sagittarius have a natural affinity to the wand cards. But you need to *slow* down your lightning responses long enough to study the images! What are those figures doing with the wands—are they using the wand as a tool, a weapon, a support staff, a flag pole to showcase a triumph? Focus on the expressions of the figures—are they at rest, or are they holding something? Wand cards can have a different interpretation for someone who likes to garden or nurture others. Those little green leaves are so hopeful!

Progress Reading

I've found this reading helpful for clients with a lot of fire in their charts, because we just keep on moving on! This utilizes the idea of Celtic cross but dealt to a reader one card at a time:

Card one (center): What is the matter at hand?

Card two (left): What (or who) is getting in the way of forward progress?

Card three (right): What do you have in your arsenal to help you keep moving forward? (Examples: patience, ability to bring other people in, courage to look for other avenues if it's a job problem)

Since wands are about "doing," when you are more comfortable, consider adding the cups, which are about feeling. This gives you twenty-six cards to work with, which is plenty!

Earth Signs and Tarot

For Taurus, Virgo, and Capricorn, the signature suit is the pentacle or disk. Many earth sign clients look at a tarot reading as an opportunity to "tune up" or to provide clarity about a situation that seems to be heading towards a crisis. Earth signs are not to be rushed, however. A reading with many low numbers suggests there is time to prepare to take action (very reassuring to earth-sign folks). The pentacles are all pretty merry cards—you won't see conflict or contentiousness as you do with the wands or swords.

Basic Reading

A sample reading for an earth sign person should definitely include some cards that reflect the past. Try this simple, three-card lineup:

Card one (left): The past. What happened in the past to bring you to this point? (Some earth signs need to really review this information for a while so that they get a handle on their own participation.)

Card two (middle): The present. What are you missing about the current situation? What is on this card that sparks your analytical side?

Card three (right): The future. Pay attention to the number here—a number between one and five suggests that revision or starting over is key; numbers six to ten or the page, knight, queen, or king indicate that resolution will be more straightforward.

Air Signs and Tarot

Gemini, Libra, and Aquarius are the air signs. Swords rule this element, and the sword cards are invariably the most dramatic. Here, you see people slain, in peril, or taking action. Does this mean that taking action (moving through space versus thinking) is the sole domain of air sign folks? Absolutely not, and one quirk of the swords is that many of the cards do not show swordplay, but rather swords at rest, as it were. However, the swords always have an underlying theme about celerity and movement—and we all know many air signs can move faster than a speeding bullet when they need to! Air signs are also highly social, and here's a sample reading that focuses on air's unique friend- and ally-making skills.

Crisis Reading

Air signs lead exciting lives and often have to react quickly and decisively. However, one aspect of being an air sign is to be paralyzed by thoughts of indecision. Any signs who sample this reading with just the sword cards may find that images depicting fighting become less fraught for them.

Card one (center): What situation or dilemma has taken center stage?

Card two (beneath): What are the circumstances (which can include people) that are causing stress or strife? What can be done about these impediments (which might also include reluctance to take action or commit to a single path)?

Card three (above): Who are the people and what are the personality characteristics that are strengths or can guide?

Optional card four (to the right of all): The final outcome.

Water Signs and Tarot

For Cancer, Scorpio, and Pisces, working with tarot cards is enormously rewarding. The cups are the suit that represents them, and water sign people invariably have deep intuitive talents—especially if they are able to separate those talents from the anxiety that unexpected insights can bring. Like their element, Cancer, Scorpio, and Pisces are happiest finding their own level and going with the flow. You can translate that to mean they don't want to be rushed, a trait they share with earth signs. However, some cards indicate stuck-in-the-mud thinking, like the number five, which portrays someone looking sadly at three spilled cups while two upright cups are unseen. Many water signs are rich in relationships, so here is a reading designed for that.

Relationship Reading

Card one (left): What do I bring to and who am I in the relationship?

Card two (right): Who is my partner, and what does this person bring to the relationship?

Card three (below left card): What are the challenges for me in the relationship?

Card four (below right card): What are the challenges for my partner in the relationship?

Card five (above all cards): How will the relationship will unfold?

For all these readings, you will want to pause between laying down cards. To get the most out of tarot—particularly as you are learning the cards—is to see how cards relate to one another one at a time. I've seen people lay out spreads with all cards up at once, but that requires a lot more attention than I have!

Practice the reading dependent on your Sun sign. And if you have a friend who is a Sun sign from another element, practice the reading that is appropriate for that element. For example, an Aries can practice the earth sign reading for a Taurus friend, and then the Taurus does a fire sign reading for the Aries.

Lunar Phases and Tarot Cards

Another factor which is both useful and entertaining when you work with your cards is the current lunar phase. When I've done large group workshops, I've taken advantage of a sweet spot between the first quarter Moon and a few days after the Full Moon. People come into the room ready to listen to something new and ready to talk. More people "get" the connections between cards after working with them briefly. Even those with "Full Moon jitters" are quickly distracted by the images in front of them.

My preference is to do readings by daylight or low light if it's after dark. Why? Consider how many moving images you view on a screen in a day, on ubiquitous sources from handheld devices to wall-sized televisions. Your brain is the

most complex structure in the known universe, according to many researchers, and my personal belief is that it will work better if you look at images that do not move. Studying one tarot card—focusing on the person or people, the colors, the action suggested, the meaning you interpret—is an exciting prospect for your subconscious. I always ask clients, "What do you see?" more than once if a card isn't obvious. Cards like Temperance and Strength are wonderfully clear, but they are outnumbered by more subtle images!

More Complex Readings

Once you are comfortable with the suit that works for your astrological element, consider adding the other suits. I have done many readings without major arcana to see the connections between the suits themselves. However, adding the major arcana is where you really can have fun with a reading. Now you are adding cards that are easier to interpret. (Can we all agree that the terrifying-looking Death card usually means "decisive transition" instead of the Grim Reaper?)

Say you have a spread that is heavy on cups, and then VIII, the Strength card (the lady with the lion), turns up. That card definitely indicates that taking the deep breath and preparing for the adrenaline that comes with emotional disturbance is in order. Or the spread might have lots of pentacles and wands, indicating a work situation is in play. And then the Tower (XVI), which represents the Tower of Babel tumbling and which immediately follows the Devil, shows up. One interpretation may be that finances at the place you work are strained, and one possibility is that the company or organization may change ownership—or that if a change is underway, it's reaching a crescendo.

However, an astrological interpretation of the above two examples also suggests that major players (which can include the querent) could be born under a sign that is in that element (cups being water signs, etc.).

Yearlong Reading

Here is a fun reading for January. You can also do it for any month, as it's a long-range reading. Record the cards, and see how they unfold. (I prefer to do this reading without major arcana.)

Lay out twelve cards in the shape of a horoscope (or a clock face), starting with a card in the position that "nine o'clock" would be in (this corresponds to the Ascendent or rising sign). Lay out card in nine o'clock, eight o'clock, seven o'clock, etc., all the way to ten o'clock, the last card.

If you are reading in December or the start of the new year, the card in the nine o'clock position represents January. The card in the eight o'clock position represents February. Look at the cards slowly, and see whether the "theme" for wands, pentacles, swords, and cups (fire, earth, air, and water) carries through for that month.

For example, January turns up the two of swords. Swords represent air signs, so there may be folks born under Gemini, Libra, and Aquarius who play a major role in your life that month. The theme would be "intellectual activity," "taking action," etc. You can also do this reading at the start of each month—give yourself a card as that month's theme!

Finally, one of the pleasures of tarot cards is a seemingly infinite array of readings as well as the range of interpretive possibilities. Start slow and move on to more complicated readings, and you will find that your self-knowledge, as well as intuition, increases.

Sky-Clad Magic:
Naturism for Shy Practitioners

by Alexandra Chauran

I have a funny-looking body. My hips are large, and my breasts are scarred from the surgical removal of multiple tumors. My belly is a little rounded and forever changed from having two babies. My daughter likes to point out my tiger stripes: "It's where I kicked you before I was born!" I'll never be a super-model, but I love my body. It is strong. My feet ran a marathon. My breasts nourished my children, and my belly cradled them. My muscles are strong enough to lift and carry things. But I didn't come to this joy and peace with my body by going to the gym, even though I do, or by staring at myself in the mirror and saying affirmations, which I definitely don't. Mostly, I learned to love my body through magic—not a single magical spell, but the conscious practice of being nude during ritual.

Let's back up a few years to chronicle my strange journey toward body positivity. It began when I decided to seek initiation into British Traditional Wicca, which is usually practiced "sky clad," or naked. As I researched local groups and met Witches, I thought anxiously about what it might be like to learn how to do magic without clothes on while in the company of strangers (at least at first). When I first attempted sky-clad rituals with others, I'd never even done one on my own. The result was anticlimactic. It was neither as weird nor as powerful as I'd hoped. I had to figure out the reason why people choose to be nude during ritual.

As I trained in British Traditional Wicca, I also moved to a new house that just happened to be across the street from a forty-acre nudist colony and family resort established in 1937. This was my crash course in what could be achieved while nude. While I wouldn't recommend weed whacking or cooking bacon, I would definitely recommend any sort of sacred ritual, from gardening to meditation and yoga. Over sixty years ago, the founder of modern Wicca, Gerald Gardner, was a nudist as well. At the time, people believed that being naked in nature promoted good health. Today, modern Wiccans carry on his sky-clad practices for several reasons: because it removes all clothing status symbols of rank or wealth, because it removes all barriers to the flow of spiritual energy between bodies, and because it is a symbol of our freedom from all of the modern prohibitions, including psychosocial ones, against nudity. In Wicca, our bodies are not just vehicles in which we drive our brains around, but working, natural batteries full of energy that can be used to manifest our magical goals.

If you choose to imbue your rituals and magic with the heightened energy flow, freedom, and power of nudity, here's how to get there. It's not always as easy as taking off clothes; some people have preexisting body issues, a past history of abuse, or cultural barriers. Here's a step-by-step plan for embracing naturism, or being nude, as a part of your spirituality.

Barefoot Grounding Ritual

Being barefoot is one step, if you'll pardon the pun, toward experiencing the power that nudity can offer so that you can decide if you want to continue with this ritual choice. Barefoot ritual aids in the grounding process. Here is one grounding technique that you can use before any ritual magic working. This ritual is best performed outdoors. I enjoy hiking barefoot, and now I hate the alternative. Shutting off my feet to the sensations of the trail would be like hiking blind to the greenery or deaf to the birdcalls—it's like removing a large fraction of the experience of nature. You don't need to hoof it on the trail to enjoy this ritual; if you can find a pleasant patch of grass outside, you will be in the ideal environment. However, this can be performed indoors as well if necessary.

Step 1: Remove your shoes and socks and face to the east, which is the home of the element of air. Feel the air on the tops of your feet. Spread your toes if you can. Take a deep breath in and breathe out, imagining any negativity leaving your body as you do so. Take deep breaths until you feel that you've rid yourself of as much negative or stagnant energy as possible.

Step 2: Turn toward the south, the direction of fire. Stomp your feet in place at least three times as you do so and then stand still. With vigorous stomping, you should feel the vibration of the blood pulsing in your veins. Become aware of the life energy within you, and visualize it in your mind's eye however it appears to you.

Step 3: Turn toward the west, the home of water energy. It is time to establish an energetic flow. Imagine that your feet are like the roots of a tree, drinking in energy from Mother Earth to fuel your magic. This energy should feel rejuvenating and refreshing.

Step 4: Turn toward the north. Feel your toes gripping the firm earth that is the element of the north. Check in with

your body. Do you feel jittery? Too much energy, so return to the eastern exercise. Do you feel sleepy? Too little energy, so return to the western exercise. With time and practice, you'll find that you hit the sweet spot and will be able to ground yourself quickly and powerfully before any ritual. I, myself, perform grounding multiple times daily.

First Nude Ritual for the Shy Neophyte

The point of this ritual is to give yourself the freedom to be nude in the privacy of your own home. It will imbue you with freedom and power, should you choose to accept it, when your barriers are safely and consensually let down. This ritual is sufficient preparation for participating in sky-clad group rituals as well, though it certainly is not a mandatory prerequisite, nor are you asked to go beyond your comfort level.

This ritual is best performed during a Full Moon. No, that's not just a pun about bare bottoms. The Full Moon is symbolic of the full revelation of power and mysteries, and can help you manifest your desires. This ritual should be performed in the dark by candlelight. All bodies are beautiful by candlelight.

Though this exercise is performed as a ritual bath in a bathroom, I suggest that you cover all mirrors even if you are happy with your body. The reason for this is that nude ritual is an expression of the sensations of the moment. When you look at your body in the mirror, you automatically adjust and change yourself. I am a student of a style of sacred temple dance called *bharatanatyam* that may be thousands of years old, and we don't use mirrors when learning to dance. In fact, when our teachers catch students looking at reflections in the window, those students are chided for not paying attention to the feeling in their bodies during the moments in the dance. Drape sheets or towels over any mirrors or turn them away so that your gaze will be directed inward.

Begin by taking a cleansing bath with three tablespoons of sea salt added to water. If you have dry skin and want to skip the salt, you can use a cleansing herb such as lemon. Three tablespoons of lemon juice will suffice. Take your bath in the darkness lit only by candles, and try to clear your mind with silent, receptive meditation during your bath. It's okay to have your favorite peaceful music playing in the background.

When you finish your bath, towel off and don some of your favorite jewelry. Jewelry is often worn in Wiccan rituals: bracelets show allegiance to people or deities, and necklaces represent the eternal nature of the Goddess. I like to wear specific jewelry that I only wear in a ritual context. It feels like I'm putting on sacred robes. It doesn't matter what type of jewelry it is (a man could easily wear a watch and a belt in a pinch), but it does matter that you are adorned. Next, anoint yourself with oil such as an oil-based perfume or olive oil. The insides of your ankles and wrists are good points to place oil so that it is warmed by the blood so close to your skin. The middle of your forehead, between and above your eyes, is the mystical location of the third eye and is a good place to put a fifth drop of oil.

Take a moment to face each direction and perform the barefoot grounding ritual, even if you are still in your bathroom. As you close your eyes and check in with your body during the final phase of grounding, say a prayer to your higher power(s) of choice. It may go something like this:

Goddess(es)/God(s)/Universe/Higher self, give me the power and the freedom to direct that power through my body as I will, for the highest good of all and with harm to none. So mote it be.

∾

This ritual can be performed as a daily devotion or as spiritual preparation before a group sky-clad ritual. Though, of course, you need never go naked in public if you don't want to do so. Do what you wish only in accordance with your own comfort level, but if your gods ask you to bare it all, I suggest that you go for it!

Magickal Soups and Salads

by Melanie Marquis

Soup and salad may not seem like the most exciting meal, but there's a reason these staple foods have stuck around throughout the ages. Simple, versatile, and clever ways to utilize whatever small scraps of food might be available, soups and salads are popular throughout the world. What's more, the vegetables, herbs, and other ingredients often included in these dishes pack a magickal punch that can be activated by preparing your meals with intention, keeping your spellcasting goal in mind as you slice, dice, stir, and mix. Once you get the hang of a few magickal cooking techniques and familiarize yourself with the energetic qualities of some common ingredients, you'll be able to prepare a wide variety of soups and salads, enchanted especially to make your wishes come true.

Magickal Soup Preparation

Dating back to ancient times, soups have a long and rich culinary history. Every culture seems to have its own signature soup, from the minestrone of Italy to the clam chowder of New England. Soups are very personal, reflective of the cook's own resources, tastes, and preferences. Recipes are great, but try to give each dish you create a personalized touch. Doing so will make the food more magickal, and who knows? You might invent a new soup that becomes a future culinary classic!

Soups might be creamy, made with a vegetable puree or dairy product such as milk or heavy cream, or they can be made with a base of meat broth or vegetable stock. For magickal purposes, vegetable-based soups work especially well, as they are less heavy and more energetically vibrant than meat or dairy-based soups. Keep in mind that different ingredients will have different cooking times, so always add the densest, largest ingredients like carrots or potatoes to your soup base first, saving any leafy vegetables or additional fresh herbs to add in last, just a few minutes before the soup is complete.

Use your spoon to empower the soup as it heats, sending whatever energy you wish to impart to the soup down your arm, through the utensil, and into the pot. You might use the spoon to trace the outline of a magickal symbol appropriate to your current goal: a heart for love, a pentacle for protection or power. Try stirring clockwise to draw in new energies and for goals focused on attracting, magnifying, or manifesting. A counterclockwise stirring motion is great for a magickal soup intended to banish or reduce any undesired energies. As the pot of soup simmers, think of your magickal goal and envision the energies of each ingredient pulsating and increasing in vibration, blending together into a powerful brew perfectly harmonized with your intention.

Common Soup Ingredients and Qualities

Here is a quick list of common soup ingredients and their associated magickal attributes. Don't limit yourself to only

these ingredients, as this is just a small sampling of the virtually endless possibilities.

Black beans: Protection, strength, defense, tenacity, the underworld

Red beans: Love, health, courage, energy, compassion, loyalty, fertility

White beans: Purity, peace, harmony, relaxation, happiness, honesty

Green beans: Prosperity, health, good luck, abundance, fertility, growth

Black-eyed peas: Good luck, health, joy, wealth, prosperity, friendship

Lentils: Health, strength, tenacity, endurance, wisdom, fortitude

Broccoli: Strength, growth, wisdom, action

Squash: Courage, defense, health, wealth, abundance, fertility

Potatoes: Prosperity, wealth, health, psychic vision, dream magick

Onions: Protection, defense, banishing, strength, courage

Leeks: Dream magick, psychic vision, flexibility, transformation

Kale: Health, strength, stamina, energy, prosperity, abundance, growth
Corn: Gratitude, abundance, energy, comfort
Garlic: Protection, purification, health, energy, passion
Oregano: Prosperity, protection, luck, concealment
Parsley: Change, swiftness, lightheartedness, new beginnings

Magickal Soups Made Easy

Try the magickal soup recipes below to get a good grasp on the basics, then experiment with your own creations. The recipes here are designed with both simplicity and magickal effectiveness in mind, and mastering these soups will give you a good foundation on which to build your skills as a culinary wizard.

Fortifying Egg Drop Soup

Eat this soup to boost your courage or energy or to bring strength and protection.

Ingredients:
4 cups vegetable stock or water
¼ cup soy sauce
¼ teaspoon salt
¼ teaspoon black or white pepper
½ teaspoon powdered ginger root
1 clove garlic, finely minced and sautéed
1 celery stalk, peeled and diced
¼ cup onion, diced
1 cup cabbage, thinly shredded
4 eggs (preferably free-range and hormone-free), slightly beaten

Heat the water or vegetable stock, soy sauce, spices, and vegetables as you envision the energies of the ingredients combining into a vibrant mixture that pulsates with your magickal intention. Stand proud as you stir, head up and shoulders back. Let a sense of power and bravery flow into the soup as it heats just to a boil. Reduce heat, then slowly pour in the beaten egg, stirring the soup very softly as you do so. The egg will immediately begin to cook. What you want is medium-sized tendrils of egg. If you stir too vigorously, the egg will completely break up, which results in an unappealing appearance. Use your spoon to just gently glide the egg through the soup as it cooks, and you'll end up with a gorgeous yet very simple and rustic dish. Let the egg cook in the soup for 1 to 2 minutes, then serve and enjoy.

Red and White Bean Soup for Happiness, Health, and Love

Use this soup to support general, all-around good health, happiness, and love.

Ingredients:
4 cups vegetable stock or water
1 can dark red kidney beans, drained (or 2 cups cooked and drained dried beans)
1 can white beans, drained (or 2 cups cooked and drained dried beans)
Several large kale leaves, chopped
Large handful fresh spinach leaves
1 clove garlic, minced and sautéed
2 teaspoons oregano
1 teaspoon basil
½ teaspoon salt
¼ teaspoon black or white pepper

Place all your ingredients into a pot and heat at low temperature. As you combine and heat the ingredients, envision all the good things you wish for in life or that you're grateful for—the things you love, your health, your happiness. Visualize the soup pulsating with a vibrant, positive energy as you stir it clockwise and affirm your magickal goals.

Passion-Boosting Squash, Tomato, and Rosemary Soup

Use this soup to increase feelings of passion and to encourage the free flow of love.

Ingredients:
3 yellow squashes, peeled and diced
2 zucchini, peeled and diced
2 Roma tomatoes, diced with seeds removed

2–3 tablespoons fresh rosemary
½ teaspoon salt
⅛ teaspoon cinnamon
⅛ teaspoon nutmeg

Boil the squash, zucchini, and tomatoes until tender; drain, cool, then puree in a blender or food processor. Pour into a saucepan and add in the remaining ingredients. Heat until the soup reaches the desired consistency, as you do so envisioning your passions rising, the energies of lust and love coursing wildly throughout the brew.

Salad Magick Basics

Nothing goes better with a bowl of magickal soup than a serving of magickal salad. Salads are easy to make, light, and refreshing, and if you prepare them right, they can be packed with nutrition as well as with magick. The magickal energies inherent in vegetables, fruits, nuts, and herbs are most vibrant in their raw and unprocessed state, making a salad a perfect way to highlight these energies with minimal fuss. As you wash, tear, slice, and dice the ingredients for your salad, focus your thoughts on the magickal effect you want the salad to produce, letting the natural attributes of the ingredients inspire you. Conjure an image in your mind of what you want, and let the feeling of having this wish come true fill your heart and overflow into each ingredient. As you mix the salad together, affirm in your mind that what you will, will be. Envision the energies of each separate ingredient working in harmony to manifest your goal.

You might also boost the magickal power of your salad with a dressing or other topper. Try sunflower seeds for a boost of happiness or to encourage friendship. Add oregano and basil-seasoned croutons to help bring prosperity. Drizzle on some honey mustard dressing in the shape of a peace sign to soothe conflict. Be creative. Your existing knowledge of cooking and of plant attributes and your natural intuition will all help you to design effective flavor combinations that are also in line with your magickal goal. You can also utilize the many books

and online reference guides that describe the various magickal attributes of different herbs, fruits, nuts, and vegetables.

Common Salad Ingredients and Attributes

Below is a small sampling of powerful ingredients you might include in a deliciously magickal salad.

Red leaf lettuce: Love, friendship, confidence, courage
Romaine lettuce: Strength, tenacity, energy, defense
Carrots: Clarity, energy, imagination, inventiveness
Spinach: Health, strength, growth, prosperity
Cherry tomatoes: Fertility, happiness, harmony, compassion, love
Sprouts: Fertility, freshness, new beginnings, rapid growth, transformation
Black olives: Love, passion, seduction, protection, psychic vision
Radishes: Passion, strength, energy, defense, stamina
Cucumbers: Peace, calm, happiness, pleasure
Mushrooms: Spirituality, wisdom, the underworld, dream magick
Avocados: Joy, satisfaction, wholeness, contentment, abundance, love, compassion, sensuality

Sunflower seeds: Joy, success, growth, friendship
Rosemary: Energy, love, happiness, luck, friendship, harmony, attraction, increase
Basil: Love, luck, prosperity, passion

Simple Salads Made Magickal

Here are a few simple salad recipes to help give your culinary creativity a jump-start. Feel free to make substitutions and adaptations as desired. Just be sure when making changes or fashioning your own creations that your recipe features at least one primary ingredient in line with your magickal goal, and avoid or minimize the use of ingredients with energies contrary to this goal.

Sesame Cabbage Salad for Wisdom and Clarity

This salad will help bring clarity and wisdom whenever you're confused or experiencing indecision. Try it paired with the fortifying egg drop soup.

Ingredients:
Red cabbage, finely shredded
Green cabbage, finely shredded
Carrots, shredded or julienned

Combine all the vegetables in a large bowl as you think of your wish for greater clarity and wisdom, then toss with the dressing below to bring extra power to your magickal salad.

Sesame Dressing for Extra Power

½ cup sesame oil or olive oil
1 clove garlic, finely minced
1½ tablespoons sesame seeds, toasted
2 tablespoons soy sauce
1 tablespoon brown sugar
⅛ cup rice wine vinegar or balsamic vinegar

In a small pan, sauté the sesame seeds and garlic in the oil until fragrant, then remove from heat. Stir in the brown sugar and soy sauce, then let the mixture cool completely. Finally, blend in the rice wine vinegar. Drizzle this dressing in the shape of an eye or a pentacle on top of your salad to add an extra burst of power and strength to your magick.

Lovely Day Salad

Eat this salad to bring a loving, peaceful energy into your day. Enjoy with the red and white bean soup for happiness, health, and love included above.

Ingredients:
Cucumber, peeled and diced into ½-inch cubes
Cherry tomatoes, halved
Fresh basil
Fresh rosemary
Drizzle of olive oil
Sprinkle of sea salt

As you prepare each ingredient, think of the people and things you love, the love you wish to share, or the love you feel for yourself. Let these feelings expand and flow from your heart and into the salad as you mix it together.

Passion-Boosting, Mood-Lifting Olive and Avocado Salad

Eat this salad to magnify feelings of passion and lower inhibitions, or to lift your spirits and bring a fresh perspective whenever you're feeling low. Try paired with the passion-boosting squash, tomato, and rosemary soup.

Ingredients:
Red leaf lettuce
Alfalfa sprouts
Black olives
Avocado
Sprinkle of salt (Himalayan pink salt or sea salt if available)

Combine the ingredients as you think of your magickal goal. Visualize yourself feeling the way you would like to feel, whether it's more passionate or more optimistic. Top with the dressing on the following page to speed along the magick and to enhance the soothing, transformative qualities of the salad.

Cucumber Dressing

½ cup plain yogurt
Splash of lowfat milk
1 cucumber, peeled and pureed or finely shredded
1½ tablespoon fresh dill
2 teaspoon fresh parsley
1 teaspoon lemon juice

Mix all ingredients until thoroughly blended. Use this dressing to initiate swift change and transformation or to calm the nerves and encourage a fresh and positive outlook.

More Culinary Magick

Cooking magickally is not only an effective form of spellwork, it's also fun. If you already enjoy cooking, designing new recipes that manage both good flavor and harmonious energies in line with your intentions can be an exciting challenge, and if you typically find cooking a rather dull chore, adding magick to the process can make it a much more pleasurable and productive experience. With so many varieties and such ease of preparation, soups and salads are a great place to start or further your journey into the joys of culinary magick. Try making big batches of both once a week, and you'll have enough for an easy-to-grab, on-the-go magickal lunch every day.

Incense: Energy Portal to Seeing and Healing

by Stephanie Rose Bird

I'm going to invite you to go on a journey with me, deep within yourself. We will travel through time and previously unexplored places, harvesting mind-altering botanicals. Don't let your mind go there—of course, we aren't going on a hallucinogenic trip. This trip is about working consciously toward opening the healer's and seer's energy portal. Vehicles for that opening up are all from a family of healers called incense trees. To tap into the magickal potential they possess, you need to be receptive. Once in a state of complete openness, the possibilities for vision quests and energy healing are infinite. So dust off a space on the ground beneath the shade of the family of incense trees. Relax, perhaps with a warm drink, and open your mind to visions that will unfold.

Seeing through the Subtle Body

We have a familiar body, related to physical being. There is also a subtle body, felt but unseen. The astral body (a subtle body) and physical body coexist. The best route to unleashing energy needed for visions and healing is opening up the astral body. Incense is a vehicle for unlocking the door. It is an activation code designed for releasing magickal potential trapped inside of you.

Soon, we will review the individual qualities of palo santo, copal, frankincense, and myrrh. For now, visualize any one of them smoldering on a portable fire before you. As it smokes and crackles, feel your senses begin to heighten. Through the foggy haze, you'll see the subtle body. It is beautiful and luminous. Don't be surprised if you see it shimmering and sparkling. The subtle body holds thoughts, develops fantasies, dreams, and has visions. It has senses of its own that are connected to divination and intuitive and psychic skills.

Features of the Astral Body

Clairvoyance (sight)
Clairaudience (hearing)
Psychometry (feeling)
Imagination (taste)
Emotional idealism (smell)

These perceptions sound similar to those senses experienced by the physical body, but they are not. These are extrasensory perceptions, unique to the astral body. Through astral body senses, we easily exit mundane existence, traveling into the domain of the spirit. In our daily astral travels, we dream, use imagination, build fantasies, and create. In some instances, we hallucinate and have visions. Through astral travel we can leave our bodies in what is known as an out-of-body experience (OBE), usually in conjunction with injury, stress, or serious illness. They also happen often in conjunction with near-death experiences.

Mainly, astral senses are useful to the objective of this journey—tapping into energy needed to venture into the great beyond. Important to opening the way for vision quests, the astral body leads the way toward healing. It is also home to powerful energy centers called chakras.

Activating Your Circles of Energy

The word *chakra* is derived from Proto-Indo-European words meaning "circle" or "cycle." Both words are helpful in gaining greater understanding of chakras. Tibetan Buddhism has a particular reverence for chakras, connecting them to all the lives we've lived and will live. Chakras are involved with birth, death, and the continuous circle of life.

Chakras are visualized as an ascending, aligned column going from the base of the spine to the top of the head. We all have these energy centers within our astral body. Engaging them ushers balance into the physical, spiritual, and metaphysical aspects of life. This is because they connect to deities, colors, emotions, and specific body parts (including glands), as well as the planets, plants, and animals. Each of the chakras is activated uniquely. We will dwell on the sixth chakra because it is stimulated into action by incense.

The All-Seeing Ajna

Without question, the eyes in our physical body are helpful. To be an effective energy healer, though, you must see deeper than physical eyes permit. Ajna, also called the third eye, is the sixth chakra and is the seat of wisdom and conciousness. The sixth chakra is sensitive to incense and shows how to see; through sight comes understanding. Associations include the pituitary gland, endocrine gland, eye, base of the skull, and brow. In the astral body it relates to intuition, imagination, psychological function, and sensitivity. Stimulation of it is provided by incense, particularly of the incense trees. These special trees that bring all the elements together yield palo santo, copal, frankincense, and myrrh.

Here is what that opening and cultivating the sixth chakra provides:

Balanced brain function: creativity and logic/analysis
Clairvoyance, which enables divination and prophecy
Dream quests, the pathway to unknown worlds
Dream interpretation, memory, and clarity of sight

The Sacred Nature of Incense

Incense has a venerable history. It has been used in ritual, ceremony, spells, incantations, invocation, blessing, consecration and as a tool for opening the way. Understanding the complex array of aspects involved with incense as medicine, positions you well to dream work and energy healing. This family of trees of our focus is the Burseraceae.

Palo santo, copal, frankincense, and myrrh are so closely aligned with magick that it's hard to decide with which one to start. In terms of their metaphysical abilities, each exists in a parallel universe. We have to begin our incense studies somewhere—no better place than holy tree, also called palo santo.

Palo Santo

Many people in need of energy healing have fallen under the influence of misfortune. Incense from the mystical palo santo (*Bursera graveolens*) is useful for those individuals. Traced back to the Inca, it encourages deep relaxation. An energy healer whose ajna is opened and then stimulated by the ancient, woodsy smell of palo santo can cure those who suffer.

This incense is typically used in South America, growing readily on the coasts and in forests of Peru. Healers use it in a practice called *sahumerio* (fumigation). Sahumerio goes back to the rites and ceremonies of the Inca. Containing age-old wisdom from thousands of years ago, palo santo's fumes and smoke capture and ground negative energy. It is returned to the universe, transformed into healing light. Even unlit, as a sacred object placed where you chose, aromatic palo santo activates the astral body. Its scent opens ajna and crown chakras. With these portals open, gifts of prosperity and good fortune flood in; healing energy takes hold.

Using Your Palo Santo Incense

Akin to the Native American smudge stick, palo santo incense is used primarily for cleansing and clearing. By working on all the physical and astral components of the body, this incense balances chakra energy, enabling peace and luck to prevail.

You'll burn it like a Native American smudge stick, smoldering but not burning. Hold it at a 40-degree angle away from your body. Light it, then let the fire die out. Smoke released from its smoldering releases healing magick for all who encounter it.

Copal

This incense is not for the faint of heart. The aroma released from smoldering copal will quickly put anyone into a trance. Due to its facility with bringing us into other worlds efficiently, it is beloved by visionaries, shamans, and energy healers.

Cultures such as the Zapotec, Lacandon, Maya, Aztec, and Zoque consider copal to be food of the gods. They work (or worked) with it in conjunction with representations of maize. As with palo santo, it has a large role in ceremonial rites.

Copal can be taken from living trees or fossils as resin; exactly which type of tree is a matter of debate. It is yielded by the family Bursereae or genus *Pinus* (family Pinaceae). Today in the Maya region of Southern Mexico, Guatemala, and Belize, copal as resin is utilized from *Bursera bipinnata*. Whatever your source, you'll be delighted by the ability of copal to open the way.

Using Copal

Once lit, copal produces copious amounts of smoke. Through that smoke you can travel at will. It's suggested, however, that you ride the billowing smoke outdoors. It's easy to get overwhelmed by copal. Completely losing your sense won't enable the best use of your visions.

Break the copal down into smaller nuggets. Put it on a lit charcoal that is already white-hot. Once the curious formations reveal themselves in the twists and turns of smoke, sit back, relax, and use your heightened senses to interpret what comes forth.

Milk of the Arabs: Frankincense

Frankincense, which comes from *Boswellia sacra* and *Boswellia carterii*, can also be known as beyo or olibanum, depending on type and origin. Attesting to its activation and energetic potential, the words "frank" and "incense" can be interpreted as "free" and "lightning." The combined words make sense: this healing medicine frees objects, spaces, and peoples from evil spirits. Its gift is purging and purification.

Frankincense is the incense for getting things started. In fact, it is even used as a fire starter. In energy healing and vision quest, you most definitely want to employ this incense. With its rich history, traced back to ancient Egyptians, frankincense facilitates the astral body's communications with divine orders you need for assistance. Those in your scope include angelic spirits, deities, and ascended masters. Burning it is a mind-altering experience which broadens your visions.

Investing in high quality frankincense is money well spent. In every occupation, you should equip yourself with the best tools for the job. Quality frankincense readily acts as a conduit for spiritual growth from released potential.

Maydi is the highest grade of medicinal frankincense and usually comes in smaller pieces. *Mushaad* is second and it is nearly transparent. *Mujaarwal* is third, also close to transparent; it and *mushaad* come in large, unbroken pieces so that you can clearly tell they are pure resin.

Myrrh: The Spiritually Uplifting, Highly Charged Incense

Like other incenses derived from the incense tree family, myrrh (*Commiphora myrrha* and *C. habessinica*) is used to open the way. Used in ancient Egypt in prayer, praise, and invocation of gods and goddesses such as Isis and Ra, this incense has always enjoyed a lofty position spiritually. Myrrh is often paired with frankincense because the two possess similar qualities and their effects are aligned. Their individual strengths are also heightened when combined.

Everyone has heard of this dynamic duo. Blessings, clearing, meditation, invocation, cleansing, healing, prayer, and even exorcisms are aided by frankincense and myrrh. When the complementary, related incenses are burned together, they invoke the powerful gods Anubis, Osiris, and Ra. Depend on frankincense and myrrh being at your side while traversing energetic planes of spirit.

Using Frankincense and Myrrh

Pound these incenses using mortar and pestle to get them down to a manageable size for your fire. Small chunks are preferred for dream quests and energy healing because they release more smoke. Work on interpreting patterns and symbols revealed by the smoke. If you're fortunate, deities and spirits might appear from the smoke. It also releases powerful medicines, opening your astral body and addressing the sixth chakra. This enables your best work to shine. Burn ground chunks of mixed incense on white-hot charcoal, making sure there are two parts frankincense to one part myrrh.

Doing the Work

As appealing as it sounds to use incense for opening the portal to vision quests, dreaming, and energy healing, it still requires work, dedication, and some skill. After understanding the various facets needing activation for opening the way, the first step in your mystical journey into the unknown is cultivating understanding through practice.

Coffee and Magic

by Tess Whitehurst

According to legend (and no one knows exactly how much fact) an Ethiopian goatherd named Kaldi discovered coffee. The story goes that Kaldi noticed that his goats became particularly wired when they grazed on a certain small tree. After relaying his findings to a local clergyman, the clergyman roasted the tree's seeds, brewed them with hot water, and served the resulting beverage to monks, who suddenly found themselves able to meditate and study until late in the night.

As you're probably aware, today coffee is big business. And, while it's a natural commodity—second only to oil in its economic value—the business is still growing! People around the world incorporate it into their lives in varying ways: as a drink, a cosmetic ingredient, a flavoring, and even a health supplement.

Below, you'll find a summary of coffee's primary magical uses, as well as some ideas for incorporating coffee into your magical work. Please note: because of unfair business practices and slave labor, please be sure to look for the "fair trade" symbol before purchasing your coffee. Additionally, coffee production is particularly hard on the environment, so buying organic when possible also helps matters to some extent.

Abundance

With creamy white blossoms that look and smell luxuriously like jasmine, vibrant red "cherries" that glow with happiness, and glossy green leaves that flutter abundantly like so many dollar bills, the lovely coffee tree undeniably resonates at the frequency of wealth. In practical terms, this is mirrored by the fact that coffee is such a huge commodity all over the

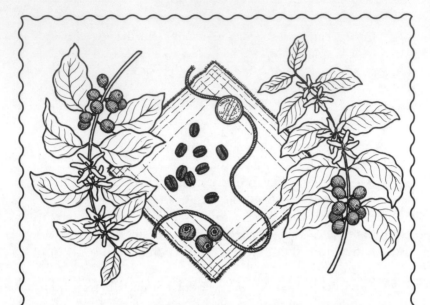

world and that literally billions of people fuel their money-making efforts with a ready stream of freshly brewed java.

If you can visit an actual coffee tree (which would probably mean that you're in Africa, Hawaii, or South America), spending time in quiet contemplation with one would be an excellent way to increase your wealth consciousness and help magnetize abundance. Just relax, breathe, appreciate the tree's unique beauty, and feel yourself receiving an energy infusion directly from the tree.

Or, to energize your wealth-production endeavors, create the following charm and place it in your wallet.

Coffee Bean Finance Energizing Charm

On a Thursday during a waxing Moon, empower nine coffee beans in bright sunlight for at least thirty seconds. Do the same with a shiny, freshly washed and dried coin and three allspice berries. Then, using hemp twine, tie all ingredients into a piece of bright red fabric. Hold it in both hands and say,

> *Wealth awaken, wealth arise;*
> *Abundant blessings energize.*

Coffee can also support abundance in the form of lush and vibrant plants and gardens. I'm talking about using coffee grounds as a natural, eco-friendly (and basically free, if you were just going to throw them away anyway) fertilizer. Simply scatter old coffee grounds in flower beds, outdoor pots, and any outdoor area where you want your plants to thrive. This, in turn, supports financial abundance and all forms of blessings: simply giving back to the earth with intention and love is a way of enlisting the earth to give back to you in the physical world. In other words, nourishing the soil is a form of sympathetic magic, as it simultaneously nourishes the soil of manifestation for you in all areas of life.

Activation

There's a reason so many of us make coffee our first priority in the morning: it gets energy moving. So simply adding coffee beans to any magical working can speed things along and jump-start your results. In many ways, coffee's magical dynamic matches that of Ganesh, the elephant-headed deity and famed "remover of obstacles" of the Hindu pantheon.

Here are some ways to incorporate coffee's magical activation properties:

Add a few coffee beans to any charm to help speed up the results.

Drink coffee before a spell or ritual to help get your own personal energy moving and to infuse your magic with clarity and speed.

Place a jar of coffee beans on your desk or in your work area. Open it up and inhale the scent to refresh your mind and senses as desired.

To cut through red tape and get a sluggish situation moving, place a small image of Ganesh on your altar, light a red candle, and request his assistance. Then place a small bowl or shot glass of coffee beans near him as an offering.

For extra activation during any spell or ritual before which you choose to cast a circle, create a visible border of your magical circle using coffee beans. After the ritual, place the coffee beans in a sealed jar to use them again for future rituals.

Clarity

You've probably heard the statistic that a cup of coffee before a test lends itself to an improved test score. Similarly, we can incorporate coffee into our magic and ritual work when clarity is required. For example, lighting a candle, setting an intention for precisely the type of clarity you desire, and mindfully drinking a cup of coffee can serve as a simple magical ritual to cut through feelings of confusion and stress and help you find precisely the divine guidance and inner quiet you seek. Alternatively, coffee flower essence can be employed as a gentle, vibrational, noncaffeinated alternative. Simply place two to four drops in a bottle of water and drink throughout the day until clarity is achieved. Or, for an extra-strength clarity boost, try the following bath.

Coffee Flower Essence Bath

Draw a warm bath and light a white soy candle in the bathroom. Place forty drops of coffee flower essence in the bathwater. Stand outside the bath, direct your palms toward the water, and visualize very bright white light coming down from above, entering the crown of your head and moving down to your heart, through your arms, and out through your palms into the water. Visualize and imagine the water pulsating with this blinding light, as if it's completely filled and surrounded in a miniature Sun. Say,

> *Clarity, I call on thee.*
> *Fill my senses, set me free,*
> *With light and bloom of sacred tree.*
> *As I will, so mote it be.*

Relax and soak in the bath for twenty to forty minutes.

Goddess Energy

One of my favorite authors, Isak Dinesen, wrote, "Coffee, according to the women of Denmark, is to the body what the

Word of the Lord is to the soul." (Incidentally, she and coffee had an intimate relationship: she owned and managed a coffee plantation for a time, as she wrote about in *Out of Africa*.) Indeed, not just the beverage, but the tree herself also possesses a seemingly divine energetic charge, with a vibration reminiscent of a powerhouse goddess such as Pele or Ishtar. And, like all plants with five-petaled blossoms, she is sacred to the archetypal Great Goddess.

Speaking of goddesses and coffee, have you heard of the coffee goddess Caffeina? It's more than likely that she's a recent addition to the roster of popular divinities, but she's quite appropriate for our modern age, wouldn't you say? If you're a coffee lover, consider creating an altar to her in your kitchen. Perhaps create and frame a postcard-sized image of a goddess rising from a cup of coffee, and hang it near the place where you prepare or enjoy your coffee. You can also take a moment to thank Caffeina and sing her praises just before partaking in your first morning cup.

And, to regularly infuse yourself with goddess energy and enhance your radiant beauty in the process, employ the following exfoliating face scrub.

Repurposed Coffee Ground Face Scrub for Goddess Energy and Radiant Beauty

At sunrise on the morning of a Full Moon, combine used, finely ground coffee grounds and a bit of sweet almond oil or jojoba oil in a small jar. Hold it in both hands and say,

> *Goddess of Morning, Goddess of Light,*
> *Share with me your beauty so bright.*

Use as you would any exfoliating scrub. Make up a fresh batch before each use, or refrigerate any unused portion between uses.

Grounding and Protection

It may seem counterintuitive that something that wires you can also ground you (no pun intended), but in many cases, it's a fact. Particularly for those of us who are sensitive and who are not naturally accustomed to being in the hustle and bustle of the modern world, a simple cup of coffee can provide the energetic adjustment we need to bring us up to speed with mainstream activities and responsibilities. It can also tighten and focus our personal energy fields in such a way that we are not as overly open to the thoughts and feelings of others. Of course, this is not ideal for every person in every situation, but it can certainly come in handy at certain moments, such as when we must drive on busy roads, run errands in frenetic environments, or brave dense crowds.

When employing coffee for this type of purpose, you might bless it beforehand by employing a ritual like the following blessing.

Coffee Blessing for Grounding and Protection

Hold your cup of coffee in both hands. Consciously send roots of white light down from your tailbone and legs deep into the earth. See these roots of light going deep into the core of the planet, and let them drink up the vibrant, golden white light they find there. Bring this light up to your tailbone and see it fill your body, protecting and grounding you in the process. Send this light through your palms into the cup, and say,

> *Sacred water and sacred tree,*
> *Combine your magic and bless me.*
> *Grounded, safe, protected, free,*
> *For your powerful magic I now thank thee.*

Drink mindfully, feeling the magic sealing up your energy field in a healthy and focused way.

Productivity

Like a gift of a single red rose given with the intention to enhance romantic love, there are some magical ingredients that are so potent, even nonmagical people make use of them. And, as modern-day workplaces are well aware, a coffee bean potion (also known as *coffee*), drunk to increase productivity, definitely works like a charm.

While coffee has many health benefits, it can also increase stress and anxiety and can cause stomach problems because of its high acidity. But did you know that cold brewing your coffee and straining it through a paper filter makes it much healthier? It cuts the acidity by up to 75 percent and removes many of the harmful components. Plus, it's delicious! Here's how to make a coffee potion that's better than the average joe:

Cold Brew Coffee Potion for Productivity and Wealth

Combine one cup of coarsely ground (fair trade) coffee with four cups of cold or room temperature water. Place in the fridge for fourteen hours. Put a basket filter in a strainer and strain. Store the liquid in the fridge and use it as a concentrate: mix one part coffee with two parts non-dairy milk. Sweeten to taste with agave nectar or maple syrup and sprinkle with cinnamon.

~

A final few words of advice: as with all good things, moderation is important! Provided it agrees with you and doesn't cause anxiety or digestion upsets, don't overdo it with the coffee drinking; one or two cups a day are plenty. And coffee dries out the body, so always be sure to drink plenty of water along with your coffee to keep a healthy hydration balance. Enjoy your coffee, and go forth, energized!